Reprint Publishing

FOR PEOPLE WHO GO FOR ORIGINALS.

www.reprintpublishing.com

THE MIRACLES OF UNBELIEF

FROM REVIEWS OF FIRST AND SECOND EDITIONS.

"From beginning to end of the book there is not a single dull passage, not a sentence obscure from overloading, not an argument skimped into shallowness, not a point ineffectively put. . . . The interest never flags; one is carried from point to point by perspicuous links of connection till all are welded together into a complete and rounded whole. . . . It is a perfect mine of quotation for men with little time for deep study, who are called, as modern ministers are, to be not only visitors and workers, but also preachers and teachers."—*Guardian.*

"The science of Apologetics is not dead. The hope of a better day wakens with the reading of a new book by Mr. Ballard. It is a full introduction to the modern science of Apologetics. The new ground is carefully chosen. In face of an enemy as hostile as ever, the opposition is uncompromising, but the warfare is less barbarous than of old. Even in the timely discussion of Haechel's 'Riddle of the Universe' there is courtesy mingled with the vigour of the refutation." . . . [Second Edition] "Mr. Ballard has made a remarkable hit. We prophesy for the book now a very wide circulation."—*Expository Times.*

"This is a well-written, reasonable, forcible piece of argument. We have been much impressed by Mr. Ballard's earnestness and acumen; his book—take it all round—is a real contribution to the large literature of Apologetics."—*Christian World.*

"A most useful volume, thoroughly up to date, clear and telling in style and thought, and very well informed. Mr. Ballard makes a capital reply to his critics in a new preface."—*British Weekly.*

"It is written by an expert in science as well as theology, a fair-minded man who faces religious difficulties, not ignores them, and one who knows how to reason out his case like an accomplished advocate, without pressing it like an unscrupulous one. Mr. Ballard has rendered valuable service to the cause of Christian truth, and given us an excellent and useful book, deserving a large circulation."—*Methodist Recorder* (Prof. W. T. DAVISON, M.A., D.D.).

"Mr. Ballard writes as a master of the subject of which he treats, and has produced something more than a good book; indeed, we think that in calling it a great book we are not far wide of the mark."—*Methodist Times.*

"We very heartily recommend Mr. Ballard's work, not only for its extremely well-reasoned arguments, but for its admirable notes and its useful list of books upon various branches of the subject. No one who reads the chapter on 'Christ, His Origin and Character,' will say that we have spoken too favourably of the Apologetic merit of the book. The Christ of the Gospels is at least possible and conceivable, but the naturalistic Christ is alike unthinkable and impossible. It is Mr. Ballard's crowning merit that he proves this with triumphant logic to the uttermost."—*Church Quarterly Review.*

"This unpretentious volume is by all odds the best apology of the Christian religion that has appeared for many a day."—*Presbyterian and Reformed Review* (edited by Prof. WARFIELD, Princeton).

THE MIRACLES OF UNBELIEF

BY

FRANK BALLARD

M.A., B.Sc., F.R.M.S., Etc.

DOUBLE PRIZEMAN IN HEBREW AND NEW TESTAMENT GREEK IN THE
UNIVERSITY OF LONDON

AUTHOR OF
"THE MISSION OF CHRISTIANITY" "REASONABLE ORTHODOXY"
"WHICH BIBLE TO READ" ETC.

THIRD EDITION
REVISED AND ENLARGED

EDINBURGH
T. & T. CLARK, 38 GEORGE STREET
1901

PRINTED BY
MORRISON AND GIBB LIMITED,
FOR
T. & T. CLARK, EDINBURGH.

LONDON: SIMPKIN, MARSHALL, HAMILTON, KENT, AND CO. LIMITED.
NEW YORK: CHARLES SCRIBNER'S SONS.

WITH REVERENT LOVE

TO A WIFE

WHOM ALL THE YEARS HAVE PROVED TO BE

INCARNATE GOODNESS

"Hold thou the good : define it well :
    For fear divine Philosophy
    Should push beyond her mark and be
Procuress to the Lords of Hell."

CONTENTS

		PAGE
PREFACE TO THIRD EDITION	. . . .	vi
PREFACE TO SECOND EDITION	. . . .	vii
PREFACE TO FIRST EDITION	. . . .	xxii
I. INTRODUCTORY	. . . . .	1
II. THE ATTITUDE OF THE CHRISTIAN CHURCH	.	11
III. STATEMENT OF THE CASE	. . . .	27
NOTES	. . . . . .	37
IV. THE REALM OF PHYSICAL SCIENCE	. .	47
V. FACTS OF HISTORY AND THEIR EXPLANATION	.	107
VI. THE REALM OF PSYCHOLOGY	. . .	175
VII. THE MORAL REALM	. . . . .	215
VIII. CHRIST, HIS ORIGIN AND CHARACTER	. .	245
IX. THE SPIRITUAL REALM	. . . .	277
X. COMPLICATION, CULMINATION, CONCLUSION	.	317
XI. SPECIAL NOTE ON ERNST HAECKEL'S "THE RIDDLE OF THE UNIVERSE"	. . . .	343
XII. APPENDIX: LIST OF USEFUL BOOKS	. .	357
ADDENDA	. . . .	363
INDEX	. . . .	365

PREFACE TO THIRD EDITION

THE speedy demand for a Third Edition of this work confirms the hope that such an appeal to reason on behalf of Christian faith as it embodies, is alike timely and valid. The present issue differs from the preceding only in the addition of a Note on p. 364 in relation to two recent and unfavourable reviews. The Author's whole and only desire is contained in the apostolic word, "Whatsoever things are true . . . these consider."

SHEFFIELD, *November* 1901.

PREFACE TO SECOND EDITION

THE demand for a Second Edition of this work so soon after its publication, suggests the hope that the labour spent upon it has not been wholly in vain, and offers a valuable opportunity for profiting by some criticisms passed upon it. No one can be more conscious of its defects and incompleteness than the author. It is perhaps an insufficient apology to plead the many interruptions and inevitable engrossments of a city pastorate; yet I humbly claim at least as much right as Haeckel (*vide* p. 348) to affirm that " my " Christian " philosophy is sincere from beginning to end, and is the complete expression of the conviction that has come to me after many years of ardent research and unceasing reflection." For the believer quite as truly as for the unbeliever, such conviction of sincerity is unshakeable, and the expression of it becomes the best contribution any man can make to the moral and spiritual welfare of his generation.

I have to thank several reviewers for pointing out a few minor slips, such as the misplacement of Schleiermacher's name, the possible overestimate of the number of early Christian martyrs, etc., all of which, together with one or two repetitions which had escaped notice, have been corrected in this edition. It is satisfactory to observe that the main positions adopted in these pages remain not only unshaken, but virtually unassailed. Some criticisms, indeed, must be disregarded, as being either unwarranted in fact or displaying an animus which is best left without reply. But a few matters appear to be of sufficient importance to merit such further consideration as is possible in a Preface.

It has been suggested that the terms "natural" and "supernatural" are not defined with sufficient philosophical precision. I must, however, be content to refer to the Preface, together with pp. 43, 151–154, as supplying all that the scope of this work either required or admitted.

Another writer represents the author as one "whose best plea for Christianity is that all other things are worse." Unfortunately the acuteness of this antithesis is purchased at the expense of truth, as both the Preface and p. 332 should suffice to show. When, moreover, the same reviewer proceeds to remark that "we could wish that writers like Mr. Ballard would pay more attention to the teaching of Jesus Himself," it becomes a little difficult to reply with placidity. Does this writer seriously wish the public to understand that only he and the school he represents, give any heed to the Gospels? When, indeed, he goes on to say, "The New Testament itself represents Jesus as refusing to work miracles," it becomes really necessary in the interests of truth that we should inquire why he does not "pay more attention" to the records with which he professes to deal? For everyone knows that, as a general statement, such an affirmation is simply untrue. To what straits writers of this school are reduced is witnessed by the following:—

"These things should at least raise the question, *Did Jesus Himself believe in the New Testament miracles?* A question which never seems to have occurred to Mr. Ballard, but which, nevertheless, is fundamental to the whole theory of miraculous Christianity. For if, when Jesus *had said that no miracles should be given*, we still believe in them, His character for truth-speaking is not improved."

The italics are mine. And it seems sufficient to add that no such question as this critic supposes could ever occur to any ordinary reader of the New Testament, unless suggested by an *a priori* theory which has previously begged the whole question, in dismissing the Gospel of John and limiting the Christian records to a sufficiently eviscerated "Triple Tradition." Though even then, as the writer on "Miracles" in Hastings' recent *Bible Dictionary* truly remarks:—

"Even if we attempt to restrict the original documents which the Synoptic evangelists had before them when compiling their Gospels, by the simple though unscientific process of rejecting everything which is not common to all three, and so arrive at a 'Triple Tradition,' we shall still find that it teems with miracle. There is no aid to faith in the mere reduction of the number of miracles."

So that as regards "truth-speaking," seeing that Jesus definitely appealed to His miracles (for, to take one instance only—and that not out of the Fourth Gospel —no other significance can be critically attached to δυνάμεις in Matt. xi. 21, 23), His character is certainly "not improved" by those who endeavour to show that there were no "mighty works" to appeal to. For in such case it must needs follow that the Jesus of the

Gospels was either deceiving or deceived. To represent Christ's own reference to His miracles as mere metaphors after the fashion of General Booth's employment of army terms, is to strain one's belief in either the intelligence or the sincerity of anyone who can make such a suggestion. For the rest, I would respectfully draw the attention of this reviewer, and those who think with him, to the quoted words of the late Professor Seeley (pp. 44, 261), as coming from one confessedly free from any orthodox bias. The thoughtful reader I would also refer to the works specified in the Appendix on the general subject of miracles, and particularly to a brief but clear discussion of the same on pp. 329 and 350 of Henry Rogers' volume mentioned on p. 112 (last edition, Hodder & Stoughton), from which, for emphasis' sake, I cannot but extract the following words:—

"If the miracles were falsely imputed to the historic Christ with His acquiescence, it occurs to ask the following questions:—(1) Did He pretend to work them, though He never did? If so, then in spite of all M. Renan's sophistical attempts to justify Him in such *tracasserie*, His conduct is at utter variance with the impressions of that intellectual and moral greatness the world has ever accorded to Him. He was equally weak and wicked."

For myself, I am happy to find the only conclusion to which I can honestly come endorsed, since the appearance of this volume, by the weighty words of Professor W. T. Davison (*London Quarterly* for April 1901, p. 309), which, in my judgement, truly sum up the whole case—

"Christianity is bound up with miracle. The supernatural is not for it a superfluous garment, which may be stripped off without loss, or perhaps with advantage. It belongs to the very essence of the Christian faith. Not thaumaturgy; not the working of wonders to make men gape and stare, but the delivery of a message from God, with credentials which give it a character and authority of its own. Christianity does not contradict, but transcend nature; it is based on a supernatural which forms, together with the natural, one vast kingdom of natural-supernatural, in which the foremost figure is the divine-human Person of Jesus Christ our Lord. We do not deny that a very real and valuable religious belief may exist without this, though it hardly deserves what it often claims, the name Christian. And this Christ is essentially one with the Christ of the Synoptics and the Fourth Gospel."

An esteemed Professor thinks that "sufficient attention has not here been bestowed upon the theory of visions" in regard to Christ's resurrection. It may be so. Yet I would respectfully plead that this volume is not a monograph upon the resurrection, and space had to be considered. Furthermore, the "vision theory" is really included in the careful consideration given to the "physical" resurrection. If there were, as I seek to show, a necessary physical objectivity in the risen body of Christ, then the vision theory is by consequence precluded. And against such physical although incomprehensible objectivity, I fail to find any valid scientific or historical objection. The only sufficient disproof would be the demonstration of the impossibility of the miraculous altogether.

The same reviewer finds it necessary to "protest against the author's frequent reiteration of the argument that if the Virgin birth is denied, Christ must have been the son of an adulteress. Even if the dilemma were correct, the latter alternative would reflect no disgrace on Jesus Himself." Such a judgement, from such a source, confessedly surprises me. I can only ask the esteemed writer to believe that every single reference to this theme was carefully considered. The pain of having to contravene the apparently sincere and manifestly erudite convictions of others herein, is to me most real. Nor has anything caused me more surprise and grief, since these pages appeared, than the hint in certain quarters that such pain was nothing to me. Moreover, if Professor Peake will forgive me, I cannot for a moment accept his verdict that "he denounces the Churches." I submit that there is no denunciation in frank and respectful expostulation, any more than in the brief mention of the Salvation Army there is the slightest disparagement of a Christian work which I have always revered and desired to help.

So as to the Virgin birth. The critic is undoubtedly warranted when he hints that the crux of the whole matter is the "authenticity of the reported sayings of Christ," and "the truth of the Gospel narratives." But it were unreasonable indeed to expect me to rehearse, or even epitomise, the whole modern discussion of this great question, in a volume written for a different purpose. All, it seems to me, that an author can do under the circumstances, is to make only such general references as are, in his judgement, warranted by the facts of the case, and to employ only such assumptions as are justified by the most recent findings of a reliable critical consensus. On these lines, then, I cannot in the present case concede that the opening narratives in Matthew and Luke are either necessarily discredited by their contents, or actually shown to be critically unreliable. Nor, again, can I at all consent to the ruling out wholesale of the

Fourth Gospel. No sufficiently overwhelming reasons have as yet been adduced for such a procedure. So that, in regard to Professor Peake's words above quoted, I am compelled to hold (i.) that the dilemma is correct as I have stated it—and it seemed necessary to state it plainly in order to do justice to its significance; and (ii.) that until the Fourth Gospel is proved unreliable, and not a few strong utterances in the Synoptics are critically jettisoned, the fact of an illegitimate birth would certainly "reflect disgrace" upon the Jesus who declared again and again that He had "come down from heaven," and from His Father, in a sense which could not have been predicated of any ordinary man, much less of one born out of the wedlock which He Himself so emphasised, in contradistinction to some religious teachers of His time. The greatest disgrace that could possibly be cast upon the Christ of the Gospels would be to fasten upon Him the stigma of personal untruthfulness.

One reviewer has complained, not unkindly, that "in his book he does not grapple with these fundamental questions." I trust he will forgive my recalling his attention to pp. 151–172, which are wholly concerned with the fundamental miracle of the "physical" resurrection. And if, as I must be pardoned for believing, the evidence is sufficient to establish such a resurrection, *cadit quaestio*. One such establishment covers all the other ground. There is nothing left to "grapple with" in the supernatural birth or ascension of the same Jesus.

It has also been suggested that in regard to the argument from the existence and history of the Jews, "a weak position" cannot be made strong. But this is surely to decide beforehand the case under consideration. Is the position really "weak"? That is the point. There are not a few, and these by no means unintelligent, to whom it seems rather that the more carefully and thoroughly this matter is considered, the stronger becomes the conviction that the purely natural factors of heredity and environment can no more account for the Jewish people, in the past and present, than they can for Christ Himself. Readers of Henry Rogers' work, referred to above, will appreciate his brief note upon this subject on p. 331.

A critic who has distinguished himself in his presentation of Ritschlian doctrines to the British public, feels justified in asking certain questions, on the ground that "a champion who goes forth to the battle with so fine a scorn for his foe, and bold a boast of his own weapons, should have no weak joints in his armour." I acknowledge the conclusion, but I deny the premisses. With all respect, I entirely repudiate both the "scorn" and the "boast," as alike foreign to my mind and unwarranted by anything here written. I cannot wonder, though I greatly grieve, at finding this misrepresentation of discourtesy copied into the Secularist press. There is really no more offensive "boast" on my part than when Dr. Ramsay—if he will pardon the reference—in his valuable monograph, *Was Christ born at Bethlehem?* says, in regard to a particular theory (p. 256), that "the theory seems to me incredible, irrational, and psychologically impossible."

However, the questions remain, and although their proper answer calls for volumes rather than a few sentences, yet out of regard for the truth and respect for the proposer, they shall receive as much attention as can here be reasonably expected.

1. "Are the birth stories as well attested as the Triple Tradition?" Well, (i.) if the "Triple Tradition" has for its sole attestation the *a priori* dismissal of the Fourth Gospel, and the mechanical elimination of all that is not common to the Synoptics, then such methods are so manifestly unscientific, and the result necessarily so forced and arbitrary, that the very least that can be said for the "birth stories" is that they *are* better attested than the "Triple Tradition." (ii.) If upon other grounds it can be established that there is a Triple Tradition which genuinely receives threefold critical corroboration, then it may be fairly alleged that the birth stories are not so well attested. But (iii.) this is not to prove that the birth stories should be rejected. Moreover, (iv.) it may be affirmed with confidence that, apart from the special contents of these narratives, there is no textual warrant for their rejection. And (v.) to dismiss a narrative, otherwise textually valid, because it contains the report of a supernatural event, is to judge by prejudice and not by evidence, which is unscientific and therefore, as a method of procedure, sufficiently discredited.

2. "Does either sound reasoning or good taste justify the alternative which the writer forces *ad nauseam* on those who question the Virgin birth, since the rejection of the birth stories disposes of any ground for such alternative?" If the alternative be correct, its repetition may be justified on the ground of importance. So that the question resolves itself into an examination of the

validity of the dilemma. It may freely be conceded that the rejection of the birth stories makes possible a "third alternative." Yet until such rejection is critically justified, that is merely the delusive cutting of a Gordian knot which cannot be untied. Suppose that the early chapters of Matthew and Luke are less strongly attested than the "Triple Tradition," at least they are better attested than the pure supposition of an ordinary paternity for Jesus, of which there is no assertion in the Synoptics —for the question in Matt. xiii. 55 is merely that of the crowd, whilst the ὡς ἐνομίζετο of Luke iii. 23 is as critically valid as it is hermeneutically significant—and against which a great deal worthy of consideration may be discovered in all the four Gospels. Furthermore, when a writer has carefully examined a debated point, and has been compelled to come to a conclusion, why should he not be permitted to avow such conclusion, and employ it as a fulcrum in his reasonings? The proper treatment of his position by an opponent is not objection to his leverage, but displacement of his fulcrum. It is precisely because it appears to me that sound reasoning not only justifies but demands the statement of the alternative in question, that it is asserted more than once in these pages. I may be wrong. But there is neither scorn nor assumed infallibility in putting forth definitely what one has been led on rational grounds to believe.

3. "Had the disciples anything to do with the conversion of Paul?" I reply first by another question— How are we to tell? In other words, are we to decide such a matter by exercising the "historical imagination" *ad lib.*, or should we be content with the sources of

information open to us in the Acts and the apostolic writings? If the former, it is, of course, open to anyone to conjecture anything. But whether we adopt the suggestion that Saul, the fiery persecutor, was cajoled into a nearer approach to Christian faith by the disciples (the questioner does not suggest any name, but it were an interesting inquiry as to which of them was most likely to attempt this), or that he was absolutely unapproachable, mere conjecture can never be worth anything as evidence. Dr. Stevens (*New Testament Theology*, quoted on p. 176, *infra*) says, I think rightly, that "no explanation tallies with all the facts which are known to us, except that which Paul himself gives us." If, then, we are to keep to this account, the supposition that the disciples had "something to do" with his conversion (in the apparently intended sense of suggested substitution of natural means for supernatural) appears to be met on the part of the apostle himself with as direct a contradiction as is expressible in human speech. To me at least it seems impossible to put any other natural construction upon his deliberate avowal in Gal. i. 11–16. Furthermore, when all the facts of the case, as set forth by Lord Lyttleton and Henry Rogers, are fairly considered, it would appear that the main principle enforced throughout the following pages would apply here also. That is to say, if the disciples "had anything to do" with Saul's conversion into Paul, so effectually as to bring it to pass on purely "natural" lines, then, in face of all the indubitable facts, the event becomes more miraculous without the supernatural agency alleged in his own account than with it. The hypothesis which is compelled to assume

Saul of Tarsus to have been a fool, or Paul the Apostle of the Gentiles a liar, would appear to be sufficiently self-discredited.

4. "Is it beyond controversy that Jesus intended the Lord's Supper to be continually repeated as a memorial feast?" In these days nothing would seem to be beyond controversy. If we follow Renan, we may make it doubtful by emphasising the silence of John. Or if we heed Strauss' representation of the Synoptics, it may be regarded as but the expression of Christ's depressed spirits. But judging for ourselves, unless the total Gospel account, together with Paul's testimony, be dismissed as worthless, there seems to be simply no room for doubt that Jesus Himself did so intend. As to differentiation of the Lord's Supper from "the common meal of heathen clubs," or from the rites of Greek and Roman mythology, detailed discussion is here impossible. But one may affirm that even if the "Agape" be shown to have some derivative relation to these, it is impossible naturally to derive from them the special significance with which first Jesus Himself and then the early Christians invested it. For a fair and forceful statement of the whole matter the reader may be referred to the discourse on pp. 174 seq. of Dr. Salmon's *Non-miraculous Christianity*, and Professor V. Bartlet's *Apostolic Age*, pp. 322–325, 465–475.

5. "Do the closing verses of Mark 'represent the earliest tradition'?" Into elaborate discussion of this also one is precluded from entering here. Yet upon further reflection I cannot concede that the expression is, on the whole, too strong. Dr. S. D. F. Salmond's

PREFACE TO SECOND EDITION

statement hereupon (*vide* article in Hastings' *Bible Dict.*), expresses fairly the finding of present-day criticism. "It is difficult to suppose that it was added by the original hand. It must have been of very early date, however, and it is not the kind of addition that can be readily explained as a work of mere invention. It embodies a true apostolic tradition, and may have been written by some companion or successor of the original author."

6. "Have we in the four Gospels independent witnesses?" As this is not my statement, I am not concerned to defend it, but I believe that what is affirmed on p. 188 is true. As to whether there is in the Gospels "such marked absence of both the personal characteristics and comments of the writers"—perhaps the word "absence" is too strong: with thanks, therefore, to the questioner, I have altered it into "repression," which is, I think, warranted by the facts, and equally suited to the argument.

7. "How could the heretical acumen of a Marcion 'prove futile in attempted alteration of the Canon' when no Canon existed in his age, and he was probably the first to attempt the formation of one?" For full answer to this I must be content to refer to Dr. Sanday's *Gospels in the Second Century*. Here I can only say that, whilst it is no doubt true, as Westcott says (*Canon*, p. 312), that Marcion's Canon is "the first of which there is any record," yet here is no disproof of the previous existence of a Canon which was none the less real for being practical rather than literary. What else can be inferred from the statement, on good authority, that Marcion "rejected" the "Acts and Pauline Epistles," and that

the "rejection of the other books of the New Testament Canon was the necessary consequence of Marcion's principles"? Surely, therefore, Westcott is justified in his summary: "There is indeed no evidence to show that any definite canon of the apostolic writings was already published in Asia Minor when Marcion's appeared; but the minute and varied hints which have been already collected tend to prove that, if it were not expressly fixed, it was yet implicitly determined by the practice of the Church." And that is quite sufficient for my argument.

8. "Can the moral hair-splittings of the Talmud be reckoned as part of the environment of Jesus?" The expression is confessedly too condensed, and I thank the reviewer for pointing it out. It should rather be "of the Pharisaic traditions which were afterwards embodied in the Mishnas and Talmuds," to quote Dr. Briggs (*The Study of Holy Scripture*, p. 429). But Dr. Angus was warranted in writing that "the traditions which compose the Talmud arose about three hundred years before Christ, and were no doubt such as met our Lord in the days of His personal ministry." And if to characterise these as "immoral hair-splittings" seems too strong language, it is only employed as summing up the estimate of Christ Himself in Matt. xxiii. and Luke xi.

These brief answers to suggested questions will, I fear, be unsatisfactory to a reviewer who definitely refrains from "expressing any judgement on the matters in dispute"—which is a perfectly safe position. I hope, however, that the few hints here given, by way of reply, will suffice to suggest that answers might be forthcoming which would at least prevent any discrediting of the main argument of these pages. With the general protest that "there should be, in apologetic literature, the greatest possible care in stating only what is certain," I most earnestly concur.

In conclusion, I cannot but repeat, with all possible sincerity, the regret above expressed that some should have found reason to wish that this work had been "more moderate and conciliatory in its general tone." It may be that in deep concern for the substance of the truth I have sometimes embodied its expression in strong terms. But every word has been weighed carefully, with the earnest desire to set forth the maximum of truth with the minimum of offence. And when one reviewer, after some kindly appreciation, adds that "some day we may hope to see the work better done by someone who will unite to Mr. Ballard's high qualifications others which are not his," I heartily endorse his desire. I can but envy those who, with richer natural endowments and larger powers of investigation, also enjoy opportunities for calm thought and pellucid expression which are denied to me. No one will rejoice more than I when the "larger man" shall come, who will make at once clear and strong and sweet to all, the truth which I have thus imperfectly sought to outline.

Meanwhile, perhaps, I may be permitted—*longo intervallo*—to repeat the word of one to whom, in common with the Christian world, I owe much. "Yet I would humbly pray that by His blessing, who is perfect wisdom and perfect light, what has been written with candour and reverence may contribute, however little, to further the cause of truth and faith, the twin messengers of earth and heaven. *In His hand are both we and our words."* (Westcott, *Gospels*, p. xiii.) F. B.

Hull, *May* 1901.

PREFACE TO FIRST EDITION

"Difficulties," in regard to Christian faith, naturally tend to increase in an age of unrestricted mental development. At a time when critical knowledge is advancing *pari passu* with scientific discovery, there cannot but arise new conceptions, new comparisons, new standpoints, which tend to bewilder if not to confound those who previously have been content with a simpler belief. The result in too many cases, especially as regards the rising generation, is a kind of practical Agnosticism. Christianity appears no longer binding upon the conscience as a personal conviction and a daily rule of life, but is regarded as a question of taste, or treated as an accident of temperament, or else dismissed altogether as a mere matter of option, even if not scorned as a delusion. How great loss accrues to the Christian Church and to individual character from this paralysis of faith, becomes ever more manifest to all who have eyes to see. The lofty cynicism of the undergraduate, the self-complacent unconcern of the busy merchant, the stolid indifference of the man in the street, are coming to be all alike defended upon the same plea. There are, it is said, so many difficulties in connection with Christianity, that no man can be quite sure of its Divine origin; whilst so many differences of opinion exist between Christian teachers and theologians, that they cannot all be right, and may possibly be all wrong.

Against this spirit, which is evidently growing in all our great cities, there is pressing need that the Churches of to-day should set themselves, with equal wisdom and love. Amongst other things it should be of some avail to utter a reasoned protest which is, so far as it goes, unanswerable. Not that it amounts to a final proof of the truth of Christianity, when we show that the difficulties of unbelief are greater than those of faith, but at least it opens the way for the appreciation of such proof as only experience and observation can afford. It destroys all presumptive objection against that actual obedience to Christ's commands, and thorough pursuit of New Testament ideals, wherein alone, either individually or socially, the benediction of Christianity can be realised.

It is something to show that the choice as regards the origin and explanation of acknowledged Christian facts is really not between the natural and the super-natural, but between the super-natural and the anti-natural. No conceivable amount of modern knowledge, no kind or degree of mental effort, can compress into the term "natural" more than the human mind is able to apprehend of this incomprehensible universe. The "natural" rightly includes all nature—both "*naturans*" and "*naturata*"—so far as we can know it. But in spite of all present-day scientific generalisations, and these based on the widest inductions possible to us, we have no warrant whatever for the assumption, that the possibilities of the universe end where our human apprehension of nature has reached its *ne plus ultra*. The acceptance of the super-natural, therefore, simply amounts to an acknowledgment of the limitations of our faculties. It is not intellectual weakness, but only the sanity of modesty, to own that there must be—

> "more things in heaven and earth
> Than are dreamt of in our philosophy."

On behalf of the anti-natural, however, no such plea can be advanced. For it directly contradicts all that we do know, so far as we can know anything, *e.g.* that we are alive, and have intellectual perceptions, together with moral capacity. If, therefore, it be reasonable because of "difficulties" to incline to reject Christian doctrine, it is equally reasonable to shrink yet more emphatically from unchristian or antichristian substitutes for that doctrine.

In a word, *Christian facts being as they are*, we are helplessly shut up to the miraculous. The only rational choice is between the miracles of the New Testament and the miracles of unbelief. It is here submitted that, so long as reason and science are anything to be regarded, the difference between these two is so manifest and significant as to be really decisive on behalf of the validity of Christian faith.

The endeavour to demonstrate this does not indeed present so much opportunity for the "originality and freshness of treatment," which constitute the *summum bonum* of the literary critic, as for the carefulness and veracity of statement which commend themselves to the genuine seeker after truth. Nor can the theme itself be pronounced novel enough to excite the curiosity of the modern Athenian, seeing that it has not seldom been hinted at, or incidentally mentioned, in works upon Apologetics. But, so far as I am aware, no frank and thorough-going examination of the whole case has yet been undertaken. Which is the greater matter for surprise, because not only does the recoil from the miracles of unbelief open wide the door for the sympathetic study of Christian evidences, but it is such as every intelligent and sincere thinker, however little skilled in dialectics, can fully appreciate.

In his little work on *The Scientific Evidences of Organic Evolution*, the late Professor G. J. Romanes wrote as follows [1]—

"Such, then, is a sketch of the evidence in favour of organic evolution. Of course in such a meagre outline it has not been possible to do justice to that evidence, which should be studied in detail rather than looked at in such a bird's-eye view as I have presented. Nevertheless, enough, I hope, has been said to convince all reasonable persons, that any longer to withhold assent from so vast a body of evidence is a token, not of intellectual prudence but of intellectual incapacity. With Professor Huxley, therefore, I exclaim, 'Choose your hypothesis, I have chosen mine,' and 'I refuse to run the risk of insulting any sane man by supposing that he seriously holds such a notion as that of special creation.' These words, I submit, are not in the least too strong. For if any man can study the many and important lines of evidence, all converging on the central truth that evolution has been the law of organic nature, and still fail to perceive the certainty of that truth, then I say that that man—either on account of his prejudices or from his inability to estimate the value of evidence—must properly be regarded as a weak-minded man."

---

[1] Pp. 76, 77.

This expression of deliberate scientific judgement certainly does not lack vigour. But if it be justified by the special quantity and quality of the evidence, then also the analogous quality and quantity of the evidence bearing upon our subject here, would seem to warrant an equally pronounced verdict. Substitute only "Agnosticism" for "special creation," "Christianity" (in the New Testament sense—including the supernatural) for "Evolution," and "spiritual" for "organic," and such incisiveness of speech is as truly justified in regard to Christian faith, as it is concerning the now generally accepted creed of modern science.

Far indeed be it from me to pronounce any individual Agnostic "weak-minded." But facts remain, and reason must rule. Hence it is the sincere purpose of the following pages to show that, at the very least, the man who rejects Christianity on account of its difficulties, is unreasonable. For he turns, and he ever must turn, not from greater difficulty to less, but from less to greater. He strains out the gnat, and swallows the camel.

F. B.

HULL, *August* 1900.

I
INTRODUCTORY

"Since writing the above remarks about the reluctance of the ablest men to be ordained, I have been told that the state of things is even worse than I had conceived at Cambridge. There, at the two largest colleges, Trinity and St. John's, I am told that of the Fellows who took their degrees between 1873 and 1879 only eight out of sixty or thereabouts took holy orders; and of those who took degrees between 1880 to 1886, only three out of sixty. Trinity is conspicuous; of the sixty Fellows who took degrees from 1873 to 1886, only two have been ordained."—*The Kernel and the Husk*, p. 353.

"But speaking generally and on principle, Christianity, and all the previous revelations of the Bible, have claimed faith, because, so far as they can be tested, they are authenticated by conscience, and because, in the points on which they go beyond our experience, they have a moral purpose and, so to speak, a moral limitation. We ask for faith, but not a blind faith."—Dr. Wace, *Christianity and Morality*, Boyle Lectures 1874, p. 274.

I

INTRODUCTORY

In his famous *Analogy*, Bishop Butler remarks that, at the time he wrote, it had "come to be taken for granted that Christianity" was "not so much a subject of inquiry," but had been "now at length discovered to be fictitious." All that remained, therefore, was "to set it up as a principal subject of mirth and ridicule, as it were by way of reprisals, for its having so long interrupted the pleasures of the world." During the century and a half which have elapsed since his day, the spirit to which he referred has in some quarters gathered strength and audacity. It reached its climax in the shameless publication of a "comic life of Jesus," with illustrations to match, which an eminent critic, himself anything but orthodox,[1] well characterised as "a disgusting failure, not so much an outrage upon Christ as upon humanity." And when he added, "it is the yell of a baffled fiend," there is only too much reason to pronounce the judgement true, as all who are familiar with the literature in question know.

But it would be glaring error to speak of modern unbelief as fairly represented by the mere ribaldry of

[1] Professor Goldwin Smith, *Contemporary Review*.

antichristian spite. It cannot, indeed, be fairly judged at all by such company. There is yet, alas! unbelief coarse enough and foul enough to reflect credit upon the faith at which it scoffs. Such assaults on Christian faith merit only pitiful disregard. But this kind of opposition is decidedly on the wane. Even amongst Secularists, who constitute, as a rule, the most vigorous and least educated of modern unbelievers, there are large numbers of thoughtful and sincere men who are far from sympathising with the rabid utterances of some of their spokesmen.

Taking a broader view, therefore, and comparing Bishop Butler's picture with the present attitude of society towards Christian verities, we cannot but mark manifest lines of difference. The great changes which have passed over the country in the matter of education, together with the vast influence of that Evangelical revival which began with Wesley and Whitefield, have effectually modified both the quality and quantity of modern unbelief. Whatever faults may justly be attributed to "Evangelicalism," its general influence on human life has sufficed to vindicate alike its character and its commission. The very revival of rationalism and tendency of sceptical thought to-day to flow in literary and scientific channels, testify that Evangelicalism has thus far accomplished its mission, in that it has transferred objections from fact to doctrine, from the Christian character to Christian belief.

It can scarcely be too plainly asserted that the last century has, on the whole, done decidedly more for Christian faith than against it. The diffusion of knowledge which has multiplied the number of minor philosophers and hasty doubters, has at the same time contributed more than any other factor in the world's history towards clearing the perceptions and correcting the judgements of men in general. Vast numbers have thus become worthier exponents of the principles of the New Testament.

Again, the very energy of that "destructive" Biblical criticism which was represented by such names as Paulus, Strauss, Baur, Renan, etc., has recoiled upon the party that fostered it. The "Tübingen" school really exists no longer. Nor is it too much to say that later assaults upon the authenticity, if not also upon the genuineness, of the Gospels, have contributed more than any preceding Christian efforts to the discovery that it is impossible effectually to discredit them. They have come out of the fiery furnace virtually unscathed, with the history of their ordeal as a guarantee for generations to come.

It is too soon as yet to estimate the final results of that "Higher Criticism" which is now concerning itself with the literary problems of the Old Testament. But we do already know enough concerning it to feel well assured that — as regards those of its general findings which are apparently beyond question—it will prove fatal only to certain *a priori* theories of inspiration for which Christianity is no more responsible than the science of optics is for Newton's Emission Theory of Light. Indeed the promise rather is that—in spite of the well meant though lamentable prejudice of some excellent people in the Churches — this effort will supplement that other just referred to, in setting Christianity free from an incubus with which it really ought never to have been weighted, and in defending it from those attacks "through the sides of Judaism" to which it has all too long been exposed.

Again, ever accumulating facts in science, though seeming sometimes to add emphasis to Mill's sensational indictment of *Natural Theology*, have yet more vividly unfolded a ceaseless mystery of good, the clearer manifestation of which cannot but "soothe and bless," in spite of all the world's tragic travailing in pain.

Finally, Agnosticism itself is a valued witness to true progress. When the real gospel was hid through mediæval fogs of corrupt and cruel ecclesiasticism, and when there was neither knowledge nor skill to penetrate beneath that surface of nature whereon she seemed "so careless of the single life"—so utterly abandoned to the callousness of absentee divinities, there was scarcely room for a middle position. A sharp line alone divided timid slaves of clerical superstition from brave but despairing men of reason. Now, however, superstition has been so far driven back that faith and reason, when avowedly antagonistic, have found room for at least an armistice, in a zone of genuine neutrality midway betwixt definite belief and actual unbelief. This debatable ground is confessedly unsatisfactory from the Christian standpoint, but it constitutes a far more hopeful region than either the dark dungeons of hierarchical fetish worship, or the black morass of dogmatic Atheism. It is real gain to have an avowal from the deliberate consensus of our clearest modern thought, that ecclesiastical fanaticism, blank Atheism, mechanical Fatalism, and despairing Pessimism, are all alike as unthinkable as they are unattractive. It is Christian advantage to have men held even in suspense by an ignorance which, in proportion as it is honest, must involve more or less of reverence as well as reason. For these are ever close akin to faith, and constitute at least the soil in which, some day, the "fruit of the Spirit" may be grown.

These things being so, it may well be asked what is left to justify the commonplace reference to "difficulties" in the way of Christian faith? For of these we still hear on every hand. Not merely in well-worn phrase from Secularist platforms, but in fluent if not flippant newspaper articles, in pungent "correspondence," in not a few contributions to our leading Reviews, as well as in the common talk of workshops, wherein it is suggested that whilst a good old-fashioned respect for religion may abide, as a sort of venerable or even useful relic, actual personal belief in Christian verities must be left to professional preachers, or be seriously held only by women and children.

Now when we inquire for the sufficient cause of all this, we find that the idea of "difficulty" is the most solid notion we can discover by way of explanation. It is not that the husband who sends his wife alone to church is a Secularist by deliberate conviction. It is not that the man in the street has proved to himself by earnest examination that the Gospels are forgeries. Nor has the youth who is content to wander about anywhere on Sundays in order to escape religion, formulated any definite reasons for his aversion. It is rather, in all these and similar cases, that our whole modern atmosphere teems with suggestions of "difficulties," with their consequent doubts, in regard to the great fundamental facts upon which Christianity manifestly rests. "If the foundations are destroyed, what shall the righteous do?"—is an ancient and significant query. It would appear that its modern answer is to the effect that the foundations of Christian doctrine are so uncertain that the unrighteous, at all events, need do nothing. Difficulties in regard to Biblical Inspiration, difficulties as to prayer and natural law, difficulties about miracles, difficulties as to the Incarnation and Resurrection of Christ, difficulties relating to the doctrines of the Trinity and the Atonement, etc., have become quite the intellectual order of the day, whenever reference is definitely made to Christian decision of character. Boldly pronounced every now and then, *ex cathedra*, by some man of repute, they are eagerly repeated by well-known journals, echoed by unthinking readers, and treasured by partisan exponents. Thus they filter down through the successive strata of the community, as well as spread abroad upon the surface of daily life, allying themselves everywhere with the endless questionings of child minds, the floating superstitions of the ignorant, and the ready shrewdness of antichristian demagogues, until such a conglomerate of unbelief is formed as Bishop Butler never conceived.

Thus it happens, that upon the vision of every honest observer of the opening century, from the Christian standpoint, there loom out large three masses of fact the portentous significance of which is unmistakable. These are—

i. That there are around the Churches on every hand, vast numbers of men and women who are manifestly "out of touch" with Christian sanctions and institutions.

ii. These are, to a large extent, not kept away from Christian associations through moral indifference, or practical hindrances, or social engrossments, so much as for reasons sufficiently intellectual to be truly described as "difficulties" in regard to "orthodox" Christian doctrine. This is especially the case with the younger portion of the better educated, in the middle-class life of to-day. It is scarcely less true of considerable numbers of artisans who shrink as really from definite Christianity as from dogmatic Secularism.

iii. The neutral and hesitant spirit thus manifest, shows every sign of increasing rather than diminishing with the advent of the twentieth century. It will certainly not be the fault of numerous writers in this generation if the "difficulties" attaching to Christian faith, fail to become more prominent and more influential. This silent weakening of the intensity of Christian conviction in the majority of our fellow-countrymen, is one of the most undeniable as well as ominous of all the religious phenomena of our day.

II

THE ATTITUDE OF THE
CHRISTIAN CHURCH

"That which is chiefly to be discerned in a survey of the state of religious thought in England and in Europe, alike among friends and foes, is a deep conviction that the Religion of the Christian nations is gravely menaced from within. The doubts thus generated are diffused far more widely than is generally avowed. That the very air is heavy with them, that they pervade alike literature and society, that they are not confined to the learned, that they perplex parents and confuse the young — these are the facts with which the apologist has in the present day to deal. It is no time for him to be contented, as in happier days, with addressing himself to the pleasant task of adorning or elaborating—he has to deal with influences, open or disguised, which are sapping the very foundations not merely of orthodox Christianity, but of Christian civilisation."—Dr. Wace, *Christianity and Morality*, Boyle Lectures 1874, p. 3.

"Now when they had passed through Amphipolis and Apollonia, they came to Thessalonica, where was a synagogue of the Jews: and Paul, as his custom was, went in unto them, and for three Sabbath days reasoned with them from the Scriptures, opening and alleging that it behoved the Christ to suffer and to rise again from the dead ; and that this Jesus, whom, said he, I proclaim unto you, is the Christ."

"Now these were more noble than those in Thessalonica, in that they received the word with all readiness of mind, examining the Scriptures daily, whether these things were so. Many of them therefore believed."

"Now while Paul waited for them at Athens, his spirit was provoked within him, as he beheld the city full of idols. So he reasoned in the synagogue with the Jews and the devout persons, and in the market-place every day with them that met with him."
—ACTS xvii. 1, 11, 16.

II

THE ATTITUDE OF THE CHRISTIAN CHURCH

ONE of the most pointed and weighty questions addressed by Christ to the men of His day was—"Yea, and why even of yourselves judge ye not what is right?"[1] The intervening centuries have rather increased than lessened its emphasis for us. It is indeed a two-edged test, in that it affects equally those who own and those who disown Him. In the following pages it is applied mostly to the latter. Yet it appears to be quite as necessary first, to call earnest attention to its bearing upon the methods of modern Christian Churches.

Peter was but echoing his Master's word when he wrote, "Sanctify in your hearts Christ as Lord: being ready always to give answer to every man that asketh you a reason concerning the hope that is in you, yet with meekness and fear: having a good conscience; that wherein ye are spoken against, they may be put to shame who revile your good manner of life in Christ."[2]

If this word had only been obeyed by all those who, since the apostle's day, have professed to accept Christ as their Master, the history of Christianity in Europe would indeed have been a different record. Even yet,

[1] Luke xii. 57.   [2] 1 Pet. iii. 15.

however, it is but partially heeded. The great principles which are here so marked, namely, that right reason should precede belief; that all rendering of reasons and enforcement of beliefs should be with the meekness and gentleness of Jesus Christ; that all profession of faith should be guaranteed by the traits of character set forth in the New Testament,—are indeed nominally accepted by the Churches of to-day, but in innumerable instances they appear to be sadly "more honoured in the breach than in the observance."

We hear much, confessedly, about the "proclamation of the gospel," and those who are familiar with evangelical "missions" know how large use is made of such phrases as "preaching Christ," "the simple gospel," "proclaiming the truth," etc. But without in the least intending to slight these good and true ideals, let us honestly ask, what, in actual fact, do they come to? They really mean public assertions by professional men from a protected pulpit. Now the very first thing that must strike an acute observer, is the direct and unmistakable contrast between this and the method of both Christ Himself and His apostles. It may, indeed, be truly said that neither He nor they ever "preached a gospel sermon," as the phrase goes nowadays. That is, neither the Master nor His earliest witnesses ever robed themselves in special attire and delivered public harangues where no man else was permitted to speak, full of assertions to be received without demur, and of assumptions which no one present might question. Yet this is a fair and true description of almost the whole of what is now known as "Christian preaching." Some few instances

THE ATTITUDE OF THE CHRISTIAN CHURCH 15

perhaps in Hyde Park, and possibly in our large provincial cities, of what is termed "outdoor work," may count as exceptions. But they are very few indeed, in proportion to the mass of Christian public services. The Salvation Army does not here come into account, because its message is all assertion, and neither courts nor permits reply from any of its myriad hearers. But Christ and His apostles always did both. He and they alike taught, indeed, "in synagogues and in the temple where all the Jews come together," but it was always definite teaching, in regard to which after inquiry was not only allowed but invited.[1] Their method could not be better described than in the words of Peter above quoted. The maxim that all things should be done "decently and in order," remains unquestioned and unquestionable. But all the legal protection that the Master and His witnesses had, was sincerity and truth. To-day, in "Christian" countries, at all events, the "proclaimer" of Christ's truth is hedged round by law which compels silence on the part of all present. Those who deem this method unsatisfactory, have but one alternative—to stay away. This is at least one reason why, in modern "Christian" England, there are four men absent for every one present at Sunday services.

But besides this ignoring of the New Testament model, is there no room for inquiry into the effect of our present stereotyped system upon preachers themselves? That they are human, will be conceded. Is it not alarmingly possible for human nature to deceive itself under such circumstances? Is it not delusively easy to argue, when

[1] Cf. Acts xiii. 15, 43, etc.

it is certain that there will be no rejoinder? And, as a matter of fact, are not statements allowed to pass unchallenged in the pulpit, which would anywhere else be subject to immediate and rigorous discussion? So has it resulted that "pulpit logic" has become a phrase at once too significant and insignificant; whilst the pulpit itself may sometimes truly, even if unkindly, be called a "coward's castle."

Paul's fearless and open appeal to men of reason upon Mars' Hill[1] was a very different affair. His bitterest opponents could never accuse him of unmanliness. How much more difficult such methods as his are than mere proclamation, every missionary knows. But if to-day all Christian preachers in foreign fields are expected—as they are—to rise to the apostolic standard, why not also those at home, in the midst of their exceptional advantages?[2]

Two remarks, therefore, appear to be really called for.

---

[1] Acts xvii. 16-34.

[2] The reply may, of course, be made that in a modern building, erected ostensibly for Christian purposes, only those are supposed to assemble who are already convinced Christians, and that these gather together for worship, not discussion. But it needs only a moment's reflection to show that this is a mere evasion of New Testament principles. The "worship" which is not altruistic enough to care for others is, as James says,* vain. The Christianity which is content to gather together its own disciples merely as a select cult for mutual congratulation, and regardless of the sin and sorrow and need of the ever-growing modern human environment, is so utterly foreign to the intention of Christ and the practice of His apostles, as to be altogether unworthy of the name. The "Christian purpose" of any Church building is quite as much the saving of the world as the edification of believers.

---

* Jas. i. 27, where $\theta\rho\eta\sigma\kappa\epsilon\iota\alpha$ really signifies worship, ii. 8, etc.

1. We know that the "common people heard" Jesus "gladly," and that the crowds of ordinary men in Asia Minor who listened to the apostles, were moved far more than the "masses" of to-day are affected by Christian preaching. If, then, the present lamentable disproportion between unchristian and Christian men is to be reduced, if the vast numbers of the artisan population are to be in any real sense "won for Christ," something more than ordinary "preaching" will surely have to be done by modern advocates of His gospel. If the men who have been educated in our Board schools are to be moved by appeal, that appeal must have manliness for its essence, and reasoned truth, not clerical assumption, for its foundation. This, however, can scarcely be the case so long as Christian teachers are content to ensconce themselves behind legal protection, and simply assume that all who differ from them are either weak or wicked.

Of course it is far more difficult to convince than to denounce. It is manifestly a much harder task to set forth, in courteous patience, clear reasons for belief in Christ and obedience to His teachings, than it is to hold Mission Services in which all statements must be by all men accepted as true upon the authority of the preacher. But it is sadly plain that the easier method is not sufficient, else why have we in London alone some four millions of human beings unassociated with any Christian Church, and a like proportion of "outsiders" in all the other great cities throughout the realm?

Every passing year shows that the harder way of, at least, supplementing earnest appeal with open reasoning, is becoming one of the most necessary methods of dealing with the men of the coming age.

So that without underrating, much less despising or discontinuing, any Evangelical effort, or humble Mission work, or regular Sunday worship, it must be manifest that there is a definite and growing necessity to add to these, other and frequent opportunities for grappling with the thoughts as well as emotions of modern men and women. The impressions likely to result from an accidental and often feeble tract, or the singing of Sankey's hymns with crude exhortations at a street corner, do not and will not, for the world of to-day, atone for the deficiencies of ordinary Christian services. These deficiencies may not be apparent to Church-members, to whom full oft the comfortable sitting, the pealing organ, the refined ethical atmosphere, together with the easy and emotional assumptions of the pulpit, constitute a perfect gospel. But modern life is making men ever more hard and keen, more shrewd and subtle, and if without these æsthetic adjuncts the true Christian Evangel won its first and most difficult foothold in a bitterly antagonistic world, assuredly it must not depend absolutely upon such means to maintain its position now or fulfil its mission to the Twentieth Century.

2. Yet further. It can scarcely be denied that the general treatment accorded to doubters and unbelievers by gospel preachers has been, and still is, to ignore them. Sermons on Christian Evidences are as rare as they are unpopular with ordinary church-goers. Such efforts are pronounced "controversial," and "lacking in spirituality," etc. etc. The preacher who endeavours

occasionally thus to teach, will assuredly be censured for "bringing doubts into the pulpit," rather than thanked for seeking to help those who already are half-alienated by "difficulties." Compared with him, the "popular" preacher who takes care to touch nothing questionable, the revivalist who assumes everything he wants, the pietist who settles all doubts by the quotation of religious poetry, will be pronounced true Evangelists, whilst younger preachers will be exhorted to take warning from the unpopularity of the "controversialist."

Yet what results from this exclusive adherence to well-worn methods? May it not be said here also—though in a sense far removed from its relation to St. Paul's Cathedral—"Si monumentum quæris, circumspice"? In England, confessedly the most Christian nation on earth, three-quarters of the population are apparently unconvinced of the Deity of Christ, with all that flows from it, especially the supreme present import of His message to mankind. All we can say of them at best is, that they are not pronounced Atheists, or avowed Secularists. It is no reply to affirm that they are merely indifferent, for what is indifference but unbelief? It is really and truly unconvincedness. Similar indifference often prevails in regard to other matters, *e.g.* as to the advisability of life insurance, or the duty of recording a vote at an election, or even the value of education at all. How then do men propose to deal with such mental inertia? Surely by earnestness and persistence in that kind of appeal which tends to produce downright conviction. Unless, therefore, Christianity be far more ultra-rational than even Mr. Kidd would have us believe, the same methods must be adopted by Christian advocates who would win men to whole-hearted decision for Christ.

Unfortunately we are all too well aware that audiences already Christian by profession, find it much more pleasant to enjoy "comforting" sermons, to listen to generalities, to admire rhetoric, to appreciate brilliant epigram, to thrill in response to pathetic illustration, than to think soberly and unselfishly in face of facts. One of the latest and most able books on behalf of Christianity[1] has for its sub-title, "Essays in aid of a reasonable, satisfying, and consolatory religion." Which is good enough, so far as it goes. But how does it comport with that maxim in which the Founder of the Christian religion Himself said:[2]—"It is more blessed to give than to receive"? It is well, truly, that we ourselves should be both satisfied and consoled, but what of that other and far greater audience outside all the Churches which makes no profession, exhibits no conviction, evinces no desire at all to know or appreciate Christian truth? Are not these also they "for whom Christ died"? Do they not need Him all the more for failing to recognise Him? Surely it is more Christian to think and care for these, than simply to satiate oneself with the luxuries of undoubting faith. No philanthropy is so real as that which seeks to redeem men from the anguish and despair typically exhibited by Strauss, when with one breath he confesses the "awful sense of abandonment" which falls upon the man who has lost all faith in God, and then with the next exclaims, "But of what avail is it to have

---

[1] Rev. A. H. Craufurd's *Christian Instincts and Modern Doubt*.
[2] Acts xx. 35, R.V.

recourse to an illusion"?[1] This tragedy of loss is far more common in our modern life than comfortable congregations permit themselves to acknowledge. There are literally thousands around the Churches to-day of whom it is true. The number is, moreover, continually growing. There is, one may truly affirm, no Church in any city of the realm that does not now reckon among its worshippers those whose faith is blighted, whose joy is dimmed, and whose character is dwarfed, by the existence of honest and even pathetic difficulty.

It is time, therefore, that we heard less as to the "mistake of argumentation" on the part of Christian teachers. The usual disparagement of "controversy" and the almost contempt for "Apologetics," are alike unwarranted and unworthy. Their real source, too often, it must be frankly said, is selfishness in congregations and indolence in preachers. It is high time, for the sake of the growing numbers who are kept away from Christian services by the chilling influences of modern doubt, that we went back to first principles, and cost ourselves any amount of labour, self-denial, pains and patience, in order to deal with honest doubters as Jesus did with Thomas. Such are neither as few nor as unworthy as is often represented. It is, moreover, as certain as the very existence of the Churches, that mere exhortation, joined with sinister hints at the moral depravity of doubters in that they do not at once accept what they are told, will only act upon them as the policy of Rehoboam did upon the tribes of Israel.

No plea is here advanced on behalf of what are called

---

[1] Strauss, *The Old Faith and the New*, p. 435.

public religious "discussions," or "debates" with Secularists. In general it may be said that such are necessarily rather harmful than helpful to the Christian cause. The mental excitement, the heated partisanship, the enforced hastiness of reference, the temptations to snatch a verbal victory even when personalities are avoided, the uncertainties and ambiguities of impromptu speech for all but the most practised disputants, together with other reasons, render this method so undesirable that it should only be employed under very special circumstances. These must be locally decided. But in every case, the conjunction of perfect self-control, in courtesy and patience, with sufficient knowledge and competent endowments of mind and speech, constitute the *sine quâ non* of such an undertaking.

The delivery of Christian Evidence lectures is not open to these objections, although in this case the lecturer must be prepared patiently and honestly to deal with questions at the close. So far, however, as practical suggestions come here within our scope, it must suffice rather to recommend the practice of taking well-advertised evidential subjects at stated intervals, on Sunday evenings, always followed by an open conference where every man may have perfect liberty to question any statement or discuss any difficulty, according to need.[1] For not only is Sunday evening by far the best, and indeed the only practicable occasion in the week for

[1] That this is entirely practicable is proved by the writer's own experience, inasmuch as for some years such a method has been adopted in his church, with nothing but good results. All that is needed is that the preacher should know his subject, and exhibit the spirit of his Master.

such a purpose, but it is also true that ordinary Christian congregations need teaching in these matters almost as much as doubting outsiders. Should any objection be raised against this method as an "innovation," it is surely sufficient to point out that it was almost always the practice of the apostles,[1] and indeed of Christ Himself.[2] It cannot be dangerous to be in such an apostolical succession, or wrong to follow the Master's own example.

Such a suggestion confessedly calls for more unselfishness on the part of Christian worshippers, and entails more labour upon preachers, than ordinary "services." But what is the Christianity worth that cannot supply these? At all events, be the trouble and self-denial involved what they may, some such effort is the only way in which to-day vast numbers of outsiders will be reached at all by the Christian message.

For there must be no blinking the fact, nor any hesitation in announcing it, that the first appeal of the gospel of Christ is not to men's feelings but to their judgement. "Why, even of yourselves judge ye not what is right?"—we have seen is Christ's own question. The late Sir Andrew Clark was therefore well warranted in his avowal of this principle:[3]—"Now the reasons, I apprehend, which influence a man in his acceptance of the Christian faith, lie in two directions, first in his head, secondly in his heart." The acknowledgment of fact must ever precede feeling arising from it. Emotion, to

---

[1] Cf. Acts xix. 8, 9, etc.
[2] Cf. the Gospels, especially the Fourth, *passim*.
[3] *A Physician's Testimony for Christ*, p. 14.

be worthy, must always be based upon judgement. Through reason, not through faith, must really come the first conviction, though not the last proof, of the truthfulness of Christ's gospel. The sooner this is frankly recognised and practically exemplified by all true disciples of Jesus, the better will it be both for those within and those without the Churches.

To insist upon this does not in the least disparage the evidence from experience. Without that, all Apologetics would be but the defence and laudation of a mirage.

It must, however, be owned that both the ethical and the experimental sides of Christianity have abundant advocates in all the religious bodies of to-day. The purity and nobleness of the Christian ideal in these respects is, happily, not likely to lack exponents. Yet all this is but as a human body without backbone, unless it be preceded and accompanied by that reasoned argument and definite teaching which, according to the Gospel records, formed so large a part of Christ's own life-work. It is especially to be noted that the Fourth Gospel, simplest, deepest, and most experimental as it is, contains the largest amount of what so many Christian people in these days disdain under the title of "controversy."

Printed books upon these themes, however numerous and valuable, no more satisfy all our modern need than did the original written sources or manuscripts of our Gospels suffice at first, without the living testimony of the apostles. The work of the Christian advocate to-day is not more arduous than theirs. But only in the degree in which he is faithful to his high commission—whatever

THE ATTITUDE OF THE CHRISTIAN CHURCH 25

it may cost him in pains and patience—has he any right to look for that which is so easy to sing about, but which seems yet so far away, namely, the "conversion of the world."

Thus we are brought to the place and use of the argument set forth in the following pages. It is not an appeal to the heart, but a challenge to the mind of every man who feels himself driven to doubt. It is no less a challenge for being expressed with the utmost possible respect and courtesy. It amounts to this, which must be openly declared without ambiguity or hesitation, that the first grave charge brought by Christian faith against all forms of modern unbelief is, not that they are plain proofs of moral depravity, but that they do unquestionably exhibit mental obliquity. The affirmation of belief is that unbelief is demonstrably unreasonable.

Now this undoubtedly constitutes the most severe indictment that can be brought against any system of thought, or method of human life. The late Professor Jevons affirmed that "we are nothing if not logical." Who, save a man in bondage to superstition or "authority," can exclaim against the "corrosive action of reason" in such an avowal? It is but to say that we must be true to what we know. And if even a Cardinal deny that, we may on various grounds respect the man, but our very manhood must sit in judgement upon his creed. When Reason, indeed, disdains the help of Faith, it becomes but a poor galley-slave aimlessly toiling at a hopeless destiny. But when Faith decries Reason, the ruin is even greater. For it wholly contemns the example of its Lord, besides bringing about its own destruction. From the lofty heights of its pious imagining it casts itself down in unwarranted presumption, only to exhibit human nature maimed by ignorance, mangled by fanaticism, crushed by despair. If there could have been a greater sin than rebellion against right reason, the gospel commission would never have been ratified by Eternal love and justice with the solemn seal—" He that believeth shall be saved; but he that disbelieveth shall be condemned."

III

STATEMENT OF THE CASE

"Modern Agnosticism is performing this great service to Christian faith ; it is silencing all rational scepticism of the *a priori* kind. And this it is bound to do more and more the purer it becomes. In every generation it must henceforth become more and more recognised by logical thinking, that all antecedent objections to Christianity founded upon reason alone are *ipso facto* nugatory. Now all the strongest objections to Christianity have ever been those of the antecedent kind, hence the effect of modern thinking is that of more and more diminishing the purely speculative difficulties, such as that of the Incarnation, etc. In other words, the force of Butler's argument about our being incompetent judges, is being more and more increased."—Romanes, *Thoughts on Religion*, p. 166.

"Materialistic philosophy is mere juggling or self-deceiving. It fancies that time, millions of years, will somehow perform the impossible. It waits for difficulties to flow away, as the simple-minded rustic in Horace waited for the stream. By distributing its stupendous miracles through endless æons, by introducing them bit by bit into the scheme of the world, Materialism hopes to make them credible and natural, and so to evade all recognition of the unfathomable primal mystery. But the fundamental laws of thought care nothing for time. They are the same yesterday, to-day and for ever."—A. H. Craufurd, *Christian Instincts and Modern Doubt*, p. 71.

"The form of belief from which the ultra-rational element has been eliminated is, it would appear, no longer capable of exercising the function of a religion."—Benjamin Kidd, *Social Evolution*, p. 114.

"Not a few intelligent and educated men who pay homage to Christ as the greatest of men, refuse to accept as correct the portrait of Him given in the New Testament. If this portrait be incorrect, these men have detected an ancient and serious error and have restored to the civilised world the true conception of God. We expect to see in them as a fruit of their important discovery some moral and spiritual superiority to those who are still held fast by the great delusion. We look in vain."—Professor Beet, article "Christology" in Hastings' *Bible Dictionary* (T. & T. Clark).

III

STATEMENT OF THE CASE

In one of His most earnest expostulations with those around Him, Christ is reported to have exclaimed, "Ye blind guides, which strain out the gnat, and swallow the camel!"[1] The reproof was unquestionably a severe one. But there are occasions when every true teacher not only may, but must be severe. Wrong that is based upon mere ignorance, or weakness, or mistake, he may treat with gentle rebuke and tender patience. He cannot, however, so pass over error that is not merely rooted in unreason, but exalts itself above all else in coarse self-assertion. There is no question that this latter was the general temper of the Pharisees, and that thus they truly merited the stern treatment they received. In these days, indeed, we should scarce have patience even to read the petty and tortuous devices by which their traditions travestied great truths and reduced holy principles to mockery.

The proverbial figure cited by Christ aptly exposed, therefore, and justly condemned, their guilty foolishness. The gnat and the camel were alike unclean, according to Levitical law, so that the comparison resolves itself

[1] Matt. xxiii. 24.

into that of insisting vehemently upon trifles, whilst giving no heed to enormities. "Ye tithe mint and anise and cummin, and have left undone the weightier matters of the law, judgement and mercy and faith." So long as morality is of any account amongst men, such doctrine and example as this must merit scathing rebuke.

But human nature persistently repeats its follies from age to age. The children of the Pharisees have proved an interminable race. The Christian Church itself has ever included some who have deserved, as completely as they have ignored, the stringency of Christ's rebuke. There are, however, good reasons for believing that such Pharisaism is becoming decidedly less in quantity, whilst its quality is ever more truly estimated.

We are free, therefore, to turn our thoughts in another direction, where, beyond the pale of the Church, very much the same wrong is still being perpetrated. As compared with Pharisaism, it would not be inapt to term this human attitude "Philistinism," seeing that it as incessantly menaces Christian truth *ab extra* as the Philistines of old did the people of Israel.

To modern ears, doubtless, the name of "Agnosticism" is much more familiar. In its freedom from all moral reproach, it is also unquestionably more agreeable to unbelievers. Nor would any thoughtful Christian advocate to-day avow that lack of faith necessarily involves deterioration of morals, or recklessly assert that doubt and depravity are one. It cannot be denied that, to an ever-increasing degree, "honest doubt" prevails around all our modern Churches. Their name is legion, who, as sincere doubters, deserve all possible sympathy from

Christian teachers. They constitute a growing class whose necessities will have to be met with increasing frankness and patience. For as each generation develops more mental power, it becomes even more necessary to do justice to the last edition of Butler's *Analogy*, than to weep over the pathos of the *Bonnie Brier Bush*. Christianity, according to Paul's conception of it, calls for "rational service" (Rom. xii. 1), and one of the finest of our modern scholars has right nobly said that " human nature craves to be both religious and rational. And the life that is not both is neither." [1]

Whilst, however, it were vain for any believer to deny either the existence or the seriousness of modern unbelief, and the growing disposition certainly is to estimate it fairly and meet it frankly, there is one widespread assumption against which an unmistakable and emphatic protest must be raised. Sometimes it is mildly hinted under the guise of a cultured Agnosticism, sometimes it is blurted out with coarse assurance by an undisguised Secularism. The substance of the assertion is the same in either case, viz. that so many "difficulties" are, in these days, attached to Christian faith, that a man may well be forgiven either his hesitation to join the Church, or even his downright scepticism. Thus it is made to appear that the best, and indeed the only way out of religious difficulties, is to relinquish all belief in Christian verities, or become at least an avowed Agnostic.

Now it is this assumption which is here openly and unhesitatingly challenged. It is the purpose of the following pages to show that, even if we dismiss all

[1] The late Aubrey L. Moore, *Lux Mundi*, p. 109.

suggestion of moral obliquity and credit every unbeliever with pure sincerity, there remains, on grounds of clear reason alone, sufficient cause to apply to modern scepticism the very same rebuke which Christ addressed to the Pharisees. It is still manifestly a case of straining out the gnat and swallowing the camel. In other words, whatever be the difficulties of Christian belief, the difficulties of unbelief are greater. Whatever mental perplexities may seem to block the path of faith, those in the way of unfaith are immeasurably worse. If Christianity be rejected because its miracles seem incredible, the miracles which unbelief is "compelled to posit" in their place, are far more incredible, both as to quantity and quality. So that if, on the whole, it be accepted as a principle of reason that men should in their convictions ever proceed upon the path of least rational difficulty, we are entirely warranted in calling upon them to become Christian. For the very ground upon which they might be disposed to refuse, viz. the existence of difficulties, ought rather to become their sufficient reason for consenting, seeing that such refusal inevitably commits them to more and greater difficulties.

In setting out to show this, it is impossible to pass without regard some recent attempts which have been made, with good intent, to reduce the supposed hindrances to Christian faith to a minimum. It must be conceded that the New Testament sets before us great and indeed unfathomable mysteries. These, in the light of our ordinary human experience, may well present "difficulties" of acceptance. But the question as to how far we may proceed, with a view to economising faith, in minimising the facts out of which such difficulties arise, is a very serious and important one. Doubtless some Christian difficulties have been unnecessary and unwarranted. They have arisen out of special theories concerning the Bible, or human nature, or eschatology, which the gospel never really authorised. These certainly call for revision, and there is little risk in affirming that evangelical Christianity to-day is being more and more purified from such adulterations, and is presented to men in more rational form than ever. The rejection of Christian truth becomes, in such case, correspondingly more irrational.

But this principle of the reduction of difficulties has definite limits. There is an irreducible minimum. When, for instance, it is suggested that if only all miracles be given up as mythical accretions, or the supernatural in general dismissed, faith would be much easier; or that the Incarnation and Resurrection of Christ may well be resolved into legendary halo—" the mere offspring of the imagination "—gathering around His ordinary birth and death, it is time to cry " Hold !" [1]

For unless we are prepared to tear the New Testament to shreds, and pronounce it either a deliberately fraudulent concoction, or, at least, an utterly unreliable collection of writings, these verities constitute the unmistakable *sine quâ non* of Christianity.[2] A man would as soon continue to live and work after his vital organs have been removed, as Christ's Christianity remain after these have been subtracted. A surgeon might doubtless engage to relieve a patient of angina pectoris by " easily " [2]

---

[1] See Note A, p. 37.   [2] See Note B, p. 38.

removing his heart; but doctor and patient alike know well that after the operation there would be left not a healthy man, but a corpse.

Even so, if the Incarnation, as brought about by the miraculous conception, be but myth, it is absolutely certain that there is no Christian salvation for men through the merely human son of an adulteress.[1] If the Resurrection be, after all, only subjective hallucination or hysterical imagining, it is the chief Christian apostle who reiterates that our "faith is vain." If there be nothing at all miraculous, *i.e.* beyond the scope of natural evolution, in the life and works and death of Jesus Christ, then indeed, *cadit quæstio*, there is left no Christianity to discuss. It is certainly true that "if the wonders related of Him are to be reduced to exaggeration, misconception, natural occurrences falsely attributed to supernatural causes, we must say that the mistake which the Church has made was made in His own lifetime, and was shared by Himself."[2]

Hence there is to be found no real help whatever towards the solution of Christian difficulties in what is often called—but really miscalled—"naturalising," unless it be also considered helpful to a man's thinking powers to remove his head. Such a proceeding would assuredly be very unnatural. But it is no less so to seek to help the Christian faith by destroying the very vitals of Christianity.[3]

No unbiassed reader of the New Testament[4] can for a

---

[1] See Note C, p. 39.
[2] Dr. Salmon's *Non-Miraculous Christianity*, p. 8.
[3] See Note D, p. 41.   [4] See Note E, p. 42.

moment doubt that its general conception of Christ and His work, includes all these elements usually classed as supernatural and miraculous, but now regarded by some as mere traditional superfluities.[1]

Unless modern *a priori* prejudice or hypercriticism be allowed to eviscerate the New Testament, as we at present possess it, the words of one able writer on these themes are thoroughly warranted—

"If we are to get rid of miracles, we must get rid of the Incarnation, the Resurrection, the Ascension, in fact of the whole Christian system altogether. Christianity is interpenetrated with miracle, and miracle is indissolubly bound up with Christianity. Miracle as an evidence may have retired into the background, now that its place has been so amply supplied by other proofs. Miracle as a fact cannot be so dispensed with. Without the doctrine of a supernatural order, capable of modifying the action of things visible at its will, Christianity must cease to exist. It is inseparably connected with the history of one who "did many mighty works, for God was with Him," and who was "declared to be the Son of God with power by the resurrection from the dead."[2]

The real question is, to-day, practically the same as that which Paul put to Agrippa: "Why is it judged incredible with you, if God doth raise the dead?"[3] Why should we shrink from accepting as true the miracle-involving accounts of Christ and His redemptive work, because of the "burdens of difficulty" with which modern scientific thought invests them? A valid answer is to be found in the following paradox. If, because it postulates the supernatural, Christianity be regarded as incredible, it is demonstrably yet more incredible without the supernatural. *The facts being as*

---

[1] See Note F, p. 43. [2] Dr. Lias, *Are Miracles Credible?* p. 258.
[3] Acts xxvi. 8.

they are, the gospel of the New Testament without miracles is shown to be immeasurably more miraculous than with them. And unbelief can only substantiate its objections to the Christian miracles, by calling into the field greater and grosser miracles of its own.

Now the more detailed be the unfolding of this paradox, the more will it be found to rest upon undeniable facts and rational inferences. In the following chapters, however, we can do little more than make a succinct summary, leaving the reader to follow out, in each section, the lines of thought suggested.

The Bible in general (and the Christian religion in particular) regards humanity as existing in several realms. These correspond alike with our simplest consciousness and our highest instincts. Physical, intellectual, moral, and spiritual elements enter into our inmost being, and constitute our daily environment. In each of these realms, therefore, we now proceed to show how the temper which rejects Christian faith on account of its difficulties, is driven by that very rejection to accept far greater difficulties. In other words, it is compelled to "swallow the camel" in its determination to get rid of "the gnat."

One assumption, and one only, must be made. *For every event there must be an adequate cause.* Such a postulate no man of reason will refuse. The only question that can arise concerning it, is as to what constitutes adequacy. For sane humanity, however, it may surely be asserted that that cause is in each case adequate which explains the fact, or the event, most easily and most thoroughly. The easiness ever makes

STATEMENT OF THE CASE 37

itself manifest when the alleged explanation agrees with rather than contradicts the working of those reasoning faculties which necessarily constitute our final guides. All this is plainly involved in Christ's own question above quoted (Luke xii. 57).

Upon such fair principles of reason, then, the position of modern unbelief is well and truly illustrated by the story of the man who is said to have been troubled by the presence of several large mounds of earth in his garden, and not a little perplexed as to how to rid himself of them, when a friend suggested that he should dig a large hole and bury them. However deep and laboriously made be the diggings for the interment of those foundation facts of Christianity which connote the miraculous, there always and inevitably results an outstanding heap of natural difficulties which, both in weight and bulk, are far harder to deal with. In removing the Christian mole-hill, there is of necessity created an Agnostic mountain.

NOTES

A. Perhaps no fairer or more typical form of this assumption, that it is easier to believe in Christ without miracles, can be found, than in the words of the amiable and erudite author of *Philochristus* and *Onesimus*. Thus in *The Kernel and the Husk* we find him describing himself as "one who has for many years found peace and salvation in the worship of a non-miraculous Christ." He cannot, however, be unaware of the fact that such an avowal contributes no more to the settlement of the actual question, than the analogous assertion of the Methodist, or Romanist, or Swedenborgian, each of whom has "found peace and salvation" in a miraculous or hyper-miraculous gospel.

When, however, he adds, that "we all feel that we understand astronomy better in the light of the law of gravitation ; and in the same way some may feel that Christianity becomes more spiritual, as well as more clear, when it becomes more natural,"—he rightly expresses the main principle upon which the present inquiry is conducted. The very essence of the thesis of the following pages is that miraculous Christianity is demonstrably far more natural than non-miraculous. Indeed, that which it especially aims at establishing, could scarcely be better stated than in Dr. Abbott's own words, "that many of Christianity's so-called difficulties fade or vanish, when what may be called its celestial and its terrestrial phenomena are found to rest upon similar principles."

B. The modern cultured and plausible method of statement is well exemplified in *The Kernel and the Husk* (p. 3): "Christ will remain for us a necessary object of worship, even if we detach the miracles from the Gospels. Now I cannot do this without showing that the miraculous accounts stand on a lower level than the rest of the Gospel narrative, and that they may have been easily introduced into the Gospels without any sufficient basis of fact, and yet without any intention to deceive, so that the discrediting of the miracles will not discredit their non-miraculous context."

But this is none the less a real for being a quiet begging of the main question. It is, of course, impossible here to digress into a detailed scrutiny of the textual worth of the miracle-containing narratives. Besides which, the argument of these pages is addressed not so much to selected scholars as to all persons of ordinary intelligence. Two notes, however, may appropriately be made. (1) As to the "easily" in the above quotation, the thoughtful reader of the English New Testament is in a position to examine and judge for himself. Of course if the miraculous element be the deadly delusion which is here assumed, every shred of it must be as thoroughly removed as every particle of cancer by the surgeon's knife. Let this be faithfully done. The residue will speak for itself as to the easiness of the operation.

Moreover, (2) the general assertion cannot possibly be passed without challenge. The assumption, indeed, made here and elsewhere, that modern Biblical scholarship, especially in the form of textual criticism, tends to give us two distinct strata of Gospel narrative, one wholly non-miraculous, sound, firm, and on a "high level"; and another miraculous, "on a lower level" and unreliable, is directly contrary to the facts of the case.

No doubt there have been critics ever since Schleiermacher's *Critical Essay on the Gospel of Luke*, in 1821, who would more or less approve such a general statement—especially the Tübingen school of "destructive" criticism represented, about the middle of the century, by Baur, Schwegler, and Zeller. But "in the heart of the Tübingen school there soon arose a series of divergences, corrections, and even retractations." It was opposed by Bleek, Meyer, Reuss, Keim, etc., and has now virtually ceased to be. [*Vide* note on p. 363.]

C. It is, of course, easy to assert, as was recently done by the editor of a well-known religious journal, that such a statement as this involves a *circulus in probando*. "It first supposes the birth stories denied, and then goes to them for the suggestion of an adulteress." The matter is not, however, quite so easily disposed of. This nebulous phrase "the birth stories," needs to be carefully defined and considered. It is in vain to refer to a "triple tradition," and to assume that whatever is beyond this—that is, whatever is outside the mechanical consensus of the Synoptics—is to be rejected. For such an assumption is critically preposterous. There is no sufficient textual reason whatever for the rejection, as unhistorical, of all mention of the relations between Joseph and Mary. Nothing that has been written concerning the "growth of the Gospels" (*vid. Kernel and Husk*, p. 170) has amounted to either critical or rational proof that these pre-infancy narratives are to be dismissed as on a "lower level" of credibility than the matters included in the "triple tradition." Dr. Salmon is entirely warranted, on the contrary, when he protests (*Non-Miraculous Christianity*, p. 11): "It would be clearly irrational if we were to imagine that—even if we could absolutely settle the words common to the three synoptic Gospels—criticism had then finished its work, and that we might jump to the conclusion that in these common words, and these alone, we had the original document. Such a process involves the assumption (the unreasonableness of which is seen the moment it is put into words), that on the supposition that such a document existed, and that it was made use of by three subsequent compilers, each of these compilers was bound to incorporate every particular of it in his work, so that an omission by any one of them condemns the part left out as no portion of the original Gospel."

Whilst, therefore, the statement that Joseph came "into Judea, to the city of David, which is called Bethlehem, because he was of the house and lineage of David: to enrol himself with Mary who was betrothed to him, being great with child" (Luke ii. 4, 5), remains firm on the same textual grounds as avail to establish the non-miraculous narratives, the dilemma naturally and inevitably arises, however much the advocates of neo-Christianity may shrink from it, that either Mary's conception was miraculous, or Jesus was born of adultery. There is no literary or rational or critical warrant whatever for dismissing certain portions of a homogeneous narrative on the ground of *a priori* prejudice against the supernatural.

It is true that the author of *The Kernel and the Husk* (p. 71) affirms: "I may with the author of the Fourth Gospel heartily believe in the supernatural incarnation while omitting from my gospel all mention of the miraculous conception." But such an assertion merits double reply.

(1) Here is an insinuation which is not warranted. "With the author of the Fourth Gospel." The half truth here—which is ever "a harder matter to fight"—is that in our Fourth Gospel the miraculous conception is not mentioned. That may pass for what it is worth. It is certainly not valid proof that John either denied or ignored the supernatural birth of Christ. *A priori*, everything throughout his record would seem to point to the contrary. And inasmuch as it is now generally conceded that John was acquainted with the Synoptics, even if he had them not definitely before him, so that his task was confessedly supplementary, it is quite as legitimate to suggest that the reason of his silence was that the remarkable event was already sufficiently recorded in the Christian writings and established amongst Christian Churches. Certainly it requires no little pre-determination of mind to warrant the assumption that the silence of John is sufficiently clear to utterly contradict and make void the deliberate record of an earlier writer, who specially affirms (Luke i. 3) that he had "traced the course of all things accurately from the first." That is, as Dr. Plummer well puts it, "he has begun at the beginning, and has investigated everything" (Int. Crit. Comm. *in loc.*). Nor would it be unwarrantable straining if, under all the circumstances, we discovered in the Gospel of John itself a definite pointer to Christ's supernatural origin when we read (John vi. 38), "I am come down from heaven, not to do Mine own will, but the will of Him that sent Me." The writer of the above extract, therefore, it is submitted, has no right to claim confirmation from the Gospel of John. One might as well affirm that Mark's abrupt beginning or comparative brevity, is proof that he denied or ignored all that is found in the other Synoptics beyond his own narrative.

STATEMENT OF THE CASE 41

(2) The actual matter in hand is whether the supernatural Incarnation which is conceded, really requires the miraculous conception to make it valid. The fact that this author asserts his hearty belief in the separableness of these two, is just a testimony to his own conviction, and nothing more. Those who would see how much can be thoughtfully affirmed in the other direction, will do well to study the statement of Mr. Griffith Jones in his *Ascent through Christ*, p. 263 ff.; and Dr. Wace's Third Lecture in his *Gospel and its Witnesses*.

Meanwhile, the double assertion holds good, that it is unscientific to object to the virgin birth as impossible, and therefore incredible ; and it is uncritical or hypercritical to stigmatise the "birth stories" of Matthew and Luke as unreliable, because a few leading critics decline, on *a priori* grounds, to receive in their case such evidence as avails for all other portions of the same narrative.

D. It is true that there is a small, perhaps a growing class of Christian thinkers, even amongst the "Evangelical" Churches, who are increasingly disposed to deny that the vital part of Christianity is the miraculous. The following excerpts are typical of this temper : " We have come through the growth of science and the scientific method, through the growth of criticism and the historical spirit, to a climate of opinion in which miracles are becoming an increasing burden to faith." "Christianity without miracles may be Christianity still." " The real truth is that the miraculous birth stories have nothing to do with the doctrine of the Incarnation, the miraculous physical resurrection has nothing to do with the doctrine of the risen Christ, and the miraculous ascension has nothing to do with the doctrine of the living and reigning Christ." (Cf. *Christian World*, July 1898.)

It does not come within the scope of these pages to enter upon such a definite and elaborate refutation of these statements as the manifest sincerity and ability of the writers would seem to merit. The reasoned reply, for instance, to *The Kernel and the Husk*, would have to be a volume of at least equal size. But thoughtful inquirers will find answers in abundance on the part of modern Christian scholarship. Especial reference may be made to Dr. Fairbairn's *Christ in Modern Theology*, Griffith Jones' *The Ascent through Christ*, Row's *Supernatural in the New Testament*, Wainwright's *Question of Questions*, and portions of *Lux Mundi*. Other works are mentioned in the Appendix. Meanwhile the statement of Strauss (*Leben Jesu*, 1864, p. 18), that "if the Gospels in general be admitted as historical records, it is impossible to eliminate miracle from the life of Jesus," remains unshaken as against that of Dr. Abbott. Dr. Salmon fairly represents the vast consensus of the Christian scholarship of to-day when he affirms that "in sum then, a non-miraculous Christianity is as much a contradiction in terms as a quadrangular circle. When you have taken away the supernatural, what is left behind is not Christianity. It is not the religion which the apostles preached, it is not that into which the early converts were baptized, it is not that for which the martyrs gave their lives." Whence it is not too much to avow that the attempts to "save" the Incarnation by rejecting the miraculous birth, to keep the risen Christ by denying the "physical" Resurrection, to confirm the reigning Christ by casting scorn upon the Ascension, are all alike worse than wasted economy.

E. No slight, of course, is here for a moment intended upon either the honesty or the erudition of those who, with the author of *The Kernel and the Husk*, lay claim to a superior reading of the New Testament in their discovery that the "miracle portions" may be safely omitted, so far as Christianity is concerned, and ought to be deleted on critical grounds. But the wish is manifestly father to the thought. And the wish, as we have seen, is derived from the desire to smooth the path of faith by removing the assumed stumbling-block of the supernatural. The truth is, however, and it cannot be too often or too emphatically reiterated, that it has yet to be shown that through "the growth of the scientific spirit, or the historical method," it is necessary to jettison the miraculous element in the New Testament in order to save Christianity from shipwreck. To assume that is simply to beg the whole question at issue.

On p. 12 of *The Kernel and the Husk* the author remarks: "I was amazed to find that little or nothing had been done by English scholars to compare the different styles, and analyse the narratives into their component parts." But what, we may ask,—even if this somewhat sweeping statement be allowed to pass,—is the special value of the "English" here specified? Surely analyses enough have been attempted by the Tübingen school and its followers on the Continent. If these all had demonstrated an exclusive "triple tradition" beyond reach of controversy, would not that demonstration also avail on this side the Channel? "After some years of work," continues the same author, "I found myself gradually led to the conclusion that the miraculous element in the Gospels was not historical." This was confessedly a personal discovery, undoubtedly subjective and sincere, but very far indeed from being a demonstration for others. Indeed there was nothing in it either new or final. The esteemed author may lay claim with all honesty to " a belief that has been fifteen years in making, and for ten years more has been reviewed, criticised, and finally retained as being historically true and spiritually reliable." But he must not forget that precisely the same asseveration has been made concerning their convictions by numbers of Romanists, Ritualists, Secularists, and others, including assuredly scholars, English as well as foreign, who are reasonably "orthodox," and whose researches have been equally thorough and equally prolonged.

F. "Supernatural and miraculous." Nothing is gained for neo-Christianity by endeavouring to set up an arbitrary distinction between these two, and so make them mutually exclusive. As when the author of *The Kernel and the Husk* asserts, " Nor does the belief in the supernatural in the least imply a belief in the miraculous also. Supernatural is the name given to the existence of God and to His creation and continuous development of all things; the Divine action being regarded not as contrary to nature but as above nature, not as suspending the sequences of nature but as originating and supporting them." The sense here attached to the term "supernatural" is somewhat unique. "The Divine creation and continuous development of all things," as known to us by observation and experience, are much rather the expression of the natural than the supernatural. Moreover, no Christian thinker to-day, meriting attention, regards the supernatural or the miraculous as being " contrary " to nature.

In another place (p. 71) the same author assumes that a miracle means that "the observed sequence of what we call cause and effect in the material world has been violated." But in his definitions we find that "miracle means a supposed suspension of a sequence or law of nature." Now it must be pointed out that these two terms are not synonymous. A suspension is not a violation. No event, therefore, can be both at once. Meanwhile we are told that " Marvel, or mighty work, means a rare sequence of nature in which great effects are produced by causes seemingly but not really inadequate." Also that the Divine action in the supernatural is to be regarded "not as suspending the sequences of nature, but as originating and supporting them." Now with the utmost respect for the sincerity and erudition of the author, it is difficult to understand how a trained mind can satisfy itself with such a general attitude as this.

(1) Are we to understand that there is an essential distinction in the New Testament records between "miracles" and "mighty works," the latter being possible though rare, but the former impossible and incredible? Certainly as Christ Himself used the terms, and in the ten other occurrences of them, there is no hint whatever at any such distinction. Nor is there any reason, critical or scientific, for suggesting this differentiation. It is a distinction without a difference. But when, as in the New Testament, miracles and mighty works are put upon the same level, they may truly be said to be "produced by causes seemingly but not really inadequate," so long as it is definitely understood that the real adequacy in the case is, as the Gospels everywhere suggest, the definite will and supernatural power of Christ Himself. The author of *Ecce Homo* did not put it too strongly when he wrote, "The fact that Christ appeared as a worker of miracles is the best attested fact in his whole biography, both by the absolute unanimity of all the witnesses, by the confirmatory circumstances just mentioned, and by countless other special confirmations of circumstances not likely to be invented, striking sayings inseparably connected with them, etc., in particular cases" (12th ed. p. ix).

(2) Neither in regard to miracles nor mighty works is there any reason to speak of them as "violations" of cause and effect in nature, for that would be assuming a scientific knowledge that we do not possess. It is indeed too much, as one of our ablest physicists has recently affirmed, to assume that we comprehend the dynamics of the simplest push. Nor is it at all necessary to affirm that miracles must be "violations of observed sequences." It is quite sufficient that they should be regarded as suspensions or overrulings of such sequences. Even if we assume that there is a natural, radical, necessary nexus between cause and effect, it is not in any such case violated, because it may be exercising its natural force all the time, as gravitation is when, in spite of it, we lift a heavy body from the ground. Moreover, (i.) we are constantly suspending such sequences ourselves, by virtue of our own knowledge and will, for sufficient reasons. (ii.) It is preposterous to assume that our little knowledge of the phenomena and noumena of nature warrants us in asserting that there can be no suspensions of sequence beyond our own experience.

(3) For aught science can say to the contrary, there is nothing

more incredible in a miracle than in an ordinary occurrence, granted the Divine intention and power. Both are alike the natural result of supernatural energy. The difference between them is merely a matter of degree. The supernatural miracle is but a higher or more vivid manifestation of that Divine energy which ever permeates the "creation and continuous development of all things," and makes possible our natural ordinary life.

(4) But the whole Gospel record assumes this Divine power and affirms this Divine intention. The mission of Jesus Christ is to reveal the holy love of an infinite and omnipotent Father, with the direct purpose of redeeming men from moral evil and its consequences, and bringing to pass an immeasurable spiritual evolution of human nature. The miraculous element, therefore, in the gospel, whatever be its quantity or quality, is neither more nor less than the manifestation of the supernatural in the greater degree necessary for the carrying out of the special design of redemption, just as the ordinary sequences of nature manifest the supernatural in the lesser degree necessary for the physical life and well-being of humanity.

And unless we are prepared to dismiss as unreliable the whole testimony of the Fourth Gospel, it is impossible to mistake the reference in Christ's own words: "If I do not the works of My Father, believe Me not. But if I do them, though ye believe not Me, believe the works." Nor, again, can we misapprehend the meaning of the writer's comment: "But though He had done so many signs before them, yet they believed not on Him."

The whole case is clearly and truly summarised in the words of Professor A. S. Wilkins (*The Light of the World*, 2nd ed. p. ix), written thirty years since: "The instances of the suspension of the laws of nature supposed to be involved in the Catholic doctrine of the Incarnation, are presenting very serious stumbling-blocks in the way of many earnest seekers for the truth. The rejection of this belief, the very sheet-anchor of hope for the Church of the world, involves the hypothesis of a no less miraculous suspension of the laws that rule in the world of mind. If the need of an adequate cause for the appearance of a phenomenon be held to exist as fully for the spiritual as for the material, then it is no longer a question of Faith or Reason which divides the Christian and the unbeliever. It is a question whether the canons of a rigid induction shall or shall not be followed for mind as well as for matter; whether we will test all truth, or only the lower and less important, by a strictly scientific method."

GARDNER'S *EXPLORATIO EVANGELICA*

THE general attitude of *The Kernel and the Husk*, quoted above, is also that of Dr. Gardner's recently published *Exploratio Evangelica*. It is impossible to study this work without admiring the tone of reverence, courtesy, and culture which pervades it. And yet one lays it down with a sigh of mingled wonder and lament. For the whole procedure adopted is precisely analogous to what might have happened a few years since in that Samoan Bay, when the *Calliope*, by means of reliable engines, fought its way through the fearful hurricane, if in the midst of the struggle some of the officers had suggested that in order to save the ship they should break up the engines and throw them overboard.

The remark of the author in regard to Mr. Gore's defence of the Virgin birth, applies generally to himself also—"All critics are at one in acknowledging the candour and sincerity of the writer, but a good deal of his argument admits of complete reply."

In his concluding summary (p. 519) we are told that "the way of regarding religion which is wholly inconsistent with the views of this book, is what I have called the way of absolute religion, the view that Christianity was sent into the world fully equipped and complete, supported by a series of miracles, and not to be approached by the ordinary principles of reason which we apply to other practical affairs of life." Upon which it seems necessary to remark, that the way of regarding religion which may be called reasonable orthodoxy, certainly does not (1) necessitate any cast-iron conception of absolute religion; nor does it (2) assume that Christianity was sent into the world "fully equipped and complete"; nor, *a fortiori*, (3) does it plead that Christianity should not be approached by ordinary principles of reason. The main purpose of these pages, at all events, is to urge that these principles should be applied alike to the whole kosmos, to human nature, and to Christian foundations. What has most to be borne in mind, as J. S. Mill long ago made clear, is that, whatever refinements of conception modern thought may introduce, God and miracle stand or fall together. To affirm (p. 262) that "the materialist circumstances of the tale of the Resurrection are now an impediment rather than a help to faith," is to confuse accident with essence in a cloud of ambiguity. The question upon which depends the validity of Christian faith, is, when the "materialist circumstances" are subtracted from the "tale of the Resurrection," what is left? How the disciples came to believe, is for us secondary to the crucial inquiry, Was what they believed true? In a word, does the Gospel rest on fact or fancy? Did Jesus rise from the dead, or not? If He did, the Christian faith is well grounded, and miracle is beyond dispute. If, now, we know that He did not, Christianity is a delusion, and nothing in science, or in history, or in "experience" can rehabilitate it.

IV

THE REALM OF PHYSICAL SCIENCE

"These discoveries effectually destroy the idea of an external self-existent matter, by giving to each of its atoms at once the essential characteristics of a manufactured article and a subordinate agent.—When we see a great number of things precisely alike, we do not believe the similarity to have originated except from a common principle independent of them."—Sir John Herschell—Address to Royal Society.

"There is in every earnest thinker a craving after a final cause, and this craving can no more be extinguished than our belief in objective reality. Our belief in what we call the evidence of our senses is less strong than our faith that in the orderly sequence of events there is a meaning which our minds could fathom were they only vast enough."—Fiske, *Outlines of Cosmic Philosophy*, p. 138.

"But as the universe in which we find ourselves is constituted, the proof of Design, which is furnished by the characteristics of beauty and sublimity that are apparent in it, is not derived from phenomena few in number or requiring to be sought out by ingenuity. Many of those who are most bitterly opposed to the doctrine to which the existence of these characteristics appears to point, nevertheless vie with those who hold it, in admiration of the startling confusion of splendour with which nature abounds."—J. H. Kennedy, *Natural Theology and Modern Thought*, p. 193.

"The Darwinian theory, properly understood, replaces as much teleology as it destroys."—J. Fiske, *Man's Destiny*, p. 109.

"The scientific conception, more or less clearly developed, is that we live in a physical universe of which the moral world forms a part. The Hebrew and Christian conception is that we live in a moral universe of which the physical world forms a part."—Dr. Wace, *Boyle Lectures* 1874, p. 302.

IV

THE REALM OF PHYSICAL SCIENCE

WE are linked, as men and women, by what is generally deemed the lower part of our nature, to all the world about us. Not only do we find ourselves definitely related to all other forms of animal life, but also and unmistakably to our whole physical environment. Our bodies are built up of the very same elements as are found in the air we breathe and the ground on which we tread. We thus form part of that whole "kosmos" which, from time immemorial, has challenged the thought of mankind to explain its origin.

Now we do not find in the Gospels that Christ made any definite attempt to inculcate and demonstrate Theism; nor does the rest of the New Testament. But the revelation of the Divine Fatherhood therein contained, manifestly postulates the most definite Theism conceivable. The consequent doctrine of Christianity is that there is one God, personal and almighty, the Creator of all things, the great Final Cause of the whole universe, no less than of this tiny fraction of it which we call our Earth. For all who do justice to its enormity, this conception is confessedly overwhelming. It is only natural that we should be baffled in every attempt we make to realise it. To that extent it may be acknowledged that Christian faith is difficult. Before, however, we reject Christianity for such a reason, it is well to ask first what we should have to face from the standpoint of Atheism or Agnosticism.

Starting, then, with the one axiom, that for every event there must be an adequate cause, it is undeniable that each day of our lives we are in contact with order, law, adaptation, harmony, correlation, beauty, in nature all around us, as well as in our own constitution. This is simple fact. As such it must be accounted for adequately. If we could take some one of these just named, and do justice to it by means of detailed illustration, as is done, say, in Sir Charles Bell's treatise on the Hand, or Helmholtz' lectures on the Eye, or Sir G. Stokes' Burnett Lectures on Light, it would doubtless make the realities of the case more impressive, and our apprehension of them correspondingly more vivid. It would indeed be great gain, if all modern doubters could be induced even to give Paley's *Natural Theology*[1] a thorough perusal. For amongst the floating fallacies of to-day, none is more delusive than the common notion, so eagerly fostered in some quarters, that such treatises as these are too antiquated to be of any value. How unjustified is the suggestion, may be left to the common sense of every careful reader. The facts pointed out by the writers above named remain facts, in whatever way we account for them. It is not too much to say that in the fair and full contemplation of either the human eye or hand, there will always be marvel enough to put to

[1] The last edition as edited by Professor Le Gros Clark.

confusion all Atheistic or anti-Theistic theories of the Universe.

If, for instance, a child should ask the modern physiologist how the human eye comes to grow at all, so as to appear duly in each newborn babe, there is absolutely no answer save that of Tennyson, " Behold we know not anything." And if the child should insist that God caused it so to do, it is utterly beyond the power of all modern science to contradict. Agnosticism, we know, professes to neither affirm nor deny. But this is one of those cases in which mental neutrality is impossible ; that is, if we desire to be rational. If we do not know that two and two make four, we do know that mathematics are not to be relied upon. The universe must either have involved mind in its origin or not. Any mean between these two extremes is unthinkable. The terms being mutually exclusive, to decline to affirm the one is virtually to affirm the other. Cultured scepticism may, indeed, avow that the Christian doctrine of God is but a hypothesis. Yet it is at least a sufficient hypothesis. Whether the kosmos results from specific creation or slow evolution, makes here no difference whatever, save as Darwin said, to impart in the latter case the grandeur of simplicity.

Now if, when every human babe was born, the eyes should be found accompanying in a separate membranous bag, which it would remain for parents to place *in situ*, that would be in itself wonderful enough, when the histological structure of the eye is taken into account. Besides which, all sorts of preadaptations and correlations, bony, nervous, and muscular, would manifestly be necessary in order that perfect vision should result. They could not conceivably be placed in the proper position without care proceeding from mind. How then, as daily recurring facts, do they come to be normally placed in the fœtus *in utero*?[1] Furthermore, whatever be our relation to other seeing mammals, we must not, for honesty's sake, blind ourselves to the marvellousness of the organ of sight as human beings now actually possess it. For assuming the eyeball to be rightly situated in the bony socket—*i.e.* with the cornea turned outwards rather than inwards, etc. etc.—what of the rest? Not only must the optic nerve be duly attached and proceed to the brain, but each eye must be provided with two delicate and exactly correlated lenses, two distinct kinds of intervening transparent media, six muscles (including a pulley passing through a socket so as to reverse the direction of the pull of two of them), ten distinct nerve layers co-ordinating with delicate fibrillæ of the optic nerve to receive and appreciate and transfer multitudinous infinitesimal impressions from the ether, together with an automatic curtain for regulating the amount of light permitted to enter (this the best modern

---

[1] Or take another example: "A most apposite comment upon the cogency of the argument suggested here, is supplied by the experience, happily rare, known to medical men as ectopic gestation. Here the ovum is diverted from its suited and preparing home; it develops up to a certain lamentable degree in its abnormal position an exile from its home, until a fatal result to mother and ovum is seldom averted, and then only by the exhibition of surgical skill brilliant among many brilliant triumphs; which is a sad but apt comment upon the interruption of design on the one hand and on the other upon the power of mind, albeit a human mind."—Dr. Walter Kidd, F.Z.S., *Journal Vict. Inst.*, No. 123, p. 201.

optical instruments have now roughly copied), and the whole enclosed in a stout protecting membrane. All this apparatus, however, goes but a little way towards explaining the mystery of sight. How, for instance, in order to the appreciation of the colour of a violet, waves of the ether must pass through the delicate lenses, without injuring them, and impinge upon the retina behind at the rate of more than eight hundred millions of millions per second![1] We have to think of this marvellous structure as being exactly duplicated for every one of all the millions upon millions who have lived, or still live, on this earth—for the exceptions in the case of the blind are so few comparatively as not to merit special notice here.[2] Then it must also be borne in mind that this whole organ of sense is but a small fragment of the marvel even of human physiology alone. In fact, examine nature where we will, take the first specimen of either animal or vegetable life that comes to hand, and we find similar wonderfulness of structure, in ever varying degrees of complexity proportioned to the grade in the scale of being. Only by

[1] It is small wonder that our greatest physicists should express themselves strongly in face of this mystery belonging to the borderland between physics and physiology. Thus Sir G. G. Stokes, speaking upon the perception of colour, says, "The subject leads us to some interesting contemplations, and one thing I think we cannot fail to be strongly impressed with, namely, the astonishing complexity of this marvellous organ, the eye, and the wonderful proof which (to my own mind at least) it gives of design in its construction."—*Journal Vict. Inst.*, No. 124, p. 264.

[2] Such exceptions belong more to the realm of theology than that of scientific apologetics, inasmuch as they relate to the character rather than the existence of a Supreme Being.

repeated efforts of careful scrutiny in every direction, can we at last form even a faint idea of all that is involved in our physical constitution and environment.

Now this immense and complex whole must in some way be accounted for. The would-be simple nescience of pure Agnosticism is mere childish fatuity, for it amounts to the sacrifice of reason, *i.e.* to the abnegation of manhood. Unable we may be to comprehend the whole, or even to apprehend it, when taken *en masse*; but we can intelligently and fairly estimate any portion of it and assure ourselves, whilst reason remains to us, that for every detail, as well as for the immeasurable totality with all its complicated correlations, there must have been and must be some adequate cause.

The modern magic word is Evolution. To utter this, however, is to say nothing, until we know whether Theistic or Atheistic Evolution is intended. The former may be regarded as both intelligible and sufficient.[1] In its simplicity as a theory of the universe we might well find its true formula in the opening words of Genesis: " In the beginning, GOD "— If, however, by reason of the alleged difficulties of Theism—which need not here be enumerated—this formula be rejected, the only rational course is to turn to the latter, and see whether or no it presents us with fewer or lesser difficulties.

Now in this case it is manifest at the very outset that all things must have caused themselves to be as

---

[1] Dr. Iverach has good reason for saying that "the Christian view of the world is the only view which does justice to all the factors of evolution, and recognises all its complexity" (*Christianity and Evolution*, p. 231).

THE REALM OF PHYSICAL SCIENCE

they are, for no cause outside themselves is alleged or allowed. Then, for such a process, both material and method are to seek. The only conclusion logically possible is that ultimately the material was nothing, and the method was chance. But truly, if chance working upon nothing has produced this universe, including ourselves, such a stupendous and absolute violation of all we know to be natural and rational has been accomplished, that all the difficulties of Theism and all the miracles of Christianity together, are literally as nothing compared with it.

But we shall do well to examine the case a little more in detail. "Evolution" really signifies mere unfolding. That is, the gradual manifestation, through development, of a pre-existing potentiality. Evolution is the process whereby that is brought out which already was latent in the matter whereof the world, or the universe, was composed. For it is certain that gradual growth, *per se*, could never evoke, in a whole eternity, anything out of either a germ or a molten globe, which was not previously and totally contained in the same. Thus Evolution always and necessarily assumes Involution, and the question of questions ever is to account for the latter, if the former is to be made even thinkable.[1]

---

[1] An instructive illustration of this may be pointed out in the words of the great modern exponent of Evolution. "If," says Mr. Herbert Spencer (*Synthetic Philosophy*, sec. 118, p. 109), "a single cell, *under appropriate conditions*, becomes a man in the space of a few years, there can surely be no difficulty *in understanding* how, *under appropriate conditions*, a cell may in the course of untold millions of years give origin to the human race." Now, apart from the entirely false assumption that any biologist "understands" the development of the fœtus *in utero*—even the mind of a child can

Now Christian thinkers have every reason for accepting Evolution as the general method of world growth, even as far as its culmination in humanity. For, besides the supreme regard for truth which the Christian law enforces, making compulsory the acceptance of demonstrated cause for manifest fact, there is absolutely nothing contrary to the highest Theism in Evolution as a working principle.[1] Dr. Lyman Abbott has well said [2]—" Does this doctrine of creation by evolution take God away from the world? It seems to me that it brings Him a great deal nearer. There is no chasm of six thousand years between the Evolutionist and his Creator. The evolutionist lives in the creative days, and sees the creative processes taking place before him."

When, however, what has been flippantly termed the " God hypothesis " is rejected, all explanation of Evolution by means of a sufficient preceding Involution is, of course, precluded. Here then we have to contemplate, not only a pyramid poised upon its apex, but the apex itself resting upon nothing. To make light of this, and then profess to find staggering difficulties in the Bible, is truly to vault over a mountain and fall headlong over a straw. appreciate such verbal jugglery as this. Given a wound reel of cotton, how easy it is to unwind it! But is it so easy if the ready-to-be-unwound reel be *not* given? Whence come the "appropriate conditions" through which alone the cell becomes a man? That is the question for a genuine thinker to face and answer.

[1] For a thorough statement of this the reader may well be referred to Dr. Iverach's *Christianity and Evolution*, mentioned elsewhere, and to Prof. Le Conte's *Evolution and its Relation to Religious Thought*. So, too, the late Prof. Drummond, "Up to this time no word has been spoken to reconcile Christianity and Evolution, or Evolution with Christianity. And why? Because the two are one" (*Ascent of Man*, p. 438).

[2] *Theology of an Evolutionist*, pp. 29, 30.

Let us, for a typical example, take the case as set forth by one of the most popular and approved advocates of the Agnostic philosophy. In Mr. E. Clodd's *Story of Creation* and *Plain Account of Evolution* [1] we find the following :—

"Of the beginning, of what was before the present state of things, we know nothing, *and speculation about it is futile.*"

This is especially interesting and noteworthy in the light of what immediately follows :—

"But since everything points to the finite duration of the present universe, *we must make a start somewhere.* And we are therefore *compelled to posit* a primordial nebulous non-luminous state, when *the atoms with their inherent forces and energies* stood apart from one another. Not evenly distributed, else Force would have drawn them together as a uniform spherical mass round a common centre of gravity, and energy, *awakened by the collision of atom with atom,* would have passed *profitlessly* in the form of heat to the ethereal medium : but *varying in position and character* with *special* gravitation towards *special centres.* All changes of state are due to the *rearrangement* of atoms through the play of *attracting* forces and *repelling energies,* resulting in the evolution of the seeming like into the actual unlike, of the shapeless into the shapely, of the simple into the more and more complex, till the highest complexity is reached in the development of living matter."

Now it is certainly instructive to be told in one breath that "speculation is futile," and in the next that we are "compelled to posit" a primordial nebulosity. For what else is this than speculation pure and simple? It is, in truth, sheer assumption, moulded and fashioned entirely with a view to the hypothesis that follows. But we must be permitted to ask, plainly, is not this "primitive nebulosity" itself definitely and necessarily the effect of a preceding cause? And if we are "compelled to posit"

---

[1] Published by Longmans, p. 137 ff. The italics are the present writer's.

the effect, are we not in all reason equally "compelled to posit" the preceding cause of it?

A moment's glance, however, suffices to show that what this writer, like not a few others, here does, is simply, by the help of the "scientific imagination," to "posit," *i.e.* to assume, an Involution of exactly what he finds necessary in order to the subsequent Evolution of the earth and man.

But this whole case requires to be set forth in other and more perspicuous language. In actual truth what does it all mean? It is a tissue of assumptions, as unscientific in substance as preposterous in audacity. For this is what it really and inevitably involves. That in the beginning matter made itself. That is, nothing created something, out of nothing. That this self-created matter first appeared as a primitive nebulosity of such tenuity that several million cubic miles of it would scarcely weigh one grain.[1] That thus the atoms composing it were the nearest approach to nothing conceivable. That in the whole universe there was no other existence. That, somehow, these atoms, being all exactly alike,—for there was no reason at all why they should be different,—proceeded to make themselves in many cases entirely different from each other. So that, through no power at all outside themselves, they suddenly—for there must have been some moment of definite change—became as utterly distinct as we now know the atoms of Carbon, Hydrogen, Nitrogen, Oxygen, etc., to be. Then again, somehow, being next to nothing themselves, and having nothing

[1] The estimate of Professor Helmholtz.

THE REALM OF PHYSICAL SCIENCE

to work with, they endowed themselves with all those potentialities—"their inherent forces and energies"—out of which all the infinite possibilities of worlds to come should be evolved. Then further, through no power at all outside themselves, these self-differentiated atoms began to move. They were "not evenly distributed," *i.e.* they distributed themselves unevenly, and manifestly with a purpose, namely, so that "Force," which came from nowhere, might not draw them around one common centre—which was everywhere—and "energy awakened by collision of atom with atom"—which collision in every case "awakened" itself—might not be "profitlessly" lost to a universe in which there was nowhere any mind whatever to appreciate, or anticipate, either profit or loss. Then all following changes were due to the "rearrangement of atoms"—it being the special function of mindless chance to "arrange" things in profitable order [1]—through the play of "attracting forces and repelling energies" which came necessarily from nowhere, and, being absolutely unguided, worked anyhow and tended nowhither. Yet, through nothing whatever beyond these infinitesimal next-to-nothing atoms, worked upon by nothing save self-created, mindless, aimless forces, the unlike came out of the like, the shapely out of the shapeless, the useful out

---

[1] Thus Mr. H. Spencer says in his Preface to *Epitome of Synthetic Philosophy* (pp. viii, ix): "Throughout the universe, in general and detail, there is an unceasing redistribution of matter and motion. *This redistribution* constitutes evolution." Just so. But is "distribution" or "redistribution" thinkable without the assumption of a guiding mind? Could not any compositor who "set up" one of Mr. Spencer's works give a valid reply?

of the useless, and finally, by one bold stroke, the living out of the lifeless.

Marvellous, indeed, was this last transformation, for if modern science be sure of anything, it is that life can and does only spring from preceding life.[1] But see now

[1] The words of an expert merit attention here. Says Professor Lionel S. Beale, M.B., F.R.S., etc.: "Life is not a consequence of the organisation of matter, but the cause. Life precedes, instead of succeeding, organisation, conversion, formation" (*Life Theories and Religious Thought*, p. 83). Again, in regard to the "Nature of Life," the same authority, after a careful exposition of the subject, concludes as follows: "Having long thought over the evidence I have been able to obtain as regards the *Nature of Life* during the past forty years,—from the study of the actual *Living Matter, the Bioplasm*, its characters, arrangement, and its relation to tissue as existing during its life, and shortly after death, in the case of organisms of very different orders, in various conditions of vital activity, in health and disease, with the aid of very high magnifying powers (up to 5,000 linear),—I now feel it a duty to publicly advocate the doctrine of the constant operation in all life, throughout the whole living world, of *Vital Power—Power* as distinct from all forces, potencies, and properties belonging to or derived from any kind, or resulting from any physical or chemical state, of cosmic matter.

"I have failed to discover any facts which would tend to cause a thoughtful student of *Living Nature* to hesitate as to the existence of *Vitality*, and so far I have been unable to discover or frame any hypothesis which could be advanced as a reasonable explanation of the facts of any kind of living matter without admitting the influence of *Infinite Power, Prevision, and Wisdom.* All my efforts to obtain evidence which in reason could be regarded as adequate to account in some other way for the facts, have entirely failed. Looking from a purely scientific point of view only, it seems to me that the *cause* of all vital phenomena from the very beginning of *Life*—in the present state of our knowledge can only be referred to the direct influence of an *Almighty Power*, and I feel confident that each succeeding advance in natural knowledge will be found to be, in the words of the Victoria Institute motto, '*Ad Majorem Dei Gloriam.*'"

So, too, Professor E. Hull, LL.D., F.R.S.: "I say that it is impossible by any reasonable hypothesis to account for the origin of

THE REALM OF PHYSICAL SCIENCE 61

what happened in the good old times. Protoplasm,[1] Sir Henry Roscoe has shown, is really not a compound at all, but a structure, built up of many complex constituents, and taxing all the resources of the latest chemistry even to partly unravel it. But, formerly, chance working on the primordial nebulosity, made it quite easy. Thus, according to Mr. Clodd—

"*Given* the matter which composes it and the play of forces and energies of which that matter is the vehicle, wherein lies the difference which gives as one result non-living substance and as another result living substance? The answer *obviously* is that *the ingredients being the same, the difference must be in the mixing.*" (The italics are Mr. Clodd's.)

"Obviously!" In very deed. To say nothing of the unblushing assumption of the first word here, in "positing" exactly the materials and forces required, the "mixing" that utterly defies the whole mind power of modern science to explain or repeat, is the simple result of blind chance, working upon a primitive nebulosity of such tenuity that millions of cubic miles of it would be required to weigh one single grain!

life on the globe without calling in the interposition of an Almighty power." Again—"When we come to deal with organised beings, so vast is the distinction between dead matter and living, I feel that we are justified in inferring, not only the ordinary guidance, but also the frequent extraordinary interposition, of Omnipotent Power, from the creation of the first living cell to man himself. The difference between inert inorganic matter and a living organism, is as vast as space itself."

It were an easy matter to multiply such deliberate utterances on the part of men whose scientific qualifications are above question.

[1] Which thirty years ago was referred to by Professor Huxley as "The basis of physical life, *or* the physical basis of life"—as if these two were perfectly synonymous!

This, however, is but the beginning of miracles. Having manufactured Protoplasm, chance proceeded further, as well it might. Without any help *ab extra*, without mind or purpose, it took in hand to produce that wonderful complexity known to biology as the ultimate cell. Thence, through nothing, absolutely nothing, but the fortuitous concurrence of protoplasmic molecules, there gradually emerged those complex aggregations of cells which, in greater or less numbers, constitute the structure of all living bodies. These, again, differentiated themselves into vegetable and animal, and without any guidance at all, produced the sum-total of all known species of each on earth, in highest as well as lowest types. That is to say, from nothing but the mindless, senseless, aimless working of pure chance upon the primordial nebulosity—which made itself out of nothing, "since everything points to the finite duration of the present universe"—there have issued not only all the order and wonder, the adaptation and harmony, the beauty and the laws of nature, but also the philosophy of Socrates and Plato, the genius of Shakespeare and Goethe, the poetry of Dante and Tennyson, the philanthropy of Wilberforce and Howard, the devotion of Wesley and Whitefield, the politics of Bismarck and Gladstone, the theology of Dorner and Fairbairn, and even the subtleties of modern Agnosticism. All from nothing wrought upon by chance! Verily, in face of this miracle, which is absolutely necessary and inevitable upon the Agnostic hypothesis, Dr. Lionel Beale is abundantly warranted in his exclamation, "*O Miraculosa credulitas!*"[1]

[1] *Protoplasm*, p. 247.

To accept all this, after rejecting Christian faith on the ground of its difficulties, is indeed to swallow a camel after straining out a gnat. For whilst the Christian doctrine of an Infinite but personal God logically and completely accounts for all, its sole difficulty is that we cannot comprehend His nature, either by extending the personal as we know it, or compressing the infinite into compass of our knowledge. This difficulty is natural. It arises naturally and necessarily from the limitations of our faculties. God who could be comprehended by man, could not be the God of the universe.[1]

But the Atheistic, or what is here the same, the Agnostic theory of the origin of all, does not merely transcend, it flatly and emphatically contradicts our reason. We see that the most skilled writers cannot even state such a doctrine, without making assumptions which either beg the whole question at issue, or set at defiance all the observation and experience of sane humanity.[2] Hence when Mr. Clodd cries out against

[1] "Say that 'in the beginning God created the heaven and the earth'—and at least you have left your disciple an universe which does not shock his very elements of knowledge.—If the existence of a Divine First Cause be admitted, it is difficult to see what *a priori* objection can be against this view of the seed-plot of life of which this globe may perhaps be but a part.

"It is not less difficult to see what ascertained facts as to life and its manifestations forbid this view, harmonious at once with Revelation, Reason, and scientific knowledge."—Dr. Walter Kidd, F.Z.S., *Journal Vict. Inst.*, No. 123, p. 199.

[2] Lord Kelvin will be accepted by all competent judges as a physicist of greater weight than Mr. Clodd. His words in this connection are, therefore, worthy of regard. "Sir George Stokes spoke of design. Is it conceivable that the luminiferous ether should throw out these effects by chance—that the colours of the

the "unverifiable assumption of dogmatic theology," he both contradicts and confounds himself. The Agnosticism that "can only confess ignorance"[1] ought not, certainly, to pronounce anything "unverifiable." Whilst to a system of doctrine which can only exalt itself into a tenable theory by wholesale and indeed outrageous assumptions,[2] it is sufficient to reply, "Cast out first the beam out of thine own eye, and then shalt thou see clearly to cast out the mote" from the eye of Christian philosophy. The words of the great Newton, summing up his profound researches, come as a refreshing contrast. "From a blind metaphysical necessity, which of course is the same everywhere and always, no variety could originate. The whole diversity of created things in regard to places and times, could have its origin only in the ideas and the will of a necessarily existing Being."

We have dwelt thus definitely and at length upon the words of Mr. Clodd, because his volume is at once popular and typical of a great deal more which is being diffused through the English-speaking world, as the latest and most exact science. How little it really deserves the name is manifest.

But before we pass from the physical realm, it is

butterfly or of a beautiful flower should result from a fortuitous concourse of atoms, and having come by a fortuitous concourse of atoms, they should give pleasure, whatever that may mean, to another fortuitous concourse of atoms constituting myself, and I should—I do not know how to express it. The atheistic idea is so nonsensical that I do not see how I can put it in words."—*Journal Vict. Inst.*, No. 124, p. 267.

[1] *Story of Creation*, p. 152.
[2] See extract at commencement of chapter x., from Dr. Momerie's *Belief in God*.

THE REALM OF PHYSICAL SCIENCE

necessary to present at least a summary of the case as it stands in regard to three other distinct lines of thought. These are (1) the argument for the existence of God from nature's manifestations of intelligent design, (2) the unmistakable exhibition of beauty and sublimity throughout the known universe, and (3) the question as to the impossibility or incredibility of miracles.

(1) From time immemorial, long ages before Paley's *Natural Theology* was conceived, the human mind inferred the existence of an omnipotent Creator from the wonderfulness of the adaptations which men could not but mark on every hand, including those manifest in themselves. The 139th and other Psalms, together with such utterances as Job xl. and xli., etc., may be taken as sufficient illustrations of this. Paley's work served the purpose of summarising these general convictions of men in succinct and vivid form. The impression it produced was naturally great and widespread. Now, however, we are informed that all such notions are "out of date," that design in nature is but an "old-fashioned conceit," and that Paley is "antiquated," deserving only to be forgotten. The extent to which such assertions as these are made and accepted by great numbers of artisans and young people, is much more serious than Christian Churches in general apprehend. Nor is it to be wondered at when we remember that in every Free Library throughout the kingdom, the works of Spencer, Darwin, Tyndall, Huxley, Proctor, Clodd, Grant Allen, Romanes, etc., are not only obtainable, but are continually being read. Let us here take but one specimen. In his *Scientific Evidences of Organic*

Evolution [1] the late Professor Romanes wrote thus, concerning the origin of nature—

> "Two hypotheses and two only are in the field. Of these one is intelligent design manifested in creation. The other is natural selection manifested through countless ages of the past. Now it would be proof positive of intelligent design if it could be shown that all species of plants and animals were created, that is, suddenly introduced into the complex conditions of their life. For it is quite inconceivable that any cause other than intelligence could be competent to adapt an organism to its environment suddenly. Thus the whole question as between natural selection and supernatural design, resolves itself into this, were all species of plants and animals separately created, or were they slowly evolved? For if they were specially created, the evidence of supernatural design remains unrefuted and irrefutable. Whereas, if they were slowly evolved, that evidence has been utterly and for ever destroyed. . . . The natural theologians can no longer adhere to the arguments of such writers as Paley, Bell, Chalmers, without deliberately violating the only logical principle which separates science from fetishism." [2]

These words have at least the merit of being clear and incisive. It is small wonder that such a statement, coming from such a source, and put into such popular form, should make deep and lasting impression upon the minds of ordinary people in this generation. And yet it cannot possibly be said too plainly, or indeed with sufficient emphasis, that it is absolutely unwarranted and untrue.

How it should come to pass that able men, equally acquainted with the facts of modern science, take en-

---

[1] "Nature" Series, pp. 12, 13, 14, 76, 77.

[2] This passage, I find, has attracted the attention also of Dr. Iverach in his valuable little volume, *Christianity and Evolution* (Hodder & Stoughton), p. 78. But as these pages were written some time before that volume appeared, it seems unnecessary to remove them under fear of apparent plagiarism. The situation will bear emphasis from independent minds.

tirely opposite views concerning its results, we are not here concerned to discuss. At least this must be said, that if it be a difficulty for the Christian believer to account for the attitude of Agnostic men of science, assuming them to be as sincere as able, it is even more difficult for the unbeliever to account for the greater number of equally eminent students of science, who do not find it necessary to give up their faith because of their knowledge.[1] It were an easy task, though it would perhaps avail little, to draw up counter lists of names. Assuredly for quantity and quality alike, the roll of Christian scientists would not be inferior to that of Agnostics. It must never be forgotten that if the opinions of many are summed up by Haeckel, when he says in his *History of Creation*—

"I maintain with regard to the much-talked-of purpose in nature, that it really has no existence but for those persons who observe phenomena in animals and plants in the most superficial manner,"[2]

---

[1] Thus says Professor J. H. Gladstone, Ph.D., F.R.S.: "Many of us Christian men of Science, recognise that there is a unity of plan, as well as of purpose, running through the works of God. We hold that the Darwinian theory of the survival of the fittest, so far from destroying the idea of a Divine purpose and plan in nature, rather confirms it, and gives us a welcome insight into the way in which this has been carried out throughout the ages, not as a series of fortuitous events, but as the result of an orderly law."

[2] "Most superficial manner!" This is, alas! by no means the only specimen of what cannot but be termed the insolence of some writers on modern science. When we call to mind the names of all those students of nature who deliberately endorse, after many years of investigation, the judgement of Sir George Stokes—"the complexity of this marvellous organ, and the wonderful proof which (to my own mind at least) it gives of design in its construction"—one is driven to conclude that a cause must be in a poor way indeed, which needs the advocacy of such downright impertinence.

he is contradicted most emphatically by leading evolutionists themselves. So that if Darwin himself felt constrained to confess in his later years, "I am conscious that I am in an utterly hopeless muddle," much more may the humble student of the writings of his followers be bewildered by such contradictions! If, therefore, it were conceded that what Huxley has called "the commoner and coarser forms of teleology" have received their death-blow, and the avowal—

> "I found him not in world or sun
> Or eagle's wing or insect's eye,"

were accepted as axiomatic truth, it is at least equally true to add—

> "Nor thro' the questions men may try,
> The petty cobwebs we have spun."

If Haeckel and Romanes[1] are right, then Huxley, and Asa Gray, and Darwin himself, are wrong. For Huxley declares that "Evolution does not even come into contact with Theism, considered as a philosophic doctrine." And when Asa Gray wrote—

"Let us recognise Darwin's great service to natural science in bringing back to it teleology; so that instead of morphology *versus* teleology, we shall have morphology wedded to teleology,"

it was Darwin himself who replied, "What you say about teleology, pleases me especially." And even in the year when he spoke of his bewilderment he says, "I am inclined to look at everything as resulting from

---

[1] In the extract quoted above. Those who are acquainted with his *Thoughts on Religion* will know how to modify this statement by his later convictions.

designed laws." Thus Professor Huxley's words may fairly be taken as the summing up of the case against Haeckel's dogmatism, when he affirms that "it is necessary to remember that there is a wider teleology which is not touched by the doctrine of evolution, but is actually based upon the fundamental proposition of evolution."

But more remains. We have only to bestow one careful glance upon each of the chief items of the popular faith in Agnostic evolution, to see that the substitution of a greater difficulty for a less, looms out large in every case.

Consider first the "suddenness" upon which Professor Romanes laid such stress.[1] What does it amount to? Really, however unintentionally, an ignoring of the facts, with corresponding evasion of their consequences. There is no gradual adaptation which is not made up of sudden changes. What does the "modification" of an organ, or an organism, mean, but the occurrence of actual, that is definite and therefore necessarily sudden, changes, in the ultimate cells of which that organism is composed? Total gradual adaptation to environment is conceivable in no other way. Nay more. If the organism, as a whole, is to be profited by the aggregate result of such changes, each one of them, however infinitesimal, must be suitable, and there must also be some co-operating co-ordination of such multitudinous microscopic changes, else the result would be confusion rather than organic advantage.

Besides which, the most ordinary intelligence can surely appreciate the fallacy of invoking suddenness in

[1] Cf. note on p. 66.

general as sufficient criterion of design.[1] That a plain deal box which can be knocked together in an hour, should be accepted as proof positive of the working of intelligence, whilst the construction of a highly-finished chronometer which would occupy a skilled workman many months, would require no intelligence, simply because it came to its intended condition more slowly, is surely a delusion transparent enough for the eyes of a child. But the truth is, that no such comparison between time and thought ought ever to have been made. The terms are utterly incommensurable. Speed and purpose have no points in contact. Slowness has absolutely nothing to do with the presence or absence of intelligence. Here again, therefore, the powers which naturally and necessarily belong to the Infinite Mind are denied, only to invest with all the attributes of Deity the fortuitous concourse of hypothetic atoms!

But further. It is not seldom the fashion, in these days, to hold up the "Design argument" to scorn as the embodiment of a "big carpenter theory" of creation. A

[1] It is instructive to note by way of contrast the utterances of other men of science equally qualified to speak. "In considering the preparation of the home for coming Man, we must not lose sight of the remarkable fact of the existence of those plants which he found ready to his hand, which he was able to cultivate as cereals, nor of the equally noticeable production of the great classes of domesticable animals. The more subtle agency which the genius of Darwin brought to light, that of earthworms, becomes of immense importance. The position here maintained is that the arguments from the slow and orderly preparation of the environments for coming life on the globe necessarily imply the existence of Design. Design, though infinitely long-drawn, is the only conceivable explanation of things."—Dr. W. Kidd, F.Z.S., *Journ. Vict. Inst.*, No. 123, p. 207.

moment's thought, however, makes it difficult to credit with sincerity either the coiner or the repeater of so false a phrase.[1] To say nothing of the quality of the science which can suggest a mechanical solution for vital phenomena, the only semblance even of force in the phrase, is due to an insinuation utterly devoid of truth. For no human mechanic ever yet either supplied himself with materials upon which to work, or perpetuated his work by conferring upon it the power of reproduction. But passing by that also, the phrase, so far as it is to be taken seriously, proves too much. For even every "carpenter" at least possesses personality and mind. If Mr. Spencer concedes these to the Author of nature, Christian faith has no further controversy with him.

Much reference is also made to "rudimentary organs," as though their presence ruled out of all further consideration the notion of design. Such an assumption is much too hasty. The dilemma can scarcely be better stated than in the words of Professor Huxley: "For either these rudiments are of no use to the animals, in which case they ought to have disappeared; or they are of some use to the animal, in which case they are of no use as arguments against teleology."[2] Seeing, moreover, that rudimentary organs may be beginnings as well as endings, and indeed all organs must have begun with rudiments, we are compelled to ask whence came the

[1] Those who care for a thorough-going examination of the whole Agnostic position as represented by Mr. Spencer, will find it in No. 68 of the *Journal of Transactions of the Victoria Institute*, in the paper by Sir E. Beckett (Lord Grimthorpe) on "How did the World evolve itself?" also in Ground's *Spencer's Structural Principles examined* (Parker & Co.).

[2] *Darwinism and Design*, St. Clair, 151.

start, and how came there to be present the potentiality in the material upon which both the initial internal impulse and the assumed outer influence of environment worked, so that both the start and its development were not only possible but co-ordinated? These greater difficulties of Haeckelian evolution are yet waiting for answer.[1]

Perhaps the most effective popular plea against the Design argument is the appeal to nature as being "red in tooth and claw with ravine." This much abused quotation has been ceaselessly pressed into unintended uses. A scientific indictment is not, as a rule, fairly couched in poetic terms. Nor is this oft repeated phrase any exception. With our wider knowledge of nature, it is true, no one thinks of denying that there is a struggle for existence and a survival of the strongest. But that is a very different thing from affirming that the amount of cruelty and suffering in nature, as illustrated, say, in the Sphex wasp, or in the habits of carnivorous animals, rule absolutely out of thought all traces of the finger of God. Paley, for instance, wrote, "This is a happy world after all. The air, the earth, the water, teem with delighted existence." This, however, is to-day said to be such sentiment as "no intelligent man could now write."

---

[1] Those, and those only, who have given to Dr. H. Stirling's *Darwinianism, Workmen and Work*, the thorough study which it richly merits, will appreciate his final sentence: "For myself, in conclusion, I must say this, I admire the naturalist and I honour the man; but I hope to be forgiven if, 'for the life of me,' I cannot but smile when assured by Mr. Darwin that there is not necessarily such a thing as design in this universe 'now that the law of natural selection has been discovered.'"

But why not, we ask? Has the "delighted existence" all ceased, so that there is no happiness worth mentioning in the life of the world as we now see it? No suggestion could possibly be more misleading. As a matter of simple fact, the whole "mystery of pain" has been grossly and sentimentally exaggerated, whilst the vastly greater mystery of painlessness has been treated as a trifle, or calmly ignored altogether. Here, once more, is the almost hysterical "straining out" of the lesser and the effortless swallowing of the greater difficulty. One would think, to listen to some authors, that every fly that is found in autumn cemented by fungus to the window-pane, represented a long-drawn death agony, putting a tragic end to a painful and abortive existence. If, indeed, this were roundly asserted, it would scarcely be more unscientific in its falsity than the frequent assumption that the pain of living and the manner of dying in the animal world, are such as to reduce conscious existence to a manifest calamity, and blot out for ever the ancient belief that "the Lord is good to all, and His tender mercies are over all His works." There is only one way in which such pessimism can be justified. That is, by magnifying the smaller part of nature's working, and intensifying its darkness beyond warrant, whilst at the same time minifying the greater proportion and treating its unquestionable "sweetness and light" as of no account.

Now we are perfectly free, as Christian believers, to acknowledge that the mystery of pain, both as to its quantity and quality, is past our comprehension. But such an avowal by no means involves either the destruction of the "Design argument," or the justification of wholesale pessimism. All that it really signifies is the limitation of our human powers of vision, which ought not, for sane men, to be so startling or repulsive a lesson. So far as the lower orders of life are concerned, we have neither the knowledge whereby to estimate accurately the actual amount of pain endured, nor the faculties to decide whether wisdom and benevolence, or their opposites, ordained that the progress upwards should arise out of a struggle for existence. It is manifestly easy for a shallow sentimentality to affirm that there ought to be no struggle at all. But the assertion has no more intellectual value than the opinion of the little child in the nursery that his father ought not to go to business on a wet day.

In regard to the nature and amount of human suffering the question is at once entangled, and that inseparably, with moral influences. In so far as human suffering is purely physical, it is shared in common with the rest of the animal world. But the existence of pain amongst men is related quite as actually to moral causes and effects. These latter may be bad. They may equally be good. Which they shall be, is largely for the individual to decide. Certain it is that pain has been the most effectual schoolmaster of the race intellectually, and the undoubted means whereby the very highest and noblest parts of our nature have been developed. Unless, therefore, these be ruled wholly out of consideration, it is no less lawful to regard them as justifying all preceding processes that lead up to them, than to see in the human form a worthy physical result of long ages of gradual upward "progress by differentiation." The confessed mystery of pain is thus by no means without its wide margins of mitigation and justification.

But whether our estimate of these be higher or lower, one vast truth remains, often ignored but incontrovertible. Whatever grade of life be considered, from the lowest insect to the highest mammal, the mystery of painlessness is ever greater than the mystery of pain. It is greater in quality, for pain is the expression of something abnormal in one organ, whilst health is the result of a balance to which thousands of separate parts contribute. It is greater also in quantity, for not only is the number of healthy creatures at any time vastly in excess of the unhealthy, but in each individual higher life,[1] taken on the average, the duration of the period of painlessness, and generally of definite happiness, is many times longer than the hours of pain. Never, indeed, throughout the whole range of poetry, has a falser impression been conveyed than by this oft quoted but utterly misleading couplet that—

> "Nature red in tooth and claw
> With ravine, shrieked against the creed,"

that

> " God was love indeed,
> And love creation's final law."

Calmly and impartially considered, nature does nothing of the kind. For the "cruelty" of nature has been

---

[1] As to the lower ranges of animal life, there are grave reasons for doubting whether the great majority of such creatures ever know or can know pain at all.

unwarrantably exaggerated by an unscientific sentimentalism,[1] which has at the same time strangely underestimated the wonder and enormity of its manifestations of benevolence.

If honest thought demands that we should face and estimate the suffering of some poor human victim of cancer or consumption, who takes twelve months to die, or the sudden (and almost painless) death of weaker animals which fall a prey to the stronger, it requires no less that we should bear in mind the longer period, sometimes amounting to twenty or thirty or forty years of healthy and enjoyable life, which has preceded.[2] To disregard this can only be an act of wilful blindness. To do it justice, as a true rule which exceptions do not suffice to annul, is to see that the denial of gracious design in nature, by reason of the mystery of pain, is but

---

[1] A brief monograph by Mr. J. Crowther Hirst, entitled, *Is Nature cruel?* (James Clark & Co.), is well worth consideration as "a partial answer" at least, founded on the "experiences of big game hunters and others while under the attack of wild beasts." The evidence shows that "in the majority of cases of attack, the tenderest-hearted person could not imagine a more desirable end to life than this. Let the physiological explanation be what it may, it is difficult to resist the conclusion that for victims of the carnivora there is in nature itself a merciful provision by a benevolent Creator for lessening the pain of death."

[2] "In the animal world what happiness reigns! What ease, grace, beauty, leisure and content! Watch these living specks as they glide through their forests of algæ, all 'without hurry and care,' as if their 'span-long lives' could really endure for the thousand years that the old catch pines for. Here is no greedy jostling at the banquet that nature has spread for them, no dread of each other, but a leisurely inspection of the field that shows neither the pressure of hunger nor the dread of an enemy."—Dr. Hudson, *Address to Royal Microscopical Society*, 1890.

another instance of ignoring the mountain and professing to be awestruck by the mole-hill.

Once more, before leaving the question of Design, it appears necessary to point out how those who reject it on account of its difficulties in the light of Evolution, do but entangle themselves in a bottomless quagmire of greater difficulties. Darwin, for instance, wrote thus concerning orchids—

"The more I study nature the more I become impressed with the conclusion that the contrivances and beautiful adaptations slowly acquired through each part varying in a slight degree but in many ways, and the preservation or natural selection of those variations which are beneficial to the organism under the complex and ever varying conditions of life, transcend in an incomparable degree the contrivances and adaptations which the most fertile imagination of the most imaginative man could suggest, with unlimited time at his disposal." [1]

Surely no words can be more emphatic than these. Here, then, is the dilemma. These wonderful "adaptations" either have or have not a guiding mind behind them. Slowness or suddenness, directness or indirectness, do not affect the case in the least. If these confessedly greater marvels do not require mind to account for them, certainly the lesser works of men do not. In that case all the instances of careful structure which we have been

[1] Note also these other utterances of the same authority. "Any young observer will be delighted at the perfection of the adaptations by which insects *are forced*, unconsciously on their part, to carry pollen from the stamens of one plant to the stigma of another. Design in nature has for a long time deeply interested many men, and though the subject must now be looked at from a somewhat different point of view to what was formerly the case, it is not thus rendered the less interesting."—Müller's *Fertilisation of Flowers*, Prefatory Notice by Charles Darwin.

accustomed to regard as proofs of human intelligence, from a chronometer to the Forth Bridge, are nothing of the kind, but simply the result of the slow and fortuitous concurrence of materials. To which one may well say, "*Credat Judæus!*" If, however, our common sense rejects this conclusion, and insists that mind must somewhere, somehow, precede these and all other such constructions, by what process of reasoning is intelligence affirmed as a necessity for the lesser marvels and coarser "adaptations," and denied for the greater and finer?

Who, again, that has ever read Professor Huxley's graphic and well-known description of the development of the tadpole in its slimy cradle, can forget or fail to see the force of his closing sentence?—

"After watching the process hour by hour, one is almost involuntarily possessed by the notion that some more subtle aid to vision than an achromatic object glass, would show the hidden artist with his plan before him, striving with skilful manipulation to perfect his work."[1]

Yet all this, according to Haeckel, is nothing more than the fortuitous concourse of atoms!

Or again. Whereas in former time the human eye was regarded as so wonderful an organ that it might fairly be taken for definite proof of design, it has become quite the fashion now to drop dark hints about its being a very "imperfect instrument"; whilst Professor Helmholtz is quoted, as a physicist of great repute, in support of such depreciation. Half a truth, however, may be equivalent to a whole lie. A few words are taken from the professor's well-known *Scientific Lectures*,[2] to the

[1] *Lay Sermons*, p. 286.   [2] P. 227.

THE REALM OF PHYSICAL SCIENCE

effect that "the eye has every possible defect that can be found in an optical instrument, and even some that are peculiar to itself"—but the rest is conveniently omitted. Let us complete the quotation—

"But they are all so counteracted, that the inexactness of the images very little exceeds the limits which are set to the delicacy of sensation by the dimensions of the retinal cones. *The adaptation of the eye to its functions is therefore most complete*, and is seen in the very limits set to its defects. *The result*, which may have been reached by innumerable generations under the Darwinian law of inheritance, *coincides with what the wisest wisdom may have devised beforehand.*"[1]

The reference to this high scientific authority is thus somewhat unfortunate for those who wish to invalidate design and deify chance. It reminds one of the attempts of Balak in olden time to get Balaam to come and curse Israel. For it really issues in fourfold corroboration. (1) Even an imperfect instrument, theoretically, may be a perfectly valid testimony to intelligent design. (2) "The very limits set to" the imperfections, testify to design in that they still more manifestly bespeak purpose. (3) Theoretic imperfection may sometimes be practically more perfect than theoretic perfection. Every piano and organ, for instance, is imperfectly tuned. If, indeed, either were perfectly tuned, it would be practically useless, for no melody whatever could be played upon it. We listen to a thrilling rendering of Beethoven or Mozart, simply because the piano has been imperfectly tuned, with a view to such practical results. In every analogous case, whether as to sight or sound, imperfection becomes a more emphatic witness to design than perfection. Extra intelligence, so to speak, is required to avoid

[1] The italics are the present writer's.

theoretic perfection with a view to practical purposes. Thus (4), the total result is coincidence with the prevision of the wisest wisdom. Such coincidence has billions to one against its being the result of unguided chance.

Furthermore, if the human eye has only become so suitable for human beings after passing through many grades of inferior stages, it is equally true that in each of those stages of inferiority it has been practically perfect for the usage of a correspondingly inferior creature. The eye of the ant, poor as it is in comparison with our own, is perfectly adapted to the habits of the insect, as also is that of the fish to its environment. "Allowing as much gradual improvement as you like by biological evolution, or the creation of small—or large—changes, adapted to changing circumstances, each creature has somehow come to be as well contrived as possible for its own work."[1]

Suppose, however, that we turn an open ear to the Agnostic plea, and ask from its best known representative for the adequate cause of all nature, including ourselves, what do we actually find? The "final formula" of Evolution is thus presented to us by its most authoritative exponent. "Evolution is an integration of matter and concomitant dissipation of motion; during which the matter passes from an indefinite, incoherent homogeneity to a definite, coherent heterogeneity; and during which the retained motion undergoes a parallel transformation."[2] To the uninstructed mind this has certainly all the merit of grandiloquence; yet one of our ablest

[1] Sir E. Beckett (Lord Grimthorpe), *Vict. Inst. Trans.*, No. 68, p. 303.
[2] Herbert Spencer, *First Principles*, p. 397.

jurists, who is equally accomplished in mathematics, does not hesitate to affirm in public and before a critical audience, that "every important word in this definition is either unmeaning or wrong, and ought to be reversed or combined with its opposite."[1] Such an estimate from such a source, at least avails to rob it of all magisterial authority, and leaves us the liberty of our own thought. A very little reflection then suffices to show that he who can accept this, in place of the postulates of Christian Theism, must have truly miraculous powers of mental digestion. For looking calmly into it, we find that not only is "matter" quietly assumed, but most convenient "matter." That is, first, matter itself is taken for granted, then, its potentiality for integration, then the process of integration itself. Whence came these three? Surely they demand an adequate cause, quite as much as anything we see around us.

But more. With all respect to a great "thinker," the terms "indefinite, incoherent, homogeneity" are themselves self-contradictory. "Homogeneity" is distinctly definite, and incoherence also is at least as definite a notion as coherence, to say nothing of the fact that, unless gravity be ruled wholly out of account at this stage—and then it has to be created at some later stage—an "incoherent homogeneity" is simply "unthinkable" on sound physical principles. In thoroughgoing scrutiny of Mr. Spencer's *First Principles*, much more might be, and indeed has been, said.[2] Enough,

---

[1] Lord Grimthorpe, *Journal Vict. Inst.*, No. 68, p. 291.

[2] Thus Lord Grimthorpe, in the paper above mentioned, forcibly comments upon some of the main Spencerian positions. *E.g.* "All

however, has here been plainly pointed out to justify the main assertion of these pages, namely, that the idea of escaping difficulties by turning from belief to unbelief, is less hopeful than flying from Scylla to Charybdis. It is indeed not one whit too strong language when the writer above quoted adds, "The very idea of power making or developing itself, is contrary to all modern science, and would not be listened to for a moment in any but the hazy regions of automatic cosmogony, for which any hypothesis seems good enough."

reasoned out conclusions must rest upon some postulate. And whoever contemplates the relation in which it stands to the truths of science in general, will see that this truth-transcending demonstration is the persistence of force." But in reply rightly says his critic, "Even if he could prove that everything may follow from the conservation of force, yet, until he proves that to be an *a priori* necessity, and not a law of nature which required a prime cause to make and to maintain it, his philosophy is nowhere. He has failed utterly on his very first proposition, and his whole case is gone. Abstract force, in no particular direction, is nonsense."

Again, when Mr. Spencer affirms that "the Absolute Cause of changes is incomprehensible," it is quite to the point to reply: "No doubt we might use the same words, only we should mean by them that the cause of all apparently automatic changes is the will of a Creator, who is Himself incomprehensible beyond what He has told us of Himself. But Mr. Spencer abandons Him for a variety of incomprehensibles of his own, which can do nothing, and are nothing but mere words expressing that he knows nothing of any of those processes which he dogmatically calls corollaries of persistent force." . . . "Perhaps Mr. Spencer, or one of his admirers who think they understand his philosophy, will condescend to explain some day how profound mysteries of experience can be necessary results and corollaries of a self-evident truth, which was itself only discovered by a long course of experimental investigation, and then how all knowledge is unified by telling us that all these things are unfathomable, and that the philosopher is hopelessly in the dark about them."

But the notion that the argument from design has been "utterly and for ever destroyed" is, thanks to some well-known writers, so widely diffused at the present moment, that it is worth while, before dismissing the subject, to quote one or two more unequivocal utterances from men whose acknowledged eminence well qualifies them to speak. Thus Lord Grimthorpe calls attention to the fact,[1] familiar to every anatomist, that

"There are cases, properly insisted on by Paley, and never answered, of holes being made in certain bones for arteries to pass through, and of sinews passed through loops in others like cords through a pulley to change their direction. It is plain that those must be all or nothing, and *could not come gradually*. And animals that live by gnawing and biting hard things, such as the rodents and elephants, have their teeth continually growing, which no others could have. What conceivable automatic process could have caused that; and that the teeth should not only grow, but be in alternate hard and soft slices vertically, so as to keep the grinding teeth always rough, and the gnawing teeth sharp, and yet not too thin? There are innumerable other questions like these, to which the Evolutionists never attempt any answer."

And it is quite worth while to adduce here his further protest,[2] that

"It is necessary to remind people that they have to choose between two only possible alternatives, according to the balance of probabilities. There is no middle way between the world, and all that is in it, having been either designed or not designed; and therefore we, *ipso facto*, believe and cannot but believe, one just so far as we disbelieve the other. A man may or may not have made up his mind which to believe. That man's opinion is worth nothing. In fact he has none. An Agnostic must be wrong, whether Theists or Atheists are right." . . . "Therefore also a man who denies design, but cannot state any other rational mode of generating

---

[1] *Journal of Vict. Inst.*, No. 68, p. 307.
[2] *Ib.* p. 302.

the universe, condemns himself. For unquestionably a designing Creator could produce the universe, and therefore must have done it, if nothing else did. And that something else must be capable of rational and intelligible description, and proof of its capacity for doing the business before we need attend to it."

This "rational and intelligible description," we have seen above, is impossible to Agnostic Evolution, without a wholesale *petitio principii*, which settles the matter from the point of view of human reason.

Professor Le Conte's [1] deliberate avowal is that

"It is simply impossible to talk about such structures without using language which implies design. The very word 'adaptive' implies it. It is impossible even to think of such structures without implicitly assuming intelligence as the cause. It makes no particle of difference how the material originated, or whether it ever originated at all. It matters not whether the adaptation was done at once out of hand, or whether by slow process of modification. It matters not whether the adaptive modification was brought about by a process of natural selection, or by pressure of physical environment, whether without law or according to law. The removal of the result from manlike directness of separate action cannot destroy the idea of design, but only modify our conception of the Designer. What science, and especially evolution, destroys, therefore, is not the idea of design, but only our low anthropomorphic notions of the mode of working of the Designer. There is still design in everything, but no longer a separate design, only a separate manifestation of the one infinite design."

In his Fernley Lecture on *The Creator and what we may know of the Method of Creation*, p. 74, Dr. Dallinger also affirms that

"Design, purpose, intention, appear, then, when all the facts of the universe are studied in the light of all our reasoning faculties, to be ineradicable from our view of the creation. Teleology does not now depend for its existence on Paleyan instances, but all the universe, its whole progress in time and space, is one majestic

---

[1] *Evolution and Religious Thought*, pp. 323, 325.

evidence of teleology. The will and purpose running through it are as incapable of being shut out of our consciousness and reasoning faculties, as its phenomena and their modes are of being rendered wholly imperceptible by our senses."

Again, Professor Le Gros Clark (F.R.S., F.R.C.S. etc.), when President of the Royal College of Surgeons, edited Paley's *Natural Theology*, and in the Introduction expresses his deliberate opinion that

"The modern doctrine of Evolution does not necessarily carry with it a confutation of the argument from the appearance of design. If this theory shall ever take its place among the universally recognised truths of science, it will undoubtedly affect what may be called the incidence of the argument, and render the application of it more remote. But a little consideration will show that the argument itself will retain its essential validity, and by no means be robbed of its force, or become antiquated or useless."

The late Kitchen Parker (Hunterian Professor of the Royal College of Surgeons) gives also his judgement explicitly [1]—

"Do not think that because Evolution has been taken advantage of to endeavour to get rid of Christianity, therefore Evolution is or means any harm, or that Darwin's Theory of the gradual origin of Species means any harm. It means nothing of the sort."

It were indeed quite easy to multiply testimonies of other acknowledged experts to the same effect. And however by some they may be pronounced inconclusive, they have at least this unquestionable force and value, that they absolutely disprove the by no means uncommon assertion that the "leaders of modern science have been compelled to give up the design argument,

[1] *Report of Christian Evidence Society*, 1889, p. 45.

and forsake the Christian faith." The utter falseness of such floating rumours is sufficiently manifest from the foregoing. But a final and unequivocal testimony may be added from Lord Kelvin, who is acknowledged by all competent to judge as the "greatest living master of natural science," and who has openly avowed, even from the chair of the British Association, that

"I feel profoundly convinced that the argument from design has been greatly too much lost sight of in recent zoological speculations. Overwhelmingly strong proofs of intelligent and benevolent design lie around us, and if ever perplexities, whether metaphysical or scientific, turn us away from them for a time, they come back upon us with irresistible force, showing to us through nature the influence of a free will, and teaching us that all living things depend upon one everlasting Creator and Ruler."

So far, therefore, as the Argument from Design is concerned, the miracle of unbelief may be fairly summarised in the forceful words of Lord Grimthorpe [1]—

"Until some theory can be invented to account for all those stages of Evolution from a microscopic particle, including its own generation, up to a philosopher, by any conceivable self-existing forces out of homogeneous self-existing matter, and also for the production of beauty—not merely a little of it—all the phrases which have been invented pretending to account for these things are nothing more than words. Natural selections, sexual selections, survivals of the fittest, atavisms, heredities, and I don't know how many more, may all be true as facts or processes, and may do what they can. But the (Agnostic) Evolutionists are at an immeasurable distance yet from showing that they can do everything. It is entirely bad logic to assume that they can do a bit more than we can prove. And, if we could prove them to be capable of doing even such inconceivable things as producing the general beauty of nature, and starting generation, the theory of spontaneous cosmogony would still be nowhere, until we could prove for them that

---

[1] *Vict. Inst. Journal*, quoted above.

THE REALM OF PHYSICAL SCIENCE 87

all the necessary forces started themselves and maintain themselves, and all their powers of transformation, according to the ascertained laws of conservation of force."

But it is necessary now to glance, at least, at other physical phenomena which equally involve the necessity of a supreme guiding Mind. No man with sane powers of perception will deny the existence of the beautiful and the sublime around us, in greater or less degree, continually. There would be much truth and no wrong in our adding to these, so as to complete the æsthetic emotions, the sense of the ludicrous. For this also, beyond all question, postulates some degree of mind, whenever and wherever experienced. But as it would merely echo and confirm the conclusions which follow from a fair estimate of our perception of the beautiful, we may omit it from further consideration here. Indeed it is for similar reasons unnecessary to dwell at any length upon the apprehension of the sublime. For although its essence may well be, as Professor Bain suggests, "the sympathetic sentiment of superior power in its highest degrees," it will suffice for our present purpose to regard it as simply the appreciation of the beautiful upon the larger scale. Its inclusion of the sense of awe in presence of the vast and terrible, will only confirm our inferences from the universal manifestations of the beautiful, and our corresponding powers of appreciation.

To most people who have not been given to abstract thought, a definition of the beautiful would be a difficult task. Yet as our appeal here is rather to common sense than to metaphysics, it may suffice to affirm that all ordinary human beings have a real and indeed a double apprehension of beauty, however much that apprehension may vary with temperament and education. Dismissing now the less intellectual of our sensations, we do at least appreciate that which is beautiful in both sight and sound. It is perfectly true, as Bain remarks, that "the source of beauty is not to be sought in any single quality but in a circle of effects." We may have a beautiful form without colour, or a beautiful colour without any precise form; but when the two are combined in some special relations, there is an unquestionable heightening of the effect. This enhanced effect reaches its maximum when the element of quantity is added. That which is beautiful when viewed upon the small scale, becomes magnificent or sublime when gathered into a vast aggregate. Illustrations are here unnecessary because they abound in all directions. The questions which concern us are whence this perception and appreciation of beauty are derived, and what they signify. Christian faith regards them as an expression of the benevolence of the Divine Mind, which has intentionally brought about such exact correlation between human surroundings and perceptions as issues in our enjoyment of the beautiful. The only difficulty attending such a causal conception, is the natural and necessary impossibility that finite intelligence should comprehend the infinite. That, however, is no contradiction to our powers of reasoning. But if faith's answer to our inquiry be rejected, what remains? Manifestly nothing but this, that the whole complex appreciation of the beautiful, both as regards our subjective faculties and

THE REALM OF PHYSICAL SCIENCE 89

the objective phenomena which so exactly correspond, is the fortuitous result of the haphazard collisions of mindless atoms through æons past. Yet no one suggests to-day that there is actually or conceivably any appreciation of beauty apart from mind. How then can that which always requires mind to apprehend it, be rationally ascribed for origin to mindless chance? The initial absurdity of such a suggestion is strongly confirmed when we look into the physical and physiological elements out of which our perception of beauty is built up.

Think for a moment of the visibly beautiful. It is an easy thing to admire a flower. It is still more easy to forget how marvellous, in its complex intricacy, is the apparatus whereby even the outer elements of its beauty are apprehended. Not to repeat what we have previously summarised, three things only need here be emphasised. First, the inexpressible wonderfulness of the physical relations involved; secondly, the unfathomable reality of the ultra-physical element in the case; thirdly, the exact and thorough-going correlation between these two.

For the first, besides the distinctly pleasurable apprehension of form—and it is to be observed that the sharp-cut angles of the crystal may be as definitely beautiful as the rounded curves of a flower—this is inseparably connected with the delight of colour. But what does this latter element mean? Only this, that in the case of a flower exhibiting the three ordinary colours of red, green, and violet, the eye must be sensitive, at one and the same time, to vibrations of the luminiferous ether, at the respective rates of 400, 700, and 850 millions of millions per second! It is the combination of this perception with that of certain forms, as distinct from other forms (for all combinations of form and colour are not beautiful), which gives rise to the ultra-physical apprehension which we call the "love of the beautiful." Now that all this should result from mere chance, involves a degree of improbability which we have no figures to express.[1] Compared with it, all the difficulties of Christian faith put together are but as an ant-heap by the side of a mountain.

Yet again, the unquestionable fact confronts us that all our own creations of beauty, without exception, are acknowledged to be results and expressions of mind. The artist or sculptor who should take his materials and persistently fling them about in chaotic heaps, in hope that somehow or other a beautiful picture or statue might emerge from the confusion, would only be regarded as a madman. The student in art is to-day more and more given to understand that his hope of success lies in the degree in which he puts mind and soul into his work. No one questions this. But what after all is the highest attainable degree of success in art? Is it not that the picture, or the sculpture, should be true to nature? Surely, then, it is none else than the veritable irony of unbelief, which can insist that the imperfect and faulty copy ever involves mind, whilst the vast original which transcends all our estimates may be ascribed to chance! How far, indeed, the beauty of

[1] Cf. Lord Kelvin's comment on Sir G. Stokes' reference to design as manifest in our human perception of colour. Note on pp. 63, 64.

nature exceeds that of our highest art, is often forgotten. But it is only the superficiality of our vision which makes such forgetfulness possible. In the matter before us, an overwhelming *a fortiori* argument arises out of the difference between our human art, at its best, and nature's realities. This difference admits of brief expression. The more we examine nature in careful detail, even to miscroscopic minuteness, the more of the truly beautiful do we find. But the more closely we investigate works of art the more do we become conscious of imperfections which, if regarded, would entirely spoil the general impression of beauty.

The beauty of a landscape, for instance, appeals to us all. But if, instead of the vast whole, we contemplate a single flower or blade of grass, or even a microscopic portion of either, we find that the beauty is often enhanced rather than lost. If, however, we take for microscopic scrutiny a quarter of an inch of any human work of art, we find at once the seeming perfection exchanged for roughness and coarseness, whilst the general sense of beauty in the whole is lost without any compensation whatever in the more closely examined part. The works of art, indeed, which are most admired, and into which it is acknowledged most effort of mind has been put, will no more bear the microscope than the back of any famous painting would bear the close inspection bestowed upon the front. But who that has ever examined microscopically the back or front alike of the leaf of an ordinary Box plant, or Deutzia, can forget the delicate wonder of the myriad stomata, or the crystal beauty of the stellate hairs?

These are but tiny types of what is everywhere to be found, in indescribable profusion, throughout nature.[1] Marvellous truly in its obtuseness then must be the philosophy which, in the confessedly faulty and imperfect can clearly recognise and freely own the evidences of intelligence, but in the wonder and beauty which are far more manifest in the infinitely great and the infinitely small, can find nothing save the results of the accidental collisions of mindless atoms!

Attempts have been made, we know, to break the manifest force of this suggestion by referring to the struggle for existence amongst living creatures, and the survival of the fittest through natural selection, as sole factors of the beautiful in nature. Thus the beauty of flowers is attributed in many cases to the gradual increase in vigour of those plants which, through possessing colours more conspicuous than the green of leaves, attracted to themselves a larger number of insects, and so secured more efficient cross-fertilisation. So, too, the beauty of butterflies is said to be due to sexual selection. Those clad in the most attractive colours were chosen for reproduction whilst others became extinct. This sounds very plausible, but the merest glance is enough to show its utter feebleness and inadequacy as an account of the beautiful in all nature. We might indeed well ask, whence came the first patch of colour, or the first conspicuous marking, which lead to

[1] "The world we live in is a fairyland of exquisite beauty, our very existence is a miracle in itself; and yet few of us enjoy as we might, and none as yet appreciate fully the beauties and wonders which surround us."—Lord Avebury (Sir J. Lubbock), *The Beauties of Nature*, p. 1.

such fruitful consequences in butterfly or flower? But many other considerations clamour for attention.

1. The manifest assumption here is that beauty and conspicuousness are one. But it is utterly false. To say nothing of those wonderful half-shades of colour in nature which defy the artist's imitation, and yet in their delicate beauty are the very opposite of conspicuous, some of the smallest and least noticeable flowers are the most beautiful. Who would think for a moment of attributing to the poppy more beauty than to the violet? Besides which it cannot be at all conceded that the beauty of the tropical flora, however striking, is more real than that of our English country lanes. There may be greater quantity, there may be more gorgeous display, but these do not constitute the soul of beauty. How easy it would be to name a score of our familiar wild flowers whose beauty is so distinctly *sui generis* that nothing can surpass them. And of these, as of numberless other beautiful things, it is true that the most actual beauty is often the most delicate, that is, the least conspicuous.

2. Again, whatever be the manifest preferences of insects, we have no warrant for attributing to them any sense of the beautiful as we perceive it. In their case, as the theory of natural selection must acknowledge, it is a purely biological impulse. They are hungry and want food, or they are urged by simple sexual instinct, nothing more. But the vision of the beautiful which flowers and insects yield to us, is certainly very much more than these. In fact it may be truly said that the sense of beauty does not come into play until these

appetites and instincts have been either satisfied or ruled out by will. Now it is this super-sensuous, ultra-physical, appreciation of beauty which has to be accounted for in ourselves, not the mere apprehension of striking form or conspicuous colour. It is the marvellous correlation between certain forms and colours—which may or may not already have served biological purpose in lower grades of life — and our own powers of perception, whence there arises in us that refined pleasure of appreciated beauty for which adequate cause must be found. To profess to do so by pointing to the appetites of insects, is to adduce a collection of sandhills as explanation of the Matterhorn.[1]

3. But besides this, we may not forget how small a portion of the beautiful in nature is touched at all by reference to biological utility. It has indeed been confidently asserted that beauty is always associated with utility in the world around us. The boldness of the assertion is, however, only equalled by its falsity.

---

[1] "It is to insects, then, that flowers owe their beauty, scent, and sweetness." . . . "It is well established that *the main object* of the colour, scent, and honey of flowers is *to attract* insects, which are of use to the plant in carrying the pollen from flower to flower." —Sir J. Lubbock, *The Beauties of Nature*, p. 66.

May be. No botanist now controverts the fact, but the question is as to its teleological significance. If the words italicised are accurate, they indicate indubitable intention somewhere. Where? In the flowers themselves? Intention inevitably connotes mind. Hence the colour, scent, and honey—and all else to the same effect in plants, *e.g.* the construction of the Salvias, in regard to which Sir J. Lubbock well says, "It is one of the most beautiful pieces of plant mechanism"—*must* mean either that the flowers themselves possess mind, or that a supreme Mind brought to pass the law of their being which they unconsciously obey. Other sane alternative there is none.

Instances to the contrary abound everywhere. Even if we agree to regard as more especially beautiful that colouring of entomophilous plants which attracts useful insects to them, there is yet left the vast realm of anemophilous plants. When it is remarked that upon the whole their colouring is less conspicuous, that does not lessen the reality of the beauty in them which appeals to us. The oak tree and the aspen are beautiful, in their own way, quite as really as the lily or the orchid.

Or if we turn from the vegetable to the animal world, even in its lowliest forms, where do we find surpassed the wondrous architecture of the Foraminifera, or the delicate symmetry of the Radiolaria, or the graceful activities of the Rotifera? But it would be absurd to talk about that beautifulness, which no human eye can help seeing in them, having anything to do with sexual selection or the survival of the fittest. How surpassingly beautiful they are, in myriads of cases, is best known to those who have spent hours in examining them. But it is a beauty which exists for our eyes alone. No other creature on earth appreciates it. Useless, apart from us, it may be called; but useful, in the biological sense, never. Thus Professor Le Conte[1] is entirely warranted in his statement that

"These and many other cases of beauty may doubtless be explained by showing that it is useful; but beauty which is without any use cannot be explained by natural selection. Now the most gorgeous beauty is lavishly distributed even amongst the lowest animals, such as marine shells and polyps, where no such explanation is possible. The process by which such beauty is originated and intensified is wholly unknown to us."

---

[1] *Evolution in Relation to Religious Thought*, p. 252.

This uselessness of inexplicable beauty, and its utter non-reference to any struggle for existence, is, however, seen most emphatically in the mineral world. We should but waste words if we attempted to describe those properties of form and colour which, from time immemorial, have made precious stones the delight of mankind. The eye of the savage has been caught and fascinated, we know, equally with the fastidious vanity of the lady of fashion. The love of jewellery appears rather to increase than grow less with the advance of civilisation. In the fervid ferment of our great European cities, as markedly as in the slow courts of an Eastern Rajah, position in society is fairly indicated by the quality and quantity of the jewels worn upon the person. Several considerations herefrom at once suggest themselves.

(1) There is no manner of doubt that it is the beauty of all brilliant gems which ever constitutes their attraction. (2) This beauty exists for men and women alone, of all creatures upon earth. The glow of the carbuncle and the flash of the diamond are absolutely nothing to the most sagacious elephant or the most intelligent dog. (3) The basis of all this mineral beauty is a process of crystallisation which has no conceivable connection with any struggle for existence, or survival of the fittest. The essence of the attractiveness, to human eyes, is a combination of form and colour which is brought to pass under special conditions in nature's great workshop. On the smaller scale we may even ourselves set the process going and watch its progress. Thus in the words of Professor Tyndall—

"By permitting alum to crystallise in this slow way, we obtain these perfect octahedrons; by allowing carbonate of lime to crystallise, nature produces these beautiful rhomboids; when silica crystallises, we have formed these hexagonal prisms capped at the end by pyramids; by allowing saltpetre to crystallise, we have these prismatic masses; and when carbon crystallises, we have the diamond."[1]

4. By mechanical processes men continually seek to enhance the beauty they find. Great part of the brilliancy of the diamond, we know, is due to its special cutting and setting. The art of the lapidary, however, with its gleaming results, seems likely to be outrivalled by that of the chemist, seeing that in our modern laboratories garnets and even small diamonds have been produced by synthesis — to say nothing of the increasing production of the imitations technically known as "paste." Now no one for a moment questions that these processes, whether chemical or mechanical, require skill guided by intelligence, and both in high degree. Yet what are all the best results which men can compass with their utmost efforts, compared with those exhibited in nature? The conditions of temperature and pressure requisite for the production, say, of a "Koh-i-noor" will, we know, never be created by the art of man. Yet if mind be manifestly necessary for the production of the lesser, by what logic is the measurelessly greater asserted to be derived from chance? It is especially interesting to observe that as our great biologist found himself unable to do justice to the wonder and beauty of a tadpole's development without invoking a "hidden Artist," so is the renowned author

[1] *Fragments of Science*, vol. i. p. 357.

of the "Belfast Address" obliged to make mention of an "Architect" in his description of the wonders of crystallography. Thus he says concerning a solution of sulphate of soda—

"Looking into it mentally, we see the molecules of that liquid, like disciplined squadrons *under a governing eye*, arranging themselves into battalions, gathering round distinct centres, and forming themselves into solid masses, which after a time assume the visible shape of the crystal now held in my hand. Here there is *an architect at work* who makes no chips, no din, and who is now building the particles into crystals, similar in shape and structure to those beautiful masses which we see upon the table." [1]

One cannot but admire the chivalrous frankness with which these prophets of Agnosticism, in their anxiety to do justice to facts, shrink not from employing phrases which cut the ground entirely from under their own philosophic standpoint. To urge that these are only figures of speech, is to forget that by such figures the most exact as well as vivid truth is ever conveyed in human speech. We are driven therefore to this conclusion, that it is simply impossible to do justice in thoughts and words to the whole vast exhibition of beauty in nature, without as definitely invoking the Divine mind for its origin as the human mind for its appreciation.

5. Such a conclusion is the more confirmed in proportion as we extend our observation. Does any one doubt, for instance, that there is such a thing as beauty of sound? Certainly we have no intellectual right to limit the beautiful to the visible. We speak with perfect truthfulness of the sweetness of some flow-

[1] The italics are the present writer's.

ing melody of Mozart, or the grandeur of Beethoven's deep and complex harmonies. These are but phases of the beautiful, in its appeal to the sense of sound rather than of sight. Where, however, in these is any room at all for natural selection, or struggle for existence, or survival of the fittest? Furthermore, it is manifest that this exhibition of the beautiful exists for human ears alone. The dog, our most intelligent animal, howls his unmistakable disapproval of it. Moreover, a trained ear is required to appreciate that which, by common consent, most truly deserves to be called "music." The rattle of the tom-toms and the wild screeching of much Oriental and all savage music, we regard with mingled amazement and pity. That is to say, music in us means mind, and the noblest music means the highest development of a distinctive capacity, potential only in primeval man. Whence, then, that potentiality? The man who should venture to affirm, seriously and in public, that the great organ in one of our cathedrals evolved itself, without any touch, *ab extra*, from an indiscriminate heap of wood and metal, would only be regarded as an imbecile. But the whole mechanism of the organ is truly a rough trifle compared with the human ear, alike in its general structure and its minute histology.

To this, however, must be added all the wonders of acoustics, together with those unalterable laws whereby certain distinct musical notes proceed from varying rates of atmospheric vibration. Even then, we are but on the threshold of the actual mystery. For no living physicist or physiologist knows, or doubtless ever will know, how it comes to pass that these vibrations are translated into consciousness, even for one single musical note, to say nothing of the enjoyment of vast and complicated harmonies, as in an oratorio.

So then it comes all to this, that the organ is pronounced, without controversy, an intricate and beautiful piece of workmanship, proving exceedingly high intelligence in its construction, whilst the actual possession of that intelligence, together with an immeasurably superior instrument, whence arises the faculty to appreciate the results of the complex man-designed mechanism, the wonderful ultra-material reality of the audibly beautiful, distinct from, yet arising out of these material conditions, and correlating perfectly with a prepared human sensorium, all have been brought to pass by sheer chance out of a primitive nebulosity several million cubic miles of which would be required to weigh a single grain! Truly the faith of Agnosticism is unbounded.

6. The two highest forms of beauty, however, yet remain. They deserve at least succinct and appreciative notice. Of all instances of visible beautifulness none can surely be more manifest than its exhibition, in innumerable cases, in the human face. That wonderful combination of form and colour which is generally termed handsomeness in men and beauty in women, has been through all ages past the constant observation of historians and the ceaseless theme of poets. What does it all amount to ? Is the beauty of the human face simply the biological expression of pure chance ? Is it ultimately nothing more than " nature's " means of sexual attraction, with a view to the continuation of the species ?

This would seem to be the inevitable though masked result of the opinions of many, and the downright assertion of an outspoken few. To find anything "Divine" in the human face, is by these philosophers regarded only as a passing dream of poetic fiction. Yet it is substantiated by all that is purest and noblest in our nature. The highest reality of the case is undoubtedly with the poet rather than the biologist. Untold myriads of men and women could be called upon to testify to the pure loftiness, the genuine spirituality, of the emotion enkindled within them by the sight of the noble brow, the speaking eyes, the mobile mouth, the cheeks suffused with healthy glow, which go to make up the fairest vision upon earth. The artist who can only approximately reproduce this, is accounted a genius. That is, his mind powers are pronounced far above the average. Yet that soul of beauty itself which he strives most of all to catch, and so often strives in vain because of its very beautifulness, is to be ascribed to the mindless clash of atoms developing aimlessly through unguided ages! May be. But in comparison with this, to insist that the *chef d'œuvre* of a Turner or a Tadema, is nothing more than a haphazard daub with closed eyes and reckless hand, is a very mild form of assertion.

7. The plain truth is that the human face may, and in the vast majority of cases does, betoken moral character. It is the expression of this expression which most baffles the skill of the artist. The fact that here and there a fair face is to be found behind which lurks a foul soul, does not invalidate the general rule that a

beautiful face at least suggests a richer and deeper beauty behind. Whenever we are assured of the contrary, there is an unquestionable feeling of disappointment or even revulsion. King Arthur's prayer concerning Galahad—

"God make thee good as thou art beautiful,"

rises in such case involuntarily to our lips. What then is this internal beauty, as indefinable as real, which not only beamed on the pure brow of Percival's sister when, looking upon the same noble knight,

" She sent the deathless passion in her eyes
Thro' him, and made him hers, and laid her mind
On him, and he believed in her belief,"

but gleams and glows in the whole "expression" of myriads more? It is quite as real as the fairness of any landscape panorama; it is much more rich than the flash of any crystal; it is more full of sweet and high suggestion than the brightest rainbow; why should it be passed over as unworthy of account? There can be no doubt whatever that it is this beautifulness, more than any other upon earth, which makes human life worth living. All that is best and noblest in human nature responds ever to the poet's deep and tender plaint when he called to mind the character-beauty of his departed friend—

" And manhood fused with female grace
In such a sort, the child would twine
A trustful hand, unask'd, in thine,
And find his comfort in thy face.

> All these have been, and thee mine eyes
> Have look'd on : if they look'd in vain,
> My shame is greater who remain,
> Nor let thy wisdom make me wise."[1]

To take wholly out of our daily environment the tender look of sympathy, the sunny smile of unselfish gladness, the winsome cheeriness of manifest benevolence, the guileless trustfulness of the eyes of little children, would be to reduce our humanity to soulless mechanism, or degrade it to the level of the tiger and the ape. The sublimest distance from such low level is found confessedly in the character of the Christ of the Gospels. As such we shall have to estimate it, farther on. Here it is sufficient to aver that moral and spiritual beauty when rooted in human nature and blooming in the "human face divine," demand adequate cause and explanation, quite as definitely as earth's fairest flowers and most luscious fruit, or their attempted representations in the pictures of "great" artists. The cultivation of orchids, we are told, is one of the most delicate and difficult as well as costly of modern arts. It would be regarded as complete proof of imbecility if any man were to suggest that these floral beauties would come of themselves, without culture, stock, or seed, in any of our gardens. How then can it be less than imbecile to assert, or assume, that the measurelessly nobler and higher beauty of human characters, with their expression in human features, which no cynic or pessimist on earth can call in question, arose simply and solely out of animal instincts which have for their ultimate essence nothing

[1] *In Memoriam*, cix.

but the satisfying of a biological craving, and even this as the chance result of the fortuitous clash of infinitesimal atoms? The bare fact that we are called upon to accept such an explanation of moral beauty in human character, shows to what desperate shifts the philosophy is reduced which rejects the Christian theory of origins.

The reality and profusion, therefore, of the beautiful throughout the wide, wide world, whether we contemplate the tender loveliness of a little flower or the glowing glory of the setting sun, whether we gaze enwrapt upon a sweet and noble face or think of the Diviner beauty of many a human character, whether we scrutinise our whole environment with microscopic minuteness or tremble before the vastness of the sublime, is amply sufficient to warrant our echoing, with all the added intensity of our modern knowledge, the reverent gratitude of the Psalmist—

"O Lord, Thou hast searched me, and known me. . . . I will give thanks unto Thee; for I am fearfully and wonderfully made: wonderful are Thy works; and that my soul knoweth right well."

It might appear to be our next duty under the head of Physical Science, to enter upon an elaborate discussion of the case for and against miracles. But it is not so. Voluminous indeed and often wearisome have been the contributions to this vexed question during the last half-century. It would appear alike unnecessary and impossible to add more. But one point of greatest import has been irreversibly established, namely, that the question as to the possibility of miracles exists only for the Atheist. For all others, including Agnostics no less than Christians, the sole matter for discussion is the sufficiency in quantity and in quality of the evidence adduced on their behalf. A few testimonies to this effect from acknowledged authorities will preclude the necessity of any enlargement upon it here. Thus Mr. J. S. Mill—

"We cannot, then, conclude absolutely that the miraculous theory ought to be at once rejected. Once admit a God, and the production of an effect by His direct volition must be reckoned with as a serious possibility."—*Essays on Religion*, p. 230.

So, too, Dr. Carpenter—

"The scientific Theist need find no abstract difficulty in the conception that the Author of Nature can, if He will, occasionally depart from the so-called Laws of Nature. I am not conscious of any such scientific prepossession against miracles as would prevent me from accepting them as facts if trustworthy evidence of their reality could be adduced. The question with me, therefore, is simply have we any adequate historical ground for the belief that such departure has ever taken place?"

The words of Professor Huxley are equally clear and emphatic—

"It is not upon any *a priori* considerations that objections either to the supposed efficacy of prayer, or to the supposed occurrences of miracles, can be based. To my mind the fatal objection to both these suppositions is the inadequacy of the evidence to prove any given case of such occurrence which has been adduced."

Principal Shairp was therefore quite warranted when, twenty years ago he wrote—

"The statement, then, that miracles are in themselves impossible, being a wholly groundless assumption, the question of their actual occurrence becomes one of purely historical evidence."—*Culture and Religion*, p. 117.

Dr. Lyman Abbott's words, in his recently published

Theology of an Evolutionist, may thus fairly stand for a summary of the whole case—

> "The question whether God answers prayer, the question whether the so-called miracles, or any of them recorded in the Bible, ever took place, are to be determined by evidence simply. If the evidence sustains the affirmative answer, there is nothing in evolution inconsistent with that answer."

In the light of the preceding pages it cannot be pronounced unreasonable that we should here assume Theism, and so dismiss at once and finally any inquiry into the physical possibility of the miraculous. That may well be taken for granted, until those who object to it have faced and solved the greater miracles which have been shown to be necessitated, when matter and chance are enthroned instead of a Supreme Mind, as the *fons et origo* of all that is.

The reality of miracles, then, so far as they are involved in Christian faith, is purely a question of evidence. This transports us at once out of the realm of science into that of history and psychology. There we shall find that the miracles of unbelief, to which denial of the evidence for Christian miracles inevitably leads, become ever more manifest and pronounced as we proceed to do justice to undeniable facts.

V

FACTS OF HISTORY AND THEIR EXPLANATION

"It is often thought that a historical revelation of God must require more than ordinary historical evidence to prove it, and that what is supernatural must needs be supernaturally attested. But this assumption is neither correct, nor helpful to Christianity."—Dr. W. N. Clarke, *Outlines of Christian Theology*, p. 38.

"The labours of the apostles and the results of those labours are unparalleled in the history of mankind. For those labours there must have been an adequate motive. To admit the truth of the story is to assign that adequate motive. To deny its truth is to leave those labours without a motive. And this is not to get rid of miracles, it is to establish them. For, that labours so unparalleled should be sustained through sufferings so severe and prolonged—without a motive—would itself be a greater miracle than any of those recorded in the story."—Dr. S. Wainwright, *The Question of Questions*, p. 157.

"The sceptic may indeed very well say, 'Do not imagine that you gain anything, as far as we are concerned, by giving up one miracle after another under the idea that what remains will be easier to accept. The motive spoils the act. You ought neither to keep nor let go with any reference to us, but simply with reference to truth. Besides, to satisfy us you must omit the supernatural altogether. When you have done that, what will be left that we do not already possess?'"—Rev. A. J. Harrison, *Problems of Christianity and Scepticism*, p. 21.

"Only to a man destitute of spiritual perception can it be that Christianity should fail to appear the greatest exhibition of the beautiful, the sublime, and of all else that appeals to our spiritual nature which has ever been known upon our earth. The most remarkable thing about Christianity is its adaptation to all sorts and conditions of men."—G. J. Romanes, *Thoughts on Religion*, p. 160.

"Miracles play so important a part in Christ's scheme that any theory which would represent them as due entirely to the imagination of His followers, or of a later age, destroys the credibility of the documents not partially but wholly, and leaves Christ a personage as mythical as Hercules."—*Ecce Homo*, 12th ed., p. 41.

"There is no aid to faith in the mere reduction of the number of miracles."—Hastings' *Bible Dictionary* (T. & T. Clark).

V

FACTS OF HISTORY AND THEIR EXPLANATION

THE gross enormities of contradiction which arise in the realm of physics from the rejection of Christian verities, have an impressive parallel in the sphere of mind. Here we are concerned no longer with the origin of inanimate nature or even the evolution of life, whether animal or vegetable, but with matters distinctively human. Dismissing now the future by reason of its uncertainty, we note that the minds of men are continually busied not only with the present, in sensation and perception, but with the past, through personal memory and written records. The former process comprises the realm of psychology, the latter that of history. This last it will be convenient to consider first.

Even when we limit the term history to the consideration of the human past, it is manifest that we can only touch upon a few salient points of so vast a theme. In every case mentioned below, however, the argument would be only strengthened by elaboration in detail.

I. Let us consider, first, the case of the Jews, in reference to their past origin, present condition, and national idiosyncrasies. Their whole history, as summarised in the Bible, forms confessedly the natural and necessary basis of Christianity. In order to appreciate this relation it is not necessary here to estimate the effects of what is now known as the "higher criticism." Its concern is with literary matters, ours with theological. Whatever may be ultimately the findings of literary criticism, they cannot seriously affect what here is the main point, namely, that the Biblical account of the origin and history of the Jewish nation manifestly involves not only the personal existence, the supreme rule, and the holy character, of God as Creator, Preserver, and Judge of all, but also the presence and working of supernatural influences [1] definitely attributed to Him.

This Biblical history, even when clarified and arranged by modern criticism, perfectly and naturally accounts for the whole of the remarkable phenomena presented to us to-day, in the striking idiosyncrasies, the modern social condition, and the apparent indestructibility, of the Jews as a people. When, moreover, the predictive element in this account is put alongside the actual facts of their history and experiences, from the Christian era to the latest European anti-Semitic development, it may safely be affirmed that there is no parallel record of anticipation and fulfilment in our whole knowledge of the human past.

Suppose, then, that the Biblical account is rejected because it is inseparably bound up with a definite Theism, and is thus pledged to the supernatural, what follows? Three plain considerations at once face us. (1) The whole Bible must, in such case, be regarded as but a mixture of delusion and fraud. (2) The complex

[1] See Note A, p. 151.

FACTS OF HISTORY AND THEIR EXPLANATION 111

and indestructible idiosyncrasies which distinguish the Jews from every other nation upon earth, must be ascribed to purely natural causes. (3) The marvellous and unparalleled agreement between predictions acknowledged to be nearly three thousand years old, and the remarkable facts of their past career and present condition, must be attributed to a merely fortuitous coincidence.

These considerations are soon enumerated, but to do them justice would require volumes. As to (1), that the whole Bible is pledged to the supernatural in the history of the Jews, no honest reader can for a moment doubt. The quantity of the supernatural deleted by modern criticism is a comparatively unimportant matter. The quality of the irreducible residuum remains unmistakable. With the hand of God in Jewish history—from Abraham to the destruction of Jerusalem by Titus—assuredly the Bible stands or falls. But if this historical basis be entirely false in its most essential part, what are we to say concerning the lofty ethics, the gracious and elevating influence, the amazing vitality of this Book of books?

These cannot honestly be denied. Few genuine thinkers will call them in question. Professor Huxley's testimony may perhaps be fairly taken as the least that can be said—

"Consider the great historical fact that for three centuries this book has been woven into the life of all that is best and noblest in English history. By the study of what other book could children be so much humanised and made to feel that each figure . . . earns the blessings or the curses of all time, according to its effort to do good and hate evil? . . . I do not say that even the highest Biblical ideal is exclusive of others or needs no supplement. But I do believe that the human race is not yet, possibly never may be, in a position to dispense with it."[1]

To do justice to the gracious and elevating influence of the Bible in all lands and ages, would require volumes of reference to facts.[2] Such testimony when it comes from believers is none the less reliable, but rather more so. For this is a case in which experience deserves to count quite as fully as observation. Upon the vitality of the Bible, moreover, not a few volumes have been written.[3] But everything about the Bible assuredly goes to confirm the main thesis of Henry Rogers' well-known work,[4] namely, that "the Bible is not such a book as man would have made if he could, or could have made if he would." Yet we are now called upon to regard this wonderful volume, which is far more truly described as a library than a book, as merely the embodiment of a colossal delusion. For such in very deed it must be, if the God of Abraham, and Moses, and Elijah, and Isaiah, be

---

[1] *Essays on Controverted Questions*, 51–53.

[2] Yet it might be fairly illustrated, and sufficiently for our present purpose, by that which is related concerning a ship wrecked off one of the Fiji islands. A boat's crew that had got ashore were terribly alarmed lest they should be devoured by cannibals. And not without reason, considering what had been known of the inhabitants. When they dispersed, for safety's sake, two of them found a cottage and cautiously sought to explore it, when suddenly one called out to his companion, "All right, Jack, there is a Bible on this table; no fear now." Cf. a brief but impressive summary in No. 67 of "Present-Day Tracts" (Rel. Tract Soc.) by Dr. Murdoch.

[3] See a convenient and able resumé by Dr. Blaikie, published as No. 23 of the "Present-Day Tracts" Series by the Rel. Tract Soc.

[4] *The Superhuman Origin of the Bible inferred from Itself*,—the Congregational Union Lecture for 1873,—a book deserving most careful study.

nothing more than the subjective idol of men given up to superstition. Yet if this be so, assuredly the Bible is more supernatural than ever. On the premisses of Atheism, the Bible both necessitates and embodies more miracles by far than when regarded as a true testimony to the Divine.

(2) But again. The task of giving adequate account of Jewish nature, idiosyncrasy, origin, religious belief, and present condition, on a purely naturalistic hypothesis, also involves decidedly greater difficulties than the acceptance of all that is reliably recorded concerning them in the Bible. The rejection of the miraculous element, which is confessedly involved in the real purpose and guidance of GOD throughout the history of the Jews, does but necessitate other and greater miracles of unbelief.

(3) Moreover, if Lord Rochester, as a sceptic of the time of Charles II., found himself unable to gainsay the argument for Christianity based upon the then condition of the Jews as a nation, much more will the Agnosticism of to-day find similar and indeed far worse difficulties.[1] For the predictions of the Old Testament, both as regards their persecution and their preservation, have in our later days gathered a force which only those who have examined it carefully can appreciate.

---

[1] If the case of the gipsies should be suggested as similar, it is a sufficient reply to compare the two cases in actual detail. So, too, if mention be made of the Maronites, or the Armenians, or indeed the Chinese, as possessing undoubted idiosyncrasies, the answer is still the same, namely, that not one of these presents the total of remarkable features which mark out the Jews in their history, nature, circumstances, and religion from every other nation under heaven.

The most remarkable passages bearing upon this are undoubtedly Deut. xxviii. and xxix., though there are others which deserve notice.[1] The fearful sufferings there predicted have been fulfilled with a lurid accuracy upon which comment would be superfluous. Take now but a portion of the solemn warning recorded—

> "And among these nations thou shalt find no ease, and there shall be no rest for the sole of thy foot: but the Lord shall give thee a trembling heart, and failing of eyes, and pining of soul: and thy life shall hang in doubt before thee; and thou shalt fear night and day, and shalt have none assurance of thy life: in the morning thou shalt say, Would GOD it were even! and at even thou shalt say, Would GOD it were morning! for the fear of thine heart which thou shalt fear, and for the sight of thine eyes which thou shalt see" (Deut. xxviii. 65-67).

Omitting here other remarkable utterances in this chapter, — though mention might well be made of vv. 52–57, and those fearful scenes in the siege of Jerusalem by Titus in which they were literally fulfilled,—compare the foregoing quotation with what has really taken place during the last nineteen centuries. The following is but a truthful summary:—

> "The history of the Jews since the Crucifixion has been one long unfolding of the scenes depicted in the pages of the Pentateuch and the Prophets. Driven out from Palestine, not allowed by Hadrian even to set foot in the Holy City, persecuted from Persia on the one side to Spain and England on the other, their lives never safe, compelled to wear a distinguishing mark on their clothes throughout the greater part of the Middle Ages, and in Persia to our own time, exiled from the Peninsula in thousands, the prey in Germany of every riotous band of marauding Crusaders, the sport of the populace and the chattel of kings, they have had one long weary

---

[1] *E.g.* Lev. xxvi.; Jer. xxiv. 8–10, etc.

FACTS OF HISTORY AND THEIR EXPLANATION 115

existence of terror and distress. Even to-day there is in some countries no real change in the feeling with which the Jews have for ages been regarded by those among whom they live. They are still as much as ever the objects of dislike and contempt. The anti-Semitism of Germany and France—markedly illustrated in the recent Dreyfus-Zola trial—is but the surface-play of a current that runs deep, and the warning of a mighty storm ever ready to break. There is no peace for the Jew of even to-day."[1]

But in the study of the Old Testament it is equally impossible to overlook the strong words which are employed to express the future restoration of the Jews. Such passages as Jer. xxx. 3, 10, xxxi. 35–37, xxxiii. 25, 26; Amos ix. 14, etc., cannot possibly be resolved into mere assurances of temporary safety, or the haze of a distant mirage. Unless they are dismissed wholly as the pious delusions of the seer, they point unmistakably to a Divinely-contemplated restoration of Israel, at some future period, to its ancient country. With modern facts and tendencies before us, it is scarcely too much to say that this restoration is already begun.

"Whereas some twenty years ago there were not more than 12,000 Jews in Jerusalem, and 30,000 in all the Holy Land, there are now about 43,000 in Jerusalem alone, and over 100,000 in Palestine. As many as 70,000 have gone there in the last few years; more by far than the 49,897 who went up with Zerubbabel from the Babylonian captivity (Ezra ii. 64, 65)."

---

[1] The whole "Present-Day Tract" (No. 77, Rel. Tract Soc.), from which the above extract is taken, well deserves consideration. It is entitled, "The Jews in their Present Condition Witnesses to the Bible," by Messrs. Burnett and Williams. Whilst these pages were preparing for the press the celebrated trial of Dreyfus at Rennes took place—than which no event of the century has more luridly illustrated the anti-Semitic feeling yet prevalent upon the Continent.

Whether this "Zionist" movement will grow into imposing dimensions or simply ebb away again, we need not venture to predict, but at present it yields no small appearance of becoming as remarkable a fulfilling of prophecy on its brighter side as all European history since the Christian era has been of the darker.

Be this, however, as it may, it is but a part of the complex whole which we are here considering. The actual correspondence between the descriptions of Jewish idiosyncrasy as illustrated in all the historical and prophetical books of the Bible, together with the predictions as to the future condition of the Jewish nation, and the actual facts of their later history and present circumstances, is too manifest to admit of denial. The Biblical, that is, the supernatural account of all this, is perfectly natural and fully sufficient. It supplies a "*vera causa*," — an adequate explanation of all the phenomena in question. To reject this, however, is to ascribe the whole vast and intricate correspondence to mere chance coincidence, and represent it as springing solely from the accidental variations of "natural" evolution. But words and figures alike fail to do justice to the enormity of the improbabilities which lie against such a suggestion. The very least that can be said is, that the man who can accept such a thesis, swallows at one gulp a veritable camel, compared with which the other alternative is but as a gnat for difficulty.

II. Let us pass on, however, from Judaism to Christianity. Here again we start with certainty. For the existence, diffusion, and influence of the Christian faith to-day is manifest beyond all cavil.

It is an immeasurable force in the present condition and future destiny of humanity. Whence then has it sprung, and how has it come to be what we now see and know? For, it must be reiterated, this is a case entirely unique, however freely we acknowledge the presence and influence of other religions in the world. It is quite true that the adherents of Buddhism alone outnumber all Christians put together. Hindus and Mohammedans also confessedly amount to vast numbers. But no one of these faiths constitutes a parallel to Christianity. For besides their totally different origins, and the well-understood methods by which Mohammedanism was propagated, they are all alike at this hour inseparably bound up with Eastern civilisations, which are not merely inoperative, but gradually and necessarily vanishing in the course of the world's progress. Whereas Christianity exercises an immeasurable and ever-increasing influence throughout the world, seeing that it is strongest in the foremost nations, such as England, America, and Germany, which show every sign of developing vitality and vigorous growth. Every now and then, indeed, we meet with sporadic prophecies that Christianity will soon be extinct, as also bold assertions that it is a "dying creed." But in all such cases the wish is so manifestly father to the thought, the Cassandra cry has become so hackneyed with vain repetition, and the confident prediction has been so flatly contradicted by the march of events, that we may pass them by with regretful compassion. All the world knows what were the oracular sentences of doom pronounced upon the Christian faith by Rousseau and

Voltaire and Paine a century ago. To-day every man is witness as to how they are being fulfilled. As a matter of simple fact, the whole world is being permeated, and great portions of it saturated, with Christian doctrine and practice. The success of Christian "missions" to foreign countries during the last century, has been far greater than the progress of the Christian Churches in a similar length of time in the apostolic and sub-apostolic days. That there are now, as then, many kinds and degrees of Christianness, does not in the least detract from, but rather add to the significance of such a fact. For it testifies to the adaptability of Christian verities to all sorts and conditions of human nature, and the wonderful vitality exhibited in their triumph over unmeasured degrees of corruption within, no less than of opposition without.

But one or two collateral certainties equally deserve notice. We do know, beyond question, when, where, and how Christianity arose. Occasional attempts to cast doubt upon the real existence of Christ and His apostles are too wild and foolish to call for serious discussion. It is historically certain, from abundant proofs, that Jesus lived, taught, and was crucified in Judæa at the period stated in our Gospels. Also that His doctrines were promulgated without force, and that from Jerusalem as a centre they soon spread everywhere throughout the then known world, in spite of their being most bitterly opposed. This general statement, however, does but scanty justice to the actual facts of the case. There is truly a triple opposition to be estimated, and a triple triumph to be accounted for in

FACTS OF HISTORY AND THEIR EXPLANATION   119

regard to the beginning of Christianity and its continuance to this hour. No one of these can be fully set forth in few words. Yet it is essential to the truth that they be fairly taken into account.[1]

1. As to the initial stages, then, of Christianity, it is only true to say that if we can imagine a lion, a tiger, and a wolf uniting in desperate effort to destroy a lamb—and failing, we should but have a fair parallel to that which actually happened in human society at the commencement of the Christian era. The practical alliance between Jewish hate, Roman might, and Greek subtlety, against the infant Christian faith, is absolutely without parallel in history. The two former of these anti-Christian factors, at least, we are considerably in danger of underrating in these days of liberty and peace.

Here it is necessary, first, to bear well in mind the whole truth concerning Jewish nature. We cannot but see how its wondrous idiosyncrasies of vitality, tenacity, fanaticism, have been writ large on the page of history, from the time of the unparalleled horrors and heroism of the war with Rome which ended in the destruction of Jerusalem, down to the latest Russian persecution. We are well able to estimate the frame of mind in which the long chain of previous wars and captivities had left them at the period when Christ appeared. Their

---

[1] The sincere reader should study carefully Storrs' *Divine Origin of Christianity*, or Pressensé's *Early Years of Christianity*, and *Martyrs and Apologists*. Brief but excellent summaries may be found in Nos. 6 and 49 of "Present-Day Tracts," published by the Religious Tract Society, under the titles, "The Success of Christianity and Modern Explanations of it," and "Is the Evolution of Christianity from mere Natural Sources credible?"

condition just then, moreover, under the Roman yoke, especially disposed them to hail with enthusiasm one kind of Messiah, and to reject with execration the opposite. Yet it was unquestionably this opposite which Jesus exemplified. So that the intensity of the national hate which He occasioned, may be measured by the shock which He administered to the popular chafing and pride and expectation then generally prevalent, as well as to all those deeply-rooted prejudices of which priests and scribes and Pharisees were the exponents. We may form some estimate of the acerbity of this national revulsion, from our own observation of Jewish characteristics as they exist in Europe to-day.

But that at first a humble few, and afterwards large numbers of Jews, including priests and elders, did believe on Him and act accordingly, is fact beyond all controversy. Now, whilst nothing is easier to understand than the rejection of Christ by the majority of His fellow-countrymen at that time, it is proportionately difficult, not to say utterly impossible, to account for the belief of His disciples on any other basis than that alleged in the New Testament. For if we reject this, unbelief is compelled to assume that they, of all people in the world, were most easily deceived, and this when their highest hopes and strongest desires, their keenest anticipations and most intense faith, together with their most fervid patriotism, were all alike being uncompromisingly contradicted.

This, however, is but an introduction to the difficulties which next arise for unbelief in connection with the origin and growth of the Christian Church. The attitude of Greeks and Romans demands also to be taken into account. The spectacle is indeed a strange one from the Agnostic standpoint. Men of the most cultured nation in the world, submitting themselves in great numbers to a transparent fraud; and citizens of the haughtiest community ever known, surrendering themselves throughout the empire to the supreme governance of the memory of a fanatic Jew, whom their own deputy had just put to a shameful death!

It is manifest enough that the only alliance possible between Jew and Roman of that age was this common determination, one from religious the other from political motives, that the followers of Christ should be exterminated and His very name blotted out. What the Roman lacked in bitterness the Jew supplied. What the Jew could not do though he would, the Roman undertook to accomplish by brute force. Both the quantity and quality of this force have to be fairly borne in mind. Here, however, we can only bestow upon the whole a single glance. It has been well said concerning those early Christians, that "as dynamite explodes at the tap of the hammer, so the whole savage empire smote them with an unutterable fierceness, and wrapped them in consuming fury." What language of earth can ever do justice either to the sufferings or the heroism of a Blandina, a Perpetua, a Potamion, a Felicitas? But by way of avoiding detailed horrors, it shall suffice to quote Mr. Lecky's summary, in his *History of European Morals*—

"We read of Christians bound in chairs of red-hot iron while the stench of the unconsumed bodies rose in a suffocating cloud to heaven : of others torn to the very bone by shells or hooks of iron :

of holy virgins given over to the lust of gladiators or the mercies of the pander: of two hundred and twenty-seven sent on one occasion to the mines each with one leg severed by a hot iron and an eye scooped from the socket: of fires so slow that the victims writhed for hours in their agony: of tortures prolonged and varied through entire days. For the love of their Divine Master, for the cause which they believed to be true, men, and even weak girls, endured these things, when one word would have freed them from their sufferings."

In estimating the quality of such maltreatment, we must not forget the quantity.

"The great persecutions," says Pressensé, "are generally enumerated as ten. This, however, is an arbitrary division. It would be an error to assert that persecution burst forth only ten times before the Constantine era. In reality it never ceased. Checked at one point, it only flamed forth afresh at another. The decree of Trajan, reinforced by many others, was not for a single day withdrawn. Persecution was therefore always lawful, and did not need a special permission."

Commencing with the innumerable and indescribable barbarities of Nero at Rome, persecution became, as Prof. Vernon Bartlet has well expressed it, "a permanent police measure" throughout the empire. It was not only intensified by the cruelties of Domitian, but everywhere savagely enforced by the people themselves. Yet as early as the time of Trajan, only fifty years after the martyrdom of Paul, we find the Roman proconsul Pliny writing to the emperor, to complain that he is so surrounded in Asia Minor with Christian converts that he does not know what to do with them—

"The superstition has spread from the cities into the country like an infection carried by the wind."

"It has seemed to me a matter worthy of consultation, chiefly on account of the number of persons in danger. Many of all ages and ranks, and of both sexes, are and will be in danger."

FACTS OF HISTORY AND THEIR EXPLANATION 123

The persecution continued none the less, and, with variations in the degree of violence, lasted on through the reigns of Hadrian, Marcus Aurelius, Septimius Maximinus Thrax, Gallus, Gallienus, until under Galerius and Diocletian, at the end of the third century, a last frantic attempt was made to "sweep Christianity from the earth." Diocletian's three edicts were promulgated throughout the empire, and "persecution rose to an almost unparalleled height of fury." In that persecution alone there perished from torture 184,000 persons in the province of Egypt, besides 700,000 in exile, or at the public works. How many more suffered elsewhere can never be known.

And now what was the result of this "long and bloody struggle"? We may find it in the Edict of Toleration issued by that very Galerius whose torturing of the Christians by slow fires is too horrible to be recounted. In that remarkable document—which we have from Lactantius, an eye-witness—the ruthless pagan confesses his utter failure to overthrow Christianity, and in the pangs of his incurable disease, concedes to Christians the right to assemble for worship, only asking them to pray for him! Thus it was that "Christianity took its place amongst the recognised religions of the empire." Fuller entrance into detail alone is necessary to confirm the conviction, that a parallel to this long-drawn tragedy has not been known in the world's history.

It is, of course, easy to say that persecution makes a cause popular and creates enthusiasm. It is just as true as to say that water makes fire burn brighter. Sometimes it does. But always and only on condition that (1) the fire is stronger than the water poured upon it, and (2) there should be such potential affinity between the fire and the water, as we know does exist in the relations of oxygen to combustion. But in the case before us, (1), the indomitable strength and unquenchable fervour of Christian conviction are the very things to be accounted for. Whilst (2), it is preposterous to suggest that there was any possibility of sympathy whatever between the unresisting meekness of the Christians and typical Roman pride,—or between Christian penitence and Greek self-complacency, — or between those who clung to a crucified Messiah alleged to have risen from the dead, and the average convictions of the Jews of that period. The flame of wild fanaticism might perhaps suffice to spread a plausible superstition. But where in this case is there any vestige of the plausible ? The Christian scheme is before us, and we have a fair knowledge of those times with their prevalent moral temper. Where is there any trace of affinity ? Did Christianity hold out any inducements likely to minister to the pride, or the expectations, or the lust, of the world as it then was ? Nay, in all sober truth, it is simply impossible to imagine a scheme of morals or an ideal of philosophy, a plan of human life or a conception of the Divine Nature, more utterly opposed than was Christianity, to the convictions and tastes of Jew, and Greek, and Roman alike. And this not merely as regards the lower classes, but equally men of high position. In fact, those who possessed most wealth and influence had ever most to lose, and were correspondingly soonest

FACTS OF HISTORY AND THEIR EXPLANATION

and most bitterly offended. Meanwhile how far removed from blind, frenzied fanaticism was the faith of the early Christians, may be well expressed in other words of the Rationalist historian quoted above—

"Christianity united with its distinctive teaching a pure and noble system of Ethics. It produced more heroic actions and formed more upright men than any other creed. It transformed the character of multitudes, vivified the cold heart by new enthusiasm, redeemed, regenerated, emancipated the most depraved of mankind."

So that when Gibbon cynically proffers, as explanation of early Christian triumphs, (1) the devotion of Christians, and (2) the power of Constantine, he calmly assumes the very thing to be accounted for. It is precisely as if one should claim to explain the cause of a great conflagration by the assertion that it was kindled by a lighted match. Which would leave unanswered the very questions that most demand answer, namely, (1) how came the match to have its potentiality of fire? (2) who struck and applied it? and (3) why? It is a belated question, and withal quite irrelevant, to ask how much Constantine did for Christianity. The actual problem to be solved is, what was it in Christianity which, in spite of all the relentless fury of preceding persecutions, had already caused it so to triumph as to make it worth the while of Constantine to seek its alliance rather than continue the manifestly useless attempts to destroy it? If, one must ask, there was such all-explaining potency in the imperial patronage of Constantine, why were the frantic and brutal and bloody efforts of Diocletian just before, as well as the civil and social efforts and energies of Julian just after, alike impotent to compass its end?[1]

We may safely conclude, therefore, that Constantine's attitude only testifies to the resistless force of that Christian devotion for which adequate cause has to be found. It is but a counsel of despair to attribute it to fanatic contagion. For whilst the plausibility of pleasing error, or the attractions of profitable fraud, may avail to fan a transient flame, they cannot and do not confer glowing immortality upon falsehood, they do not and cannot cause a system of lofty and difficult ethics to take on such vitality in human society as not only to defy extinction, but gather strength with passing ages and become in the end the mightiest "power that makes for righteousness" in the greatest nations of the world.

One need not here dwell upon the "wisdom of the Greek" save to affirm that it was, in some respects, a more formidable foe even than persecution. But a pertinent question may be put with emphasis. If Christ were only a Galilean impostor, seeking to establish a borrowed system of morals upon a fraudulent or fanatical basis, so clumsily, moreover, that to-day the eye of the mind can easily detect His fallacies over a vista of eighteen centuries, how came it to pass that all the subtlety and force of the Greek intellect could not, there and then,

---

[1] "The first of these laws (of Julian) prohibited the children of Galileans—for this was the name he gave to Christians—from being instructed in poetry, rhetoric, or philosophy." Such is the testimony of Theodoret. And it is confirmed by Ammianus, who was a pagan sympathiser with Julian: "His forbidding masters of rhetoric and grammar to instruct Christians was a cruel action, and one deserving to be buried in everlasting oblivion.'

expose the whole, even as the Coulombs recently exploded *in situ* the Blavatsky frauds in India?

So far, however, from succumbing to this threefold opposition, which assuredly was such as no other religion on earth has ever experienced, we see that from each and all of these opposing sources, Jewish, Greek, and Roman, the ranks of the early converts were continually recruited, until they became the ever victorious army which included the whole world in its triumphal march. The first manifest triumph of Christianity, therefore, was over its enemies.

2. The second, hardly less significant, has been over its friends. For as history records in regard to Hannibal's famous struggle with Rome, that "Capua was the Cannæ of Carthage," by reason of its enervating luxury, so may it be averred that the freeing of Christianity from persecution and contumely, and the flooding it with imperial wealth and privilege, constituted a far more real and potent danger than the previous ordeals of fire and sword. From this time, indeed, it must be owned that the history of the Christian Church, in its main features, becomes alike perplexing and saddening. As a matter of lamentable fact, during the subsequent generations when external persecution had ceased, Christians in all too many cases began to do exactly contrary to the teaching and the spirit of the Master whose name they bore. The details of the degenerating process through which the "light of the world," obscured more and more by ecclesiastical pride and corruption, sank into the darkness of the Middle Ages, must be sought elsewhere. It is often and truly

said that Church history is sad reading. But in the heart of the confession a question lurks which must not be overlooked, namely, how came it to pass that such internal poison did not succeed in accomplishing what external violence had failed to do? Germ diseases, we now know, are the most deadly of all, both as to dire effect and difficulty of cure.[1] Why, then, did not Christianity die of the fevered un-Christianness which so soon and so virulently permeated its whole extent? Such triumph over the corruption of its friends bespeaks —if it be a merely human development based on delusion—a greater moral miracle even than its refusal to succumb to the onslaughts of its enemies.

3. A third triumph might also justly be specified, namely, that over the definite and vigorous unbelief of the last century. The detailed history cannot, of course, be here attempted. It is sufficient to recall the early vigour of Continental Deism with its English echo, followed by the development of Atheism and Secularism in this country *pari passu* with the "destructive criticism" of Germany and the widespread influence of Strauss and Renan.[2] It certainly appeared as if Christianity had but a short time to live. Yet to-day, in spite of Agnosticism, which appears, under the influence of modern education, to be taking the place of Secularism and Atheism, it is simply true to say that Christianity is not only as vigorous as ever, but has taken on fresh vitality, and exhibits definite promise of

[1] Mr. H. G. Wells is perfectly justified in his *War of Worlds* in representing the dreadful and resistless Martians as succumbing at last to Bacterial attack.

[2] An able summary of the case in regard to modern Secularism will be found in Rev. H. Footman's *Reasonable Apprehensions and Reassuring Hints* (London: Field & Tuer).

FACTS OF HISTORY AND THEIR EXPLANATION

becoming at once purer and stronger than during all the preceding centuries. Its present activity throughout this country is too manifest to call for comment. When all fair allowance has been made for differences of opinion between the various sections of the Church, it yet remains true that there is to-day more devotion and influence in the world than ever before which must be definitely pronounced Christian, whilst all kinds of Christian workers are more numerous and more energetic than ever. Missionary operations alone exhibit a degree of disinterested zeal never before equalled in the whole course of history, and the results of these labours surpass even those of the first century of Christian propagandism.[1] The more perplexing, therefore, and disappointing the history of Christianity may be when tried by the high standard of the New Testament, the greater is the marvel of its indestructible vitality and perpetual rejuvenescence. Unless, indeed, the foundations of the Christian faith are true, this marvel becomes a veritable miracle. For upon the theory of unbelief, all this triumph, all this unparalleled diffusion, this strength of conviction which has manifestly defied empires, this inner spring of purity which has prevented even internal corruption from issuing in destruction, this whole complex, immeasurable, irrepressible reality of growth, and permanence, and vigour, originated in fraud or delusion, or a sinister

[1] Take a typical comment from an unbiassed source. Says the *Daily Chronicle* of July 4, 1900: "'Is Christianity a failure?' was the subject of a correspondence pursued in this paper some years ago. The answer has come in a tremendous reawakening of the Churches in the direction of practical life; and in America this has been visible with perhaps more distinctness even than in England."

admixture of both! Can any process of thought whatever render this either reasonable or credible?[1]

To sum up, then, we are warranted in affirming that if the whole past and present of Christianity can be attributed to myth, to ignorance, to hysteria, to fanaticism spiced with fraud, or to any conceivable combination of all these, then it is not enough to liken such an attribution to a pyramid poised upon its apex, for the apex itself rests upon nothing. Thus is involved a miracle indeed, as much more stupendous in the quantity of its supernaturalness as more sinister in quality, than all those recorded in the New Testament. It is undoubtedly true, as Mr. Lecky has frankly acknowledged, that

"Amid all the sins and failings, amid all the priestcraft, the persecution, and fanaticism which have defaced the Church, it has preserved, in the character and example of its Founder, an enduring principle of regeneration."

But if only a character so high and an example so potent be conceded as a necessity of the case, unbelief answers itself (as will be presently more fully shown), and rationalism is hoist with its own petard. We are entirely warranted, therefore, in borrowing the words of Hume and saying, in regard to the New Testament account of the rise, progress, vitality, and influence of the Christian religion, that "its falsehood would be more

[1] The origin and history of Mohammedanism or Buddhism may well be acknowledged to be remarkable. But no one fairly acquainted with these can for a moment allege them as a parallel to Christianity. Rather they exactly illustrate the present contention. For in regard to each of these we are able to discover clear and sufficient natural causes for their diffusion. But in the case of Christianity, the more such are sought the less they are found.

miraculous than the fact which it endeavours to establish."

III. We proceed now to notice another testimony in the same direction, namely, that arising from the present existence, significance, and origin of the Christian rite known as "The Lord's Supper," or the "Eucharist," or "The Communion of the Lord's Table." The particular name adopted, or indeed the specific theological conception of the meaning of this service, does not here concern us. The argument is the same either from the High Anglican or the Free Church standpoint. It is not affected by the adoption of the Romish, or Zwinglian, or Lutheran conception of this rite. We can, indeed, only now sketch in outline that which richly merits closest attention. But we will at least start once more with certainty. Throughout the whole world, wherever Christianity is known, this rite is observed. With what degree of complexity or variation as to method, is here irrelevant. The simple and sufficient fact is that this observation of a unique service has always been part of the Christian religion. It is no less significant, though we may not here pause to dwell upon it, that somehow, wherever it has prevailed, living sacrifices for sin have ceased, and at the same time the sense of sin has been greatly intensified.

For our present purpose we are only concerned to demand an adequate cause for this unique institution. The New Testament account of its origin, intention, and promulgation is at once simple, reasonable, and sufficient. If, however, this be rejected, on the ground that it involves the truth of Christ's resurrection, as a supernatural and therefore incredible event, what follows? Such rejection disposes of none of the facts. The features of the case which may be fairly said to be beyond controversy are these—

1. That this rite has been sacredly observed by all Christians without exception and in every part of the world, without a break, for the last eighteen and a half centuries.

2. That it could not possibly have been derived from Judaism, seeing that it entirely ignores the very heart of the analogous Jewish rite, namely, a living animal victim for sacrifice.

3. That, on the other hand, the bare notion of a Messiah making Himself a sacrifice, could only shock and horrify the pious Jew.

4. That there was nothing in Greek or Roman mythology from which this rite could be derived, nor was there any reason at all why any such borrowing should be even contemplated. It was, indeed, a puzzle alike to Jewish and Roman persecutors.

5. That it was definitely instituted by Christ Himself, and manifestly intended by Him as a memorial service to be continually repeated from that time forth.

6. That not only has it been so observed, unbrokenly, from that day to this, but it is more and more repeated every year by means of Christian Foreign Missions, and promises to become known ere long absolutely throughout the whole world.

Now upon the assumption of unbelief, namely, that Christ was simply a human reformer, murdered and left in some known grave like other men, two questions

FACTS OF HISTORY AND THEIR EXPLANATION

at least demand an unevasive answer. First, what could be the motive for the institution of such a service by Christ Himself? Secondly, how came it to be universally accepted as a distinctive Christian rite, and continually prevalent thenceforth to the present hour?

For, be it clearly observed, on the assumption that the Resurrection is false, this service could only be, from the very first, the perpetuation and proclamation of an utter failure, as well as the absolute contradiction of Christ's own most emphatic assurance and definite promise. It would also be, in such case, the manifest stultification of all that the apostles afterwards so earnestly taught. Over and over again Christ asserted that He would not only be killed, but "the third day rise again from the dead." Now upon the hypothesis of unbelief, He must either have known or not have known that this prediction of His was utterly delusive. In the former case, He must be regarded as a deceiver; in the latter, as deceived. What then becomes of that character which, as will be presently shown, unbelief has extolled almost as highly as belief? The same dilemma, however, also applies to all the apostles. For whilst we know that they went everywhere preaching "Jesus and the resurrection," they also insisted, in every Church, upon the observance of this service, which, if Christ were not risen, utterly mocked their teaching and called attention to its foundation falsehood, seeing that all men were thereby continually reminded of what they themselves also knew, namely, that the dead body of the Christ of whom they spoke lay rotting in some Jewish grave.

And strangest of all, this most glaring of all contradictions arose on the very spot where the events in question took place; thence as from a centre developed itself throughout the world; and now, after the lapse of nearly nineteen centuries, has stronger hold than ever upon the reverent affections of the noblest men and the foremost nations of modern civilisation! Well indeed has Ebrard said that "in the whole sphere of criticism there is no absurdity more uncritical than the idea that a rite which universally prevailed should have grown up accidentally and gradually, especially a rite of such marked peculiarity." But when to this is added the inference which necessarily follows from the assumption of Christ's non-resurrection, namely, that the whole rite was but the mark of an utter delusion, or a manifest fraud, combined with unmeasured failure, we have in truth a miracle of unbelief, which, in modern parlance, is simply and utterly "unthinkable."

For the more we strive to avoid the supernatural by assuming Christ's non-resurrection, the more vainly do we ask how it came to pass that the Master Himself instituted such a service; or what could induce the first disciples to perpetuate the memory of a death which proved them to be either deceivers or deceived; or what could possibly have led others of all temperaments and positions from the very midst of their opponents and persecutors, to join in the continuance of this rite, and the deification of an impostor who had broken his most emphatic promise and disappointed every hope that he had raised?

The actuality of the Resurrection, on the other hand,

as a sign and seal of the divineness of Christ's life and death, is a simple and sufficient explanation of all the facts. But if that be rejected, then the institution of such a rite, at such a time, and under such circumstances, together with its unbroken and ever-increasing perpetuation to this day, is more inexplicable upon natural principles, and therefore more miraculous, than the Resurrection itself.

IV. It is time, however, that we faced unflinchingly, and upon its merits, the whole modern case for or against Christ's actual Resurrection. It has of late years become more and more apparent, that the key of the entire Christian position is in the reality, or otherwise, of the Resurrection of Christ from the dead. Mr. Row, in his lecture before the Christian Evidence Society, stated the case with emphatic frankness when he said, "Above all, let unbelievers not carp at minor details about miracles, but join issue in the truth or falsehood of the Resurrection of Jesus Christ, with the truth of which miracle the writers of the New Testament affirm that Christianity stands or falls."

It cannot be said these words are too strong. If this greatest of all miracles be true, there is no more question about the reality of the supernatural. If this be false, the whole representation of the New Testament is a delusion, and there is left no Christianity to defend. We cannot be surprised, therefore, that a special attack has been made upon this central position of the Christian faith. It was also to be expected that equally concentrated attention, by way of reply, would be paid to it by Christian apologists. Many monographs have thus appeared upon this theme.[1] Here it must suffice for us to attempt a fair estimate of the facts which confessedly remain, after all the winnowing criticism of the present day has done its utmost. Abundant reasons may be supplied for the following general affirmations :—

1. That the witnesses on behalf of the Resurrection were entirely competent.[2]

The further possible suggestion that they were wanting in moral character will be met presently. The only valid proof of incompetence as witnesses would be the demonstration that all the apostles and early preachers were insane, which suggestion is its own sufficient refutation.

2. That they were sufficient in number.

3. That they commenced their zealous testimony immediately upon the occurrence of the events recorded in the Gospels. Time for growth of a myth is, thanks to modern critical research, entirely out of the question.

4. That believers in the Resurrection multiplied at once in the very place where it was alleged to have occurred, and thence, as from a centre, it spread until the world of that day was filled with the doctrine.

[1] For ordinary readers the best modern statement of the case is undoubtedly that of Dr. J. Kennedy's little volume, entitled, *The Resurrection of Jesus Christ*, published by the Religious Tract Society. For a succinct summary of the whole position see *Reasonable Orthodoxy*, by the present writer.

[2] The suggestion that the early witnesses of the Resurrection were lacking in the critical and scientific faculty is quite irrevelant. For it is plain that neither of these faculties was necessary for the clear apprehension of the fact that Christ was risen, or the truthful representation of that fact to others.

FACTS OF HISTORY AND THEIR EXPLANATION 137

5. That the early developments of party differences, on other matters, between the first believers, prevented all possibility of dishonest collusion in regard to this great fundamental conviction and declaration.

6. That the number of backsliders and perverts, through persecution, is sufficient guarantee that there was no guilty secret to be kept, or it would most certainly have come to light.

7. That from the belief in the Resurrection there sprang a moral and spiritual impetus which set in motion the mightiest forces for righteousness known in human history.

8. That this mighty and holy impulse has not only lasted until now, but is still developing fresh energy year by year, in the diffusion of Christianity throughout the world.

Now all this, and more that might truthfully be tabulated, has to be rationally accounted for. These facts, as such, demand a valid explanation and an adequate cause. They can no more have arisen out of nothing, or come about by chance, than our great modern railroad system could have arisen spontaneously in a land where iron was unknown, or have been developed without the brain of a Watt and the genius of a Stephenson.

In other words, if all this weight of testimony, this enormity of actual, wonderful, and holy result, could have sprung either from nothing or from fraud, aided only by delusion and superstition, a greater psychological and moral difficulty is involved than any mental or physical difficulty attendant upon the actuality of the Resurrection as recorded in the Gospels.

In order, however, to bring out into due relief the weighty truths thus summarised, let us briefly survey the dilemma of unbelief. That *something* happened which gave rise to the great foundation belief of Christianity, may be postulated as incontrovertible. What was that something? The choice is necessarily restricted to one of the three following:—

1. Christ did actually rise from the dead,[1] substantially as recorded in the New Testament, thus at once creating and explaining the new impulse of spiritual life, fervid zeal, and triumphant hope, in the disciples.

2. Or else, the indisputable and rapid spread of Christian belief throughout all the early Churches, with its continuance and influence until now, resulted solely from the superstitious and weak-minded delusion of a small band of Jewish men and women who were given over to credulity and fanaticism.

3. Or else, the whole Christian result rests upon well-known and cunningly concocted fraud.

Now of these, if (1) be accepted, everything is not only adequately accounted for, but explained as naturally as supernaturally. If this, however, be rejected, we must look to (2) or (3) for the sufficient cause of the whole result. But the more searchingly this is done, the more does it become manifest that such a proceeding is but an overwhelming case of straining out the gnat

---

[1] The question as to the nature of His Resurrection, whether "physical" or "spiritual," is here irrelevant, but will be considered at the close of this chapter. See Note B, p. 155.

FACTS OF HISTORY AND THEIR EXPLANATION 139

and swallowing the camel. The difficulties which at once and inevitably arise, are incomparably greater than those which on the side of Christian faith are regarded as incredible.

For in this case one of two statements must be true. (1) Either Christ did die, but did not really rise again; or (2) He did not really die, and so only seemed to rise from the dead.

Now the latter alternative can scarcely be better despatched than in the words of Strauss himself. Such a witness should surely suffice, even apart from other incredibilities. Thus he says—

"It is impossible that a being who had stolen half dead out of the sepulchre, who crept about weak and ill, wanting medical treatment, who required bandaging, strengthening, indulgence, and who still at last yielded to his sufferings, could have given the disciples the impression that he was a conqueror over death and the grave. Such a resuscitation could only have weakened the impression he had made upon them in life and in death. It could by no possibility have changed their sorrow into enthusiasm, or have elevated their reverence into worship."

All this seems so self-manifest that it would appear scarcely worth while to take further notice of so puerile a hypothesis. And yet, strange to say, this very supposition is that which has most recommended itself to the late President of the Royal Society, Prof. T. H. Huxley. How a man of his scientific acumen and polemical skill could bring himself to such a choice in the dilemma, is not ours to say. One must, however, avow that it is sheer scientific pedantry to refuse to believe that Christ really died, "unless careful thermometric observation proved that the temperature of the body had sunk to a certain point, or unless the cadaverous stiffening of the muscles had become well established."

But whatever we may think of such a proposition, the difficulties which immediately arise upon denying the reality of Christ's death have to be honestly faced. They have been sufficiently put by Keim in his *Jesu von Nazara* (vol. vi. p. 330)—

"And what impossibilities meet us, from the rolling away of the stone to the restless travelling, those long journeys between Jerusalem and Galilee with his utterly exhausted vital force, even if we grant to Dr. Paulus that his feet had not been pierced. Then there is the most impossible thing of all ; a poor sick, weak Jesus, with difficulty holding himself erect, in hiding, disguised, and finally dying, this Jesus an object of faith, of exalted emotion, of the triumph of his adherents, a risen conqueror and Son of God ! Here, in fact, the theory begins to grow absurd, worthy only of rejection, since it makes the apostles either miserable victims of deceit, or with Jesus themselves deceivers. On these grounds the theory of apparent death has in recent times been rejected by critics almost without exception."

It has been reserved for England's foremost son of science to endeavour to resuscitate this moribund hypothesis. Certainly one would have said that if modern science really had anything worth regarding against the Resurrection of Christ, an abler advocate of its findings could not be found than Thomas Henry Huxley. But, in good sooth, if this is the best that even he has to advance, then Christianity is firmly based indeed.

Dr. Sanday[1] has but expressed the final finding of modern criticism—after the most exact and prolonged scrutiny—when he avows that both this suggestion of only pseudo-death, and the theory that the early witnesses

[1] In the recent *Dictionary of the Bible*, edited by Dr. Hastings (T. & T. Clark).

to the Resurrection might have been wilful deceivers, are dead and done with, so far as further present-day consideration is concerned.

If we turn instead to the second supposition, namely, that Christ did really die but did not really rise, we have first to consider Strauss' own belief, that mythical theory upon which he spent so much cultured ingenuity, and which was afterwards so embellished by the rhetoric of Renan.

According to this, the spring and centre of the whole Christian doctrine of the Resurrection was the hysterical imagination of Mary Magdalene. Jesus did die indeed, but did not rise. Mary simply thought she saw Him, and made all the rest of His former disciples think so too. Out of their conjoint " elevation of mental and nervous life "—in plain statement, out of their weak-minded and credulous fanaticism, sprang the Resurrection narratives with all their following results. Thus, according to this suggestion, the real foundation of the apostolic Christianity which overran the world, was mere hysteria plus credulity !

Well, one thing assuredly follows. If this be so, it is at all events a greater miracle by far than the Resurrection itself. If such a result from such a cause be deemed credible, there need no longer be any objection to the supernatural, for here we have thrust upon us that which is not only beyond but utterly opposed to all that we know to be natural. Let us, however, see clearly to what this mythico-visionary supposition commits us. There are certain facts of the case which may be pronounced indisputable. These are as follows :—

1. The Resurrection was confessedly entirely contrary alike to the fears and the hopes of the disciples. There

is, therefore, no reason whatever to call in question the representation of them which we find in the Gospels, as being astounded at something which followed upon the Crucifixion, sceptical as to the reality of a resurrection, "slow indeed" to believe that it was actually true.

2. By their final conviction that it was true, and the consequent undertaking of a world-wide propaganda, they had nothing whatever to gain, but everything valuable to lose. All hope of personal advantage in this life was reversed. All that they had naturally held precious up to that time, was utterly lost. Everything that human nature finds hardest to bear and most seeks to avoid, shame, persecution, martyrdom, stood out luridly before them as their inevitable prospect.

3. The first converts were from amongst the Jews, including priests and other Mosaic devotees, of whom Saul of Tarsus stands out as a prominent specimen. If any man is disposed to think that such men as these are easily moved from their venerable traditions, it is open to him honestly to prove it to-day, whenever he will, by trying to compass the same results in the case of any ordinary Jewish Rabbi.

4. From Paul's unchallenged — or perhaps rather challenged and confirmed—letters, namely, those to the Romans, Corinthians, and Galatians, we do know that the full and unhesitating belief in Christ's real Resurrection was established amongst all Christians throughout the then known world within about twenty-five years after the Crucifixion. That is, during a less period of time than has elapsed between the passing of the Education Act of 1870 and the present day. Is this, then, suffi-

cient time for the development of a "myth," at the centre of which was a sheer delusion, into the strength of a conviction which was more than conqueror over the bitter prejudice of the Jew, the stubborn pride of the Roman, and the cultured conceit of the Greek? Should this, indeed, be accepted as true, we need go no farther. The supernatural—in sinister fashion—is proved to demonstration.

5. Again, Keim repudiates the "vision theory"—after prolonged and friendly consideration—on the ground that it "leaves the main facts unexplained, and indeed subordinates what is historically attested to weak and untenable views." He also acknowledges that the belief in the Resurrection was "directly accompanied by astonishingly clear perceptions and resolves." But this acknowledgment surely connotes more than the author of it appears to perceive. "Clear perceptions" could not but distinguish between the sight or touch of the body of their risen Lord, and a "telegram from heaven" in the shape of some misleading impression made upon their brain, whereby they mistook the subjective for the objective. Dr. Bruce well asks [1]—

"If the resurrection be an unreality, if the body that was nailed to the tree never came forth from the tomb, why send messages that were certain to produce an opposite impression?"

---

[1] *Apologetics*, p. 393. This "telegram theory" is well criticised and dismissed by Dr. Bruce, but calls for no special consideration here, inasmuch as it concedes the supernatural. Dr. Bruce forcibly remarks, "it is simply a question whether what was seen was the body that was laid in the tomb, or a vision bearing the likeness of that body, produced for the benefit of His disciples by the still living spirit of Jesus."

Out of the "main facts" which are "historically attested," rises, however, the real question of importance. Whence did the disciples draw the influence which made them, almost immediately after the Crucifixion, the very opposite to what they had been before? Not only have we abundant evidence of their previous narrow-mindedness and dulness of spiritual apprehension, but we know that these characteristics remained right up to the time of their Master's betrayal and death. Whilst, indeed, He was yet with them, and when He most of all needed their support, they were so craven-hearted that they "all forsook Him and fled"; one of them afterwards denying with oaths that he had been in His company.

Yet see what now follows. The Master whom they had so long timidly followed is absolutely overwhelmed by Jewish hate working through Roman might, is helplessly subjected to shame and suffering, and finally put to death in the most ignominious way as a common malefactor. Thus He is utterly taken away from them, and with His removal every high hope that they had cherished is wholly lost, every chance of renewed inspiration is gone for ever. The *natural* result of all this we know—if we know anything at all about human nature—would be that broken-hearted, crushed in spirit, scattered in all directions, they should sink into obscurity, leaving only the record of another prophet's failure to be reckoned with that of Theudas, and Judas of Galilee, and similar sporadic flashes of Jewish fanaticism.

But instead of this what do we actually find? The very men who whilst their leader was with them were arrant cowards, now that He is taken away become bold as lions. The disciples who when they had their Teacher daily in their midst were dull in mind and "slow of heart," selfish in aim and craven in spirit, now stand forth before the whole world, clear-toned in their mission, fervent in zeal, defiant alike of the religious spleen of the Jew and the political animosity of the Roman. And whereas, formerly, they were chiefly anxious to know how much each would gain in this world by becoming the followers of the Prophet of Nazareth, now they care nothing for aught of riches or honour that men can bestow, but have their whole soul-vision intently fixed upon the present approval of an invisible Lord, and the assurance of reward from Him hereafter. Thus the very same individuals who a little time before, in cowardly haste to save themselves, fled and left their Master to His fate, now openly avow themselves His disciples; paying no heed to the malignant threats of scribes and Pharisees, or the maledictions of priests and elders; bearing shame with perfect equanimity; making light of the sufferings that came through persecution; and treating death itself as but a trifle; so only that they might bear witness everywhere to their Lord, and to the gospel which they conceived they were commissioned from Him to preach.

This is indeed a sudden change in human nature, as manifest in fact as unparalleled in history. The events cannot be called in question, either as to their reality or their rapidity. Yet this whole phenomenon, with all that flowed from it and is inseparably connected with it, is to be explained by hysterical imagination working upon weak-minded infatuation! Those who can believe this should, in simple modesty, surely be the last in the world to make mention of the "difficulties" of Christian faith.

But the difficulties of unfaith in this case are by no means yet exhausted. The tissue of absurdities to which denial of the Resurrection of Jesus inevitably commits us, is far from complete. Another question remains which is generally overlooked, but merits fair and full examination. We are bound to ask what actually became of the body of the crucified Teacher, in the event of His not having risen again? If we assume the substantial reliability of the New Testament narrative, such a question is at once simply and sufficiently answered by the reality of the transformation of the "natural" body of Jesus the Crucified into the glorified body of the Risen Christ.

But if not this, then what? Would not the production of that body have been perfectly easy for the authorities to have arranged? Would not such production have ended, necessarily and at one blow, the whole mission of the men who went everywhere proclaiming "Jesus and the Resurrection"? One open procession in the streets of Jerusalem, one public proclamation inviting verification, one exhibition of that mangled form—so well known to all—and the new faith would have been strangled in the birth. Such palpable proof of delusion would unquestionably have sufficed, at once and for ever, to convict of manifest falsehood all those who throughout Judea were making Christ's Resurrection the unvarying basis of their strange and obnoxious doctrine. Is it conceivable that neither the fertile cunning of the Jew nor the astute shrewdness of the Roman, was capable of suggesting such an effective *coup de grâce*, when priests and rulers alike were incensed and baffled by the newborn zeal of the Christians?

"But might not the body have been stolen?" It might, possibly. But in such case certain other questions at once demand answer. (1) By whom should this theft be compassed? By the craven band that had just executed such a *sauve qui peut*? Were these the men to outwit the lynx-eyed watchfulness of the Jews, or surprise, or overcome, or bribe, the stolid Roman guards? The puerility of the suggestion, "Say ye, His disciples came by night and stole Him away while we slept," is only equalled by its barefaced assertion of the manifestly incredible. (2) For, we must ask, why should this insignificant band of weeping women and panic-stricken men attempt such a foolhardy feat? It is not in human nature to undertake such a rash and risky venture without reason. Yet there is absolutely no single valid reason that can here be suggested. There was nothing whatever of comfort, or hope, or guidance, or inspiration, to be gained, even if such a fanatic attempt should succeed. (3) Moreover, one may surely add, that if they had succeeded in stealing a mangled body, that would in itself have availed them nothing, unless there had also been the conjoined, universal, and life-long perpetuation of what they knew to be a lie. But in that case other difficulties immediately arise. If the ceaselessly proclaimed resurrection were thus only a guilty lying secret, how came it to pass that from such a source there emanated the ethics of the New Testament? Or how did it happen that out of all the thousands of early Christians, so many of whom, we know, proved backsliders and renegades, not one was found to betray this ghastly trust and explode the colossal deception by revealing where the body really was, or what had actually been done with it? Has any secret society known to us or to all history, kept its oaths so effectually, in the perpetual concealment of outrageous falsehood? (4) The very fact that, in order to dispose of this difficulty, some have suggested that the body of Jesus might have been swallowed up in the earthquake recorded by Matthew [1] serves to show how hard pressed is the modern scepticism which can have recourse to such a shift. (5) But let this also pass. Suppose that, without either courage or reason, the disciples did somehow elude the Jews, overpower the Roman guard, and possess themselves of the corpse. What then? Then, in view of facts which cannot be disputed, the following consequences inevitably ensue. That this same band of cowardly but successful thieves, knowing themselves to be such, went forth (maintaining a miracle of silent conspiracy amongst themselves) and gave themselves up (at the cost of everything enjoyable and precious, with a reward of pain and shame and suffering and death) to the ceaseless advocacy of truth by the tireless promulgation of what they knew to be a lie. By their main falsehood they converted a keen and zealous young Rabbi, who (being conversant with all the facts) at first bitterly opposed them, and then became suddenly the ablest and most influential of all their co-workers in the self-same mission. Together they victoriously defied the

[1] Matt. xxviii. 2.

venerable traditions of Judaism, the all-conquering might of Rome, the subtle intellectual pride of Greece. Thus, upon the corrupting body of a deluded enthusiast, they proceeded to build up, by means of ignorance, fanaticism, delusion, and fraud, the whole fabric of the Christian Church as outlined in the New Testament, with its undeniable sanctions of truth and goodness, a system of ethics to whose loftiness the greatest unbelievers have ever borne ungrudging witness, as well as the most worthy hope of blessed immortality that has ever stirred the hearts of men.

Verily, those who can believe that such results sprang from such causes, can believe anything. But, to ordinary minds, the difficulty of accepting this wholesale monstrosity, as compared with that of acknowledging the Resurrection of Christ to be true, can only appear as an enormity by the side of a trifle, alike illogical and incredible.

Dr. Kennedy is therefore well warranted in saying that [1]

"The utter collapse of all attempts to explain the facts which unbelievers acknowledge, while denying the main, the supernatural fact, adds not a little to the force of the evidence."

No doubt Dr. Bruce is right [2] that "the physical resurrection remains a great mystery." Mystery, however, is no bar to faith. In this case it may freely be affirmed that mystery is far more reasonable than perspicuity. Besides which, it must be borne in mind that every vision we have of a friend, every intelligent conversation we hold, every simple thrill of consciousness,

[1] *The Resurrection*, R.T.S., p. 172.   [2] *Vide* p. 172.

nay, the life of every gnat that flits in the summer sun, and of every infinitesimal bacterium that fulfils its function in the soil, all alike embody mysteries as utterly unfathomed and unfathomable by our latest and most exact science, as the Resurrection of Jesus Christ.

To sum up the whole case, therefore,[1] we are driven

[1] Other testimonies similar to that of Dr. Bruce might, of course, be multiplied. As it is sometimes of value to know the definite judgement of those who occupy leading positions and have earned their reputations, we may here quote the deliberate utterance of Dr. Maclaren of Manchester : "And so we are shut up—in spite of people who do not accept that great truth—we are shut up to the old alternative, as it seems to me, either Jesus rose from the dead, or the noblest lives that the world has ever seen, and the loftiest system of morality that has ever been proclaimed, were built upon a lie. And we are called upon to believe that, at the bidding of a mere unsupported, bare, dogmatic assertion that miracles are impossible. Believe it who will, I decline to be coerced into believing a blank, staring contradiction and psychological impossibility in order to be saved the necessity of admitting the existence of the supernatural. I would rather believe in the supernatural than the ridiculous. And to me it is unspeakably ridiculous to suppose that anything but the fact of the resurrection accounts for the existence of the Church, and for the faith of this witness that we have before us."—On the First Epistle to the Thessalonians.

The clear straightforwardness of this statement contrasts very distinctly with the mazy verbal shufflings of some who pose as advanced Christian teachers, but profess to have grave intellectual doubts concerning the reality of the supernatural. One of these recently, whilst affirming his belief in the Resurrection, explains it thus : "We believe that Jesus rose from the dead when His gracious spirit returned to His Father's care." Surely only ordinary intelligence is required to put this side by side with the New Testament and see that, as a professed exposition of the force of Christ's own words and the definite assertions of the Apostles, it is even worse than "ridiculous." Such an invertebrate and eviscerated Christianity has no honest claim to the name. Whilst as to "difficulties," it doubles rather than relieves them. For it is weighted both with those of faith and those of unfaith.

to affirm that, in view of all the related facts which are incontrovertible, *somewhere and somehow in this connection the miraculous is inevitable.* The facts and laws of psychology are just as real, just as sure, as those of any other branch of science. If, therefore, on grounds of biology, or physics, the actual and historical Resurrection, as narrated in the New Testament, be rejected, then immediately, upon equally valid grounds of psychology, that rejection must itself in turn be rejected. By no "natural" possibility whatever, can hypocrisy flood the world with sincerity. No brainless fanaticism can naturally enforce universal sobriety. Fraud cannot, save by miracle, build up through all the ages the pure and lofty temple of truth. Weak-minded and heartless selfishness cannot naturally give birth to an unquenchable world reform, the very essence of which is rational but self-denying devotion to the "strong Son of God" who is "immortal love."

Thus are we warranted in the conclusion, that if the Christian account of the Resurrection of Jesus Christ involves solemn mystery, the un-Christian invokes utter impossibility. The miracles of faith are credible and justifiable. The miracles of unbelief are incredible monstrosities. Between these two, for every reasonable mind, the choice is plain.

NOTES

A. The unsatisfactoriness of the attempt to establish any substantial difference between the supernatural and the miraculous has already been noticed (p. 43). It seems necessary, however, to give a moment's heed to the shyness with which the very term "supernatural" appears to be increasingly regarded, even by estimable thinkers and speakers inside the modern Christian Church. Is there after all any real ground for this? The author of *The Kernel and the Husk* apparently thinks not: "In the supernatural, every rational man must believe, if he knows what is meant by the term; for every rational man must acknowledge that the world either had a beginning or no beginning, a First Cause or no First Cause; and either hypothesis is altogether above the level of natural phenomena, and therefore supernatural. The Theist and the Atheist alike are believers in the supernatural."

This, however, is rather to cut than to untie the Gordian knot. Reasons have been given above for regarding the "supernatural" of the Atheist as really and emphatically the anti-natural. And when our author carefully spells "super-natural" with a hyphen, in which he is quite justified, it is manifest that then the true connotation of the term necessarily depends upon the significance of the word "natural." In his interesting chapter upon "What is Nature?" two general meanings are suggested: (1) "the ordinary course of things apart from us and from our intervention"; (2) "the ordinary course of things in ourselves, not in our bodies but in some other part of us, but still apart from our deliberate intervention." Such a definition, however, scarcely grasps the attitude of modern science in this matter. According to scientific thought to-day the essence of the natural is to be found in the continuity and uniformity which appear to be everywhere exemplified around and within us. Hence "the idea of the supernatural, *i.e.* of a region on this earth closed to science, where continuity ceases and uniformity cannot be assumed," is said to be a "monstrosity which scientific thought cannot for a moment tolerate." Thus "wherever science goes there can be no supernatural." Now in some cases these postulates of continuity and uniformity are carried to such an extent that what is termed "natural" becomes merely a synonym for physical. But such an ignoring of moral and spiritual phenomena cannot be allowed to pass, even if it were permitted under the term "physical" to include vital and intellectual realities, in all the myriad degrees in which they are manifest around as well as within us. "Natural" must certainly mean more than "physical."

On the other hand, although "it is now by the advance of the physical sciences no longer possible to draw any sharp line of distinction between the natural and the super-natural," yet the absence of the "sharp line," and the substitution of a borderland wherein much is indeterminate, does not abolish the reality of the distinction between the two. Nothing is gained for truth by overweighting the term "natural" with an artificial connotation. When, for instance, instead of signifying, as scientifically it should do, the sum-total of our actual modern knowledge concerning ourselves and the universe — which may be ever growing, but beyond which no one can rationally deny that there may be something—it is made to assume an acquaintance with the universe within and without, beyond which there shall be nothing, plainly by the "natural" is really connoted the infinite. So that when we are told that there can be no supernatural, the assertion is tantamount to saying that there can be nothing beyond the infinite. Which avowal is as unnecessary as it is irrelevant.

But "everything in this universe within our ken is according to law." May be. Yet there are two things, at least, which such a statement does not prove. (1) That the universe contains nothing beyond our ken. (2) That the only working laws within our ken are those which human science at present recognises. Furthermore, what are we to understand by "law"? "An order of nature which is based upon universal and invariable experience."[1] More and greater fallacies could hardly be packed into as many words. "Invariable" means that which cannot be broken. Even this, applied to nature, must signify by any power at our disposal. But what has science to do with specifying that which cannot be? Nothing at all. And until the whole experience of prophets, martyrs, saints, and Christian heroes has been definitely proved to be delusion or insanity, how can there be a "universal" experience against the basis of faith?

But more. How can any order of nature, as an objective reality, be "based" upon human experience at all? Our experience has nothing whatever to do with it, save to witness, appreciate, and submit to it. It is based, and can only be based, upon that which causes it to be order and not chaos. If that cause be nothing, then nature is self-ordered, which puts an end to reasoning. If that cause be something, it must at least be something independent of, that is, beyond, the nature which is ordered. That is, it must be supernatural.

If, then, there be a "nature" to be recognised, it is because of the order which manifestly prevails. For the very conception of nature excludes chaos. This order means a continuity and uniformity in the succession of phenomena, which, so far as we can see or work, are unvarying. But they can only be accounted "laws" by regarding them as expressing the will of a Lawgiver. To assume that

---

[1] *Supernatural Religion*, vol. ii. p. 210.

there cannot be a rational will outside or beyond the human organism, is the greatest *petitio quæstionis* conceivable.[1]

It is, however, asserted that the supernatural can only work by "interfering" with the natural, and that all such interference is unscientific. But even this is too much to affirm. For "there may not have been a single link in the chain of biological progression which—for aught science has proved to the contrary—might not have required special intervention to cause it to be precisely as it was."[2] There is no scientific warrant whatever for representing the natural sphere as so solidly exclusive that it is utterly impervious to the supernatural. Whilst we are assured that physically no two atoms of matter are actually in contact, so that there is room everywhere for the all-penetrating ether, how can either rational analogy or the scientific imagination consistently pronounce that vision a mirage which exhibits the natural as everywhere suffused and saturated with the supernatural?

The scorn, therefore, poured upon this term by some "advanced" scientists is quite uncalled for; nor is there any substantial reason why the Christian teacher of to-day should throw this word as a sop to the modern Cerberus. For the "natural" is neither a closed circle shutting out the supernatural save when it "interferes,"—as possibly some unwise advocates of faith might represent,—nor is it a circle whose radii are infinite, so that its limiting circumference is nowhere, as some overweening advocates of science would postulate. Rather is the supernatural at the very heart of the natural, extending thence by ever spreading concentric circles of influence all through it, and measurelessly beyond. It is thus distinct though always present. Though super-natural it is often most "beyond" when most near. It is ever real, though not amenable at will to our ordinary physical or mental tests. It is under law, indeed, but under His law Who is the Author of nature, though not necessarily those fragments of His law which our science has thus far unveiled. Reason no less than faith thus echoes the ancient estimate—"Lo, these are but the outskirts of His ways; and how

---

[1] See review of *Supernatural Religion* in the *Church Quarterly Review*, April 1876. See also *Lectures on the Cumulative Evidences of Divine Revelation*, by L. F. March Phillips (Lond.: Chris. Evid. Soc.); an underrated book, which honest inquirers would do well to study.

[2] The late Mr. R. A. Proctor, in *Knowledge*.

small a whisper do we hear of Him! But the thunder of His power, who can understand?" (Job xxvi. 14).

B. The words of Baur[1] are here worth quoting: "The question as to the nature and reality of the Resurrection lies outside the sphere of historical inquiry. History must be content with the simple fact that, in the faith of the disciples, the Resurrection of Jesus came to be regarded as a solid and unquestionable fact. It was in this faith that Christianity acquired a firm basis for its historical development. What history requires as the necessary antecedent of all that is to follow, is not so much the fact of the Resurrection of Jesus as the belief that it was a fact." But although this may be true as far as it goes, assuredly, as Strauss saw, and every honest mind must also see, it does not go far enough. History itself here becomes useless, if it is not concerned to know whether the fact of the disciples' faith rested upon reality or upon delusion. Upon that, not upon the mere endurance and development of a belief, depends the worth of Christianity to every individual soul as well as to humanity at large.

Sooner or later the question must arise, What do we mean by the "actual" resurrection? We may be well content to accept Strauss' strong utterance (p. 139) as the *coup de grâce* of the suggestion that Jesus did not really die, which Prof. Huxley was pleased to bless with his approval, whilst as to the theory of "visions," the words of Keim himself[2] may suffice: "After all that has been said, it must be allowed that the theory of visions which has of late become so popular, is only a hypothesis: that, while it explains some things, it fails to explain the main substance of the narrations to be dealt with: nay, that it leads us to look at facts historically attested, from a distorted and untenable point of view." Nor does the further concession that such visions must have been divinely caused, with a view to producing their exact effect, serve to rehabilitate this theory.

What then is left for ordinary Christian faith to-day? With the plain New Testament in hand there will probably be little hesitation in avowing that reality, in this case, involves both the revivification and transformation of the veritable body of Christ which had been so carefully and tearfully buried in the tomb of Joseph of

---

[1] *Church History of the first three Centuries*, i. p. 42.
[2] *Jesu von Nazara*, iii. p. 600.

Arimathea. This is generally known as the "physical" resurrection, because there is undoubtedly a physical side to it which would constitute such an event the miracle *par excellence* of the Christian gospel. But it is precisely this which creates the "difficulty," in the eyes of that pseudo-scientific school of criticism, which approaches the Gospel narratives with an acknowledged predetermination to eliminate miracle. The echo of this avowal and the reflection of this attitude are manifest amongst those Christian thinkers who are confessedly bent upon the utmost economisation of the miraculous element in the New Testament, if not even upon its unsparing excision. Hence the efforts with which the Churches are becoming more and more familiar, to jettison every trace of the "physical" and establish instead what is termed a purely "spiritual" resurrection.

This is done with no little ingenuity and confidence by the author of *The Kernel and the Husk*, in a chapter especially devoted to the theme. It is certainly interesting to find so sincere and erudite a writer saying on one page — in reply to the supposed retort, "You are ready enough to attack other people's notions about the semi-material resurrection, but you are not equally ready to explain your own notions about a spiritual resurrection. You cannot even tell us what a spiritual body is."—"Precisely so, I am *quite ignorant*. Yet in my knowledge of this matter"—which is a remarkable kind of ignorance—"I am superior to a very great number of other theologians. For they think they know, whereas I know that neither I nor they know." After this refreshingly emphatic humility, within a few lines we are told: "For my part, I am now *quite certain* of Christ's spiritual Resurrection, and in that conviction" (certainty?) "I am far happier and *far more trustful* than when I at first *mechanically* accepted upon *authority* and *evidence* the belief in the Resurrection of Christ's body, and subsequently strove to retain that belief, *against the testimony of my intelligence and my conscience*." This sentence is fairly typical of the whole chapter; and as it is impossible here to examine the latter in detail, it may be worth while, by means of the italics and a few notes, to call attention to the former.

How any thinker can be, concerning the same matter, at once "quite ignorant" and "quite certain," constitutes an initial puzzle. It is, we know, frequently solved by those who know all because they examine nothing; but Dr. Abbott cannot be included in this category, so that the puzzle must remain. Yet the clothing of such an attitude in the apparently modest garb of a personal conviction, by no means conceals the fine scorn (which is so general a characteristic of the school represented) for all other poor benighted theologians who have "mechanically accepted," etc., "against the testimony of intelligence and conscience." These innuendoes are surely unworthy. "Mechanical acceptance" of evidence and authority has yet to be shown to be an essential part of reasonable orthodoxy. And it ought to be conceded, if it is not, that those who still find reasons for believing in the real Resurrection of Christ's body, have neither forfeited their intelligence nor strained their conscience in so doing. In the end it may appear that the believer in a "spiritual" resurrection is, in a sense not to be admired, "far more trustful" than those from whom he differs.

It would certainly seem, at the outset, that Dr. Milligan is warranted in his estimate of the view that "the Resurrection of our Lord is to be understood in a spiritual not in a literal sense," namely, that "it is not necessary to ask whether a clear and definite idea can be attached to this view. One thing is obvious—it is not that given us in Scripture." [1]

The most recent effort in this direction is confessedly the attempt to confer a nebulous objectivity upon this "spiritual" resurrection, which is said to be warranted in somewhat the same sense as when we read, "Blessed are the pure in heart: for they shall see God." But even though we freely concede that such purely mental-spiritual objectivity is possible and actual in this latter case, it is assuredly no parallel to that which is before us. And the following reasons may be outlined on behalf of the conviction that this effort, under fear of the modern prejudice against the miraculous, to "spiritualise" the recorded and necessary foundation facts of the Resurrection, shares the fate of almost all similar attempts springing from hyper-timidity. It increases rather than diminishes the difficulties it undertakes to remove.

1. The utter ignoring of the human body which is implied in the "spiritual" theory of the Resurrection, is emphatically contrary to the plainest utterances both of Christ Himself and the apostles. The well-known passages in John ii. 18-22 and 1 Cor. xv. 35-50, may be taken as typical and sufficient.

It must be averred that some of Dr. Abbott's words are strange reading.[2] Thus—

"A heartfelt conviction of the spiritual resurrection of Christ

---

[1] *The Resurrection of Our Lord*, p. 7.
[2] *The Kernel and the Husk*, pp. 256, 257.

affords more comfort than your old belief—based largely upon historical evidence, and brain-felt rather than heart-felt—in His physical resurrection. For the former unites us with Christ, the latter separates us from Christ. If Christ rose a material body from the grave—that stirs no hope in us. But if, while His body remained in the grave, His spirit rose triumphant to the throne of God, then we see a hope indeed that may suit our case and give us some gleam of consolation. The bodies of the dead may lie there and decay, but what of that? Even so was it with the Saviour; but the spiritual body is independent of the flesh, and shall rise superior to death."

It is, indeed, marvellous how any writer at once so erudite and sincere can satisfy himself with this verbal jumble. One may make bold to say, with all respect, that he could not possibly do so, but for the predetermination against miracle with which he avowedly starts.

What means, for instance, this semi-sneer at "historical evidence," seeing that this is the very evidence upon which the author bases his own *a priori* rejection of the miraculous element in the Gospels? How can the same evidence be valid for the wholesale rejection of miracle, and at the same time invalid for the establishment of plain facts of seeing and hearing? As to "brain-felt rather than heart-felt," is he not himself deciding against the "traditional" account of the Resurrection upon brain-felt grounds? And did not Christ Himself appeal to brain-felt evidence when He remonstrated with the Jews: "Yea, and why even of yourselves judge ye not what is right?"[1] Is not, moreover, the initial apprehension of the whole gospel, and of Christ Himself, always and necessarily brain-felt?

Again, as regards the attempted antithesis between the material and the spiritual body, it is really necessary to ask definitely which are we called upon to accept, a "spiritual" resurrection, or a "spiritual body" resurrection? The author, as it pleases him, treats these as synonymous. Can it be that he does not see that here is the crux of the whole question? At one moment he says, "But if, while His body remained in the grave, His spirit rose triumphant to the throne of God,"—upon which we are bound to ask how pure "spirit" can "rise triumphant" at all, much less when a definite and almost spatial direction is appended? But the next moment we are told: "Do not imagine that the spiritual body is one whit less real than the material body." Now it is easy to

---

[1] Luke xii. 57.

add, by way of mental legerdemain, that "as to the relation between the material body and the spiritual body we know nothing, and we need know nothing." But if that be so, surely this whole discussion is only "much ado about nothing." For if we know nothing, we do not know that these two are antithetical at all ; we do not even know that they differ. So that for aught we know, all that is true of the material body may be equally true of the spiritual body. In which case *cadit tota quæstio*, and we are all agreed about everything.

But, speaking soberly, one must submit that three notes at least ought to be made hereupon. (i.) "Spirit" is not the same as "spiritual body." If a spiritual body is "a real body," then by all that reality it is differentiated from pure spirit. And it must be plainly avowed that the whole of the New Testament is one in the doctrine that from the mere continuance, or "rising," of the "spirit of Jesus," no *resurrection* whatever can be predicated. The reality of the Resurrection depends upon the reality of the resurrection body, whether we know much or little as to the nature of that body.

(ii.) Again, the author entirely assumes, not proves, his contention that Christ's body remained in the grave and decayed. There is not only no hint whatever in our Christian records as to any such thing, but the absolute contrary is affirmed as didactically and emphatically as language permits.[1] Nor is it a matter which can be resolved by the elimination, on critical grounds, of a few inconvenient and isolated passages. It is the doctrine of the whole New Testament that Christ's body did not remain in the grave, and did not see corruption. If, then, a new "Christian" theory can only be substantiated by flat contradiction of the Christian Scriptures, we should surely know what to think of its Christianness.

(iii.) Furthermore, it is not true that a "spiritual" resurrection unites us with Christ, whilst a "physical" resurrection separates us from Him. For we no more think of a physical resurrection—in the crass material sense of Professor Tyndall—either for Christ or for ourselves, than the New Testament does. Besides which, are not the terms "physical" and "material," as applied to the Resurrection, synonymous? And is not their significance precisely the same as Paul's word "natural"?[2] How then should we posit or desiderate a "natural" resurrection, when he assures us that such is not the Christian doctrine (and we ourselves heartily agree

---

[1] Cf. Acts v. 31.   [2] 1 Cor. xv. 44, ψυχικόν.

with him) in his solemn assertion that "flesh and blood cannot inherit the kingdom of God"?

Whilst as to the assertion that a belief in the "physical resurrection of Christ commits us also to belief in a local, spatial, and therefore unthinkable heaven"—it is sufficient to reply that it is simply untrue. No Christian thinker worth taking into account contemplates such a purely physical resurrection. For that were manifestly as clear a contradiction of New Testament testimony as is a purely spiritual resurrection. The true contents of the term "physical" in this connection, are, revivification and transformation as applied to the body of Christ, and as constituting all the essentials of actual resurrection. Here is no more committal to a spatial heaven than in the words of the apostle himself.

No more do we look to be united with Christ hereafter in a "spiritual" resurrection. For there is no such thing possible, either for our Lord or for ourselves. If it be a resurrection, it is more than spiritual. If it be not more than spiritual, it is no resurrection at all. For in His case as in ours, the spirit does not die and therefore cannot rise again. And whatever difficulty there may be to us to conceive of a "spiritual body" (surely no greater, comparatively, than that which a caterpillar might find in conceiving of a butterfly body), the whole promise of the future life that begins with the "resurrection from the dead" is the promise of a life associated with a body. To eliminate wholly the idea of a body, is to dismiss for ever the notion of a resurrection. It is difficult to imagine how human language could express this more clearly and emphatically than that employed by the apostle in writing to the Philippians: "The Lord Jesus Christ, who shall fashion anew the body of our humiliation that it may be conformed to the body of His glory, according to the working whereby He is able even to subject all things unto Himself."[1] Whether this be a "physical" conception or not, assuredly it is the only Christian one.

Certainly such words, if at all authoritative, make manifest that it is by means of a spiritual body (which we are assured is also a "real" body), not by a merely "spiritual" resurrection, that we are linked, alike for comfort and hope, with the risen and living Christ. His Resurrection is undoubtedly put forth as the pledge and earnest of our own. Such as His was, ours will be. If His "rising from the dead" was purely spiritual, without any nexus at all,—call it physical, material, corporeal, or what we may,—with His pre-resurrection body,

---

[1] Phil. iii. 21.

FACTS OF HISTORY AND THEIR EXPLANATION

then not only is our resurrection rendered unthinkable, but the whole New Testament conception and doctrine concerning the future are falsified. In regard, therefore, to the relation between Christ and ourselves, when His risen life is considered as the true type of our own, the words of Dr. Westcott sum up the true Christian doctrine : " Thus the Resurrection answers, as completely as it can be answered, the first great question by which we are met. In the person of Christ we see the whole man of man, His body and soul, raised together from the grave. No part is left behind. The whole complex nature is raised and glorified. It is not that the soul only lives ; nor yet that the body, such as it was before, is restored to its former vigour. The Saviour, as far as we regard His manhood, is 'not unclothed,' to use St. Paul's image, but 'clothed upon.' Nothing is taken away, but something is added by which all that was before present is transfigured. ' The corruptible puts on incorruption ; the mortal puts on immortality.' "[1]

Or, in the words of one of the most thoughtful of recent writers upon these themes, " In a word, we are made to feel as we read the strange story, that the body of our Lord after His resurrection was a 'glorified' or 'spiritual' body, and that while it was as real as ours, it was possessed of certain attributes which we cannot predicate of our own. It was a body such as we can easily conceive ours would be if it were released from the laws of decay and death, and the trammels of locality and infirmity. It was indeed a type of the spiritual body which is the heavenly heritage of those who die in faith."[2]

2. All the records agree that the Christ after the Resurrection was, in a true and reliable sense, the same as before. Dr. Milligan is warranted in his statement that "whatever difficulties may attend the conception of the fact, one thing is clear, that the apostles and early disciples of Christ did not think of His resurrection state as simply spiritual, but that the very substance and essence and peculiarity of their faith was this, that the same Son of Man with whom they had companied during the years of His ministry, had been brought back by the glory of the Father from the grave." Whilst as to Christ Himself, " there can be no doubt that He Himself wished to be recognised by them as essentially the same as ever, and that they acknowledged Him to be so." This being the case, it is difficult to know how to understand Dr. Abbott's

---

[1] *Gospel of the Resurrection*, 6th edition, p. 164.
[2] *The Ascent through Christ*, by Rev. Griffith Jones, p. 343.

avowal: "The movements of the risen Saviour appear to me to have been the movements of God." This much, however, seems to be warranted in our thought. According to the apostolic conception, the identity between the risen and the pre-crucified Christ was so real and far-reaching, that if after the Resurrection He was nothing more than spirit, we are helplessly committed to the old Docetic heresy, that also before His death He was never really, but only apparently, man.

It has, we are aware, been stated that the facts of His life and death and resurrection were not facts " of the same order, inasmuch as (i.) His works and the crucifixion were apprehensible by anyone possessed with ordinary faculties, whereas the resurrection was only manifested to and appreciated by believers; and (ii.) Christ's death was His own doing, but the resurrection was God's doing to Him." But in regard to the first of these, whilst it may be generally true that "a fact which demands special fitness or faculty to appreciate it, is not of the same order or sense as ordinary facts," yet in the present case, that which is assumed is not only that which should first be proved, but something which cannot be proved because it is contrary to fact. The Resurrection certainly was not at the outset appreciated by "believers," but by unbelievers, with only ordinary faculties. For we are given distinctly to understand that none of the original witnesses either expected Christ to rise again, or, at first, believed that He had risen. Moreover, the words in the Acts which state so plainly that "Him God raised up on the third day, and gave Him to be made manifest; not to all the people, but unto witnesses that were chosen before of God," add also the significant statement, "even to us, who did eat and drink with Him after He rose from the dead."[1] Such words at least assert that it was not a purely spiritual resurrection to which the witnesses were to testify.

As regards the second suggestion, it is no doubt in accord with the verse just quoted, as well as with other similar expressions, but it must not be forgotten that Christ Himself said, "I have power to lay it down, and I have power to take it again."[2]

Even if, therefore, it were conceded that the facts of the Crucifixion and the Resurrection were not "of the same order," it is surely an insufficient foundation upon which to build up a theory of a resurrection whose objectivity was purely spiritual, as against the trans-

---

[1] Acts x. 41.

[2] See Dr. Westcott's note on this passage in the *Speaker's Commentary*.

formation of the dead physical body, which yet (according to the New Testament) left it objective on occasion to ordinary ocular perception.

3. This, however, brings necessarily before us the right employment of the two terms—"objective" and "subjective"—which are capable of contributing so much towards the formation of opinion in this matter. It has been well said [1] that the ultimate question herein is, "What was the nature of the experience which convinced the apostles that the Lord had risen? Was it something that happened only in the region of the spirit, or of physical sensations? Three possibilities, and only three, are conceivable: (i.) that their experience was purely subjective; (ii.) that it was objective and spiritual; (iii.) that it was objective and material." Now of these the first may be dismissed, as being to-day finally discredited. The second is said to have its stronghold in the Epistles, and the third in the Gospels. But we must ask, Is it so clear that these two latter conceptions are utterly distinct and mutually exclusive? Does the "spiritual" resurrection which is suggested admit of being considered thus unequivocally objective? And does the objectiveness of the Resurrection, as recorded in the Gospels, compel us to regard it as in the ordinary sense of the word "material"? Both these questions would seem to be most truly answered in the negative.

It is suggested that the true solution of the question should begin with the experience of the Apostle Paul, because his Epistles antedate the Gospels; that his experience, to quote Dr. Abbott, "must have been of the nature of a vision, and in a sense subjective"; [2] and that his experience was essentially the same as that of all the other apostles. Whence it would follow that their experience was also "in a sense" subjective, and the Resurrection was purely spiritual and non-objective. Now there can be no doubt—to quote Dr. McGiffert—that "Paul believed that at a particular period in his life the risen Christ appeared to him, and to that appearance he owed his Christian faith." [3] But is it demonstrated that this whole "appearance" was subjective, or only spiritually objective? The narrative in the 9th chapter of the Acts certainly does not commit us to this, and it might well be asked whether there is not rather the suggestion of both the objective and the "material" in the statement

---

[1] In a thoughtful paper read at a Theological Conference at Lancashire College, June 1900, by the Rev. Eric Lawrence of Halifax.

[2] *The Kernel and the Husk*, p. 244.

[3] *History of Christianity in the Apostolic Age*, p. 121.

that "straightway there fell from his eyes as it were scales." At least Prof. Vernon Bartlet is warranted in his judgement that in Paul's words in 1 Cor. xv. 1, etc., "the explicit statement, 'and that He was buried,' coming between 'He died' and 'He was raised,' proves Paul's belief in a highly objective resurrection, including a bodily somewhat, though of a non-fleshly order. It was the prototype, in fact, of the spiritual body in which the believer is clothed at resurrection, in contrast to the sensuous body committed to the grave. And this confirms the view, often confidently challenged, that the 'empty grave' was an element in the original apostolic witness, not a later supplement."[1]

Seeing, moreover, that there is no sufficient reason, on chronological grounds, for preferring the testimony of Paul to that of the Gospels,[2] it would rather appear that we are justified in deciding the objectivity of Paul's vision from the undoubted objectivity of the Gospel accounts. Hereupon Mr. Griffith Jones rightly points out that[3] "our Lord is distinctly spoken of as having risen from the dead in a real objective sense.—There is abundant evidence of the impression of both identity and corporeality in the Resurrection body of Jesus; so that His disciples, *i.e.* those who knew Him best, and could not possibly be deceived by any fancied resemblance between Him and a pretender who might have personified Him, were left in no manner of doubt that He was the Jesus whom they had known and loved during His earthly life."

This objectiveness, then, being considered beyond dispute, the question that remains is whether it was purely "spiritual," or whether it involved also other elements which, for the moment, we may call material?

On behalf of the former view we are asked what Christ meant by "Blessed are the pure in heart: for they shall see God"? Or what we intend when we speak or read of a "vision of the glory of God"? Are not these at once spiritual and objective? It may be freely conceded that they are. But it must at the same time be insisted that they constitute no parallel to the case before us, and therefore yield us no guiding analogy. In these cases there neither is nor could be any suggestion of a corporeal or material element; whilst as to the Resurrection of Christ, the suggestion—to say the least—of such element is so vivid that the ordinary reader generally

---

[1] *The Apostolic Age*, p. 4.
[2] Cf. Keim's estimate, quoted on pp. 140, 143, 155.
[3] *The Ascent through Christ*, p. 341.

takes it for the whole, and the modern attempt to rule it out only arises under the pressure of the prejudice against the miraculous which at present prevails. The being of God and the risen Christ are, indeed, "facts of a different order," much more distinctly than the Crucifixion and the Resurrection, as alleged above. In the one case it is as necessary to empty the conception of all material appeal to the senses, as in the other case—according to the narrative—it is manifestly intended to put into the conception as real an appeal to the ordinary faculties as is compatible with all the other assertions made in reference to the same event. It may well be that our powers of speech and thought are here inadequate ; that "objective" is too strongly redolent of the material, and inevitably suggests "this too solid flesh" which will not "thaw and resolve itself into a dew"; whilst "subjective" is equally misleading, in suggesting the purely internal and immaterial, and eliminating wholly all appeal to those faculties by which the disciples had always known their Lord before He died, and were ready to recognise Him if He arose.

That there was something more than this "purely spiritual," subjective objectivity, seems to be really involved in the fact that the conviction that Christ was definitely and objectively before them came so often collectively, as Paul narrates. Upon this the author of *Supernatural Religion* has, we know, alleged that [1] "if we turn to the inquiry whether a similar subjective impression can be received by many persons at one time, and be mistaken by them for an objective reality, an equally certain reply in the affirmative must unhesitatingly be given." But the instances he alleges in support of this are singularly feeble and inadequate as parallels. As Mr. Row remarks,[2] "It is easy to say that these enthusiasts communicated their enthusiasm to the rest. But this little sentence conceals behind it whole mountains of difficulty." And we shall do well to remember that Paul's assertion concerning the five hundred brethren at once "is boldly made in the face of the powerful party who denied his apostleship. If this assertion was false, nothing was easier than for the opponents of the apostle to refute it. However common the belief in ghost stories, it would be impossible to find a case of several hundred persons who believed that on some one definite occasion when they were all assembled, they had seen the ghost of a person who had recently been executed, appear before

---

[1] Vol. iii. p. 532.
[2] *The Supernatural in the New Testament*, p. 460.

them, and on the strength of this belief constituted themselves into a new society — a society which has endured through eighteen centuries. However cynical our views may be, it is impossible to believe that human nature is a lie."

On the whole, therefore, we are driven to the conclusion that the "objective and spiritual" estimate of the apostolic experience cannot be substantiated, and does not satisfy the conditions of the inquiry.

4. But other matters also demand notice. If, for instance, the Resurrection were purely spiritual, not only is there no sufficient nexus between the Christ who "died and was buried according to the Scriptures," and the risen Christ, but there is no basis whatever for the universal Christian doctrine, surely warranted by the New Testament, that Christ has glorified our humanity in retaining the Resurrection body henceforth and for ever. In this connection the following is worth quoting as a fair summary.[1] "As a matter bearing vitally on our special inquiry, it should be noticed that it is not taught us in the analogy of our Lord's resurrection that the future life is a disembodied state. The future life is not to be one of pure spirit. We are to be like our Lord, and He ascended into the Unseen in possession of a body like ours, only glorified and made free from the law of sin and death. Though this does not make a belief in a future life more easy in itself, it does take away that difficulty which is felt by many who cannot realise how the soul can exist without some kind of an organism with which to act." No doubt, as Dr. Westcott says, "it is vain for us to speculate on the nature of that transformed human body";[2] but for that matter it is no more insoluble a mystery than the growth of a flower, say a poppy, from a tiny seed in which lie potentially all the beauty and wonder of the future. At all events the spiritual body, and not the purely spiritual resurrection, is the doctrine of the Christian records.

5. According to John's account, Christ Himself definitely appealed to His Resurrection body in order to satisfy the doubts of Thomas, and so at least represented it as objective enough in its reality to answer to the proposed physical tests of the doubting disciple. It is, of course, easy to dismiss this incident as not finding a place in the "Triple Tradition," but there is manifestly no textual warrant for such an arbitrary proceeding.

6. Again, the references to the "third day" are too definite and

---

[1] *The Ascent through Christ*, by Rev. Griffith Jones, p. 358.
[2] *Gospel of the Resurrection*, p. 163.

too often reiterated to be put aside as an unimportant detail. All the accounts point to something remarkable happening on the third day, as a distinct beginning of appearances, which, so far as we can gather from a record that is avowedly imperfect, continued with startling vividness for a comparatively short time, and then wholly ceased. Nothing less than this can be inferred from Paul's public avowal.[1] "He was seen for many days of them that came up with Him from Galilee to Jerusalem, who are now His witnesses unto the people." The restoration of the word "now," according to the best authorities, adds emphasis to this definiteness. But it is impossible to think of a purely spiritual resurrection, which would necessarily be quite as much subjective as objective to all witnesses, thus beginning and ending suddenly. No such limit manifestly is set to the other spiritual gifts which are conspicuous in the same records.

7. An equally important consideration in this regard, is the question as to what became of the Lord's body. It is not a new inquiry, but one must be forgiven for saying that all the attempts to deal with it from the anti-miraculous standpoint, display a startling amount of tergiversation. A lively imagination is also called in to help out the difficulty, as when we are told[2] that "possibly some of the enemies of Jesus had themselves removed the body. Being almost surprised in the act, they may not have had time to replace the great stone at the entrance of the tomb, when the women arrived. If so, the action of Christ's own enemies prepared the way for the belief in His Resurrection by exhibiting to the sorrowing disciples the stone rolled away and the empty sepulchre. First came the cry, 'He is not here,' and that prepared the way for 'He is risen.'"

It is surely a hard pressed Christian (!) theory which leads ultimately to the assumed thievish malignity of Christ's enemies, as the true basis of that belief in His Resurrection which inspired the early Church. The suggestion that the body "might have been swallowed up in one of the recorded earthquakes" cannot be any more highly appraised, seeing that it only substitutes accident for fraud. No answer, indeed, has ever been given worthy of serious thought to the plain consideration, resting on indubitable fact, that, whether the body were left to decay in the tomb or were stolen by enemies, the production of it in any way to the people would have silenced for ever all the witness to the Resurrection. Whilst the suggestion that the friends of Christ may have stolen

---

[1] Acts xiii. 31.   [2] *The Kernel and the Husk*, p. 243.

and disposed of it, might do very well [1] for the malignant elders and callous soldiers, but is utterly useless to-day. The idea of the emanation of the ethics of the New Testament from a coterie of conscious deceivers, is now too preposterous to be even thinkable. Every theory of a "purely spiritual" resurrection finds an insuperable difficulty in the dead body which it ignores.

8. The Ascension has also to be fairly considered. But it is in no sense a fair consideration simply to dismiss it with a wave of the critical hand, and say with Dr. Anderson,[2] that "the miraculous Ascension to heaven has nothing to do with the doctrine of the living and reigning Christ." This attitude is taken because of "all the difficulties connected with the belief in miracle" in general, and with the Resurrection in particular. There is, however, no textual warrant for such an evisceration of the Christian gospel, nor has any modern destructive criticism justified the elimination from the Christian records of such statements as are found in Acts i. 6–11; Eph. iv. 9, 10; John xx. 17, etc. And even if the closing verses of Mark's Gospel be adjudged a separate document, it must, at least, be conceded that they represent the earliest tradition, and are not rightly to be ruled out of all further regard.

The true doctrine of the Ascension is in no degree affected by such remarks as those of the author of *Supernatural Religion*:[3] "The bodily Ascension up the sky in a cloud, apart from the miraculous nature of such an occurrence, seems singularly to localise Heaven, and to present views of cosmical and celestial phenomena suitable certainly to the age of the writer, but which are not endorsed by modern science." The objection here, it would appear, is that there is not enough miracle, but that another should have been performed in causing the writers of that age to anticipate the findings of the science of to-day.[4] But the very economy of miracle in the Christian gospel is no slight testimony to its genuineness. Even the writers of that day, however, do not use such an expression as "the bodily Ascension up the sky" (!), nor do they by any means necessarily imply it. For them it was enough, as it may well be for us, that "a cloud received Him out of their sight." All hints and innuendoes, that we are hereby committed

---

[1] Cf. Matt. xxviii. 12–15 and p. 147 *supra*.
[2] *Christian World*, May 1898.   [3] *Vid.* iii. p. 473.
[4] See note on p. 270 of *The Ascent through Christ*, by Rev. Griffith Jones.

to-day to a localised or spatial heaven, are neither endorsed by the New Testament, nor by modern reasonable orthodoxy. The miraculous nature of the occurrence is assumed, which is perfectly permissible until miracles are shown to be incredible and impossible. Whilst all reference to the "body" is unmistakably to the spiritual body, which, according to the accounts given, had already vanished on previous and lesser occasions. But, as Dr. Abbott assures us, it was a "real" body; and we may venture to assure him that it was also objective enough to warrant those who were present in "looking steadfastly" with their bodily eyes. For the conception of a group of sincere and sensible men looking consentaneously with closed eyes at one and the same subjective cerebral creation, is as unimaginable as that they should be constrained to gather in order to gaze unitedly into vacancy. The reality of the Ascension, therefore, may be said to show that the Resurrection was not purely spiritual.

9. It is certain that the first opponents of the Christian faith, of all nationalities, knew nothing about a purely spiritual resurrection. Such a doctrine as that already quoted,[1] that "while His body remained in the grave His spirit rose triumphant to the throne of God," or that "the essence of the resurrection of Christ is that His spirit should have really triumphed over death," *i.e.* that He still lived in the spirit world, was assuredly neither what the apostles preached nor their hearers so often disbelieved. The attitude of both preacher and hearers at Athens[2] may be taken as a typical case. "When they heard of the resurrection of the dead some mocked." But neither Jew nor Greek could have mocked at the doctrine of the continuance of the life of the spirit, as apart from that of the body. It is not even needful to quote proofs of this. The real objection of the thinkers of that day was precisely the same, *mutatis mutandis*, as that which weighs on anti-supernaturalists at the present, viz. the allegation of a bodily resurrection. And one cannot but feel that the ancient sceptics deserve our sympathy rather than the modern. For their crude conceptions of the nature and laws of matter may well have prevented their acceptance of the apostolic doctrine of a spiritual body. But our modern scientific assurances that "matter is a double-faced somewhat" of which spirit is rather to be regarded as the cause than the effect, should dispose us in the opposite direction. The ever-enlarging revelation of the potentialities of

---

[1] *The Kernel and the Husk*, p. 256.   [2] Acts xvii. 32.

the ultimate atom are, moreover, such as to make the Christian conception of a spiritual body comparatively easy. But it was in regard to a bodily resurrection, unquestionably, that Paul wrote: " Whether then it be I or they, so we preach and so ye believed " —or disbelieved.

10. It has been said [1] that the Gospel narrative, rightly considered, "strongly supports the theory which regards the resurrection as belonging to spiritual things, to be spiritually discerned." Also,[2] that the certainty of the apostolic conviction was "that kind of certainty which is bred from faith and hope. And this sort of certainty, and no other, appears to me that which was intended to be produced by the Resurrection of Christ." " As in the life of Christ, so in the Resurrection of Christ, conviction appears never to have been forced on any entirely unwilling unbeliever." Upon this last sentence we may remark that, as it stands, it is an irrelevant truism. For conviction to be such, cannot be forced upon anyone, save by manifest preponderance of indubitable evidence. That there is sufficient evidence to convince everyone open to conviction, is assumed in the general formula, " He that disbelieves shall be condemned." But if it be intended here that only those believed who already possessed some germs of " faith and hope" in the risen Christ, such a statement would seem to be so contrary to the plain facts of the establishment of the primitive Church as to need no refuting.[3] Is it not also true that the spiritual discernment rather followed than preceded the acceptance of the reality of the Resurrection, in the case of the original witnesses ? [4] Doubtless "there was a spiritual side to the manifestation of the risen Christ which could only be discerned spiritually."[5] But was it the apprehension of this spiritual side which first convinced the early disciples that their Lord had actually risen? Is there any evidence at all that the men and women who came to the tomb, or gathered together in frightened conference, were any quicker in spiritual discernment than the men who in terror forsook Him and

---

[1] Paper by Rev. Eric Lawrence, referred to above.

[2] *The Kernel and the Husk*, p. 248.

[3] Matt. xxviii. 17 ; Acts vi. 7, xvii. 32, xxvi. 9, 10, 11, etc.

[4] Dr. Westcott says concerning the apostle himself, "We find an appearance granted to St. Paul, which carried with it immediate conviction to an unbeliever." Note on p. 158, *Gospel of the Resurrection*.

[5] *Gospel of the Resurrection*, p. 158.

fled, or the women who clung to Him out of sheer despair during His last agony? The whole consensus of the Christian Scriptures appears to be that it was the apprehension of the reality of His Resurrection, which first opened the eyes of their heart to the true nature of their Master's mission, and the kind of service to which He had called them as His witnesses.

11. The term "spiritual," as applied to a theory of Christ's Resurrection which especially sets itself to oppose all reference to the physical body, is distinctly misleading. "Spiritual" in Christian terminology has a definite connotation, and is, in accordance with New Testament usage, antithetic to "carnal" not to "physical." When resurrection signifies, as in Paul's doctrine, the revivification and transformation of the dead body, there is confessedly the concept of an altered and glorified body which may be called "spiritual" and set over against the physical. "If there is a natural body there is also a spiritual body." But the theory which is now suggested under the guise of a "spiritual resurrection," expressly excludes the body, asserting that this "remained in the grave and decayed." Its whole concern, therefore, is with the spirit, and the proper appellation for it is manifestly "spirit resurrection." But as this has been shown to involve a contradiction in terms, it must be dismissed altogether. If we agree to leave out of account the "objective and material" view of what transpired, there is left for our acceptance, not the "objective and spiritual," but the "objective and transformed material," which is not rightly named "spiritual."[1]

12. Upon the whole, it must be alleged that the attempt to reduce the miraculous element in the Resurrection to a minimum, however well intended, is but wasted economy. The whole genius of Christianity and the total witness of the New Testament endorse what Dr. Westcott said hereupon some years since.[2] "The Resurrection is either a miracle or it is an illusion. Here there is no alternative, no ambiguity. And it is not an accessory of the apostolic message, but the sum of the message itself. Its unique character is the very point on which the first teachers of Christianity support all their arguments. It claims to be the opening of a new life to the world." Its mystery may be great, although for that

---

[1] For a thoughtful and suggestive study hereupon cf. "The Problem of the Resurrection" in the volume entitled *The Imperfect Angel*, by Rev. T. G. Selby.

[2] *Gospel of the Resurrection*, p. 52.

matter it is no more inscrutable to modern science than is the life of a gnat. But to take away this mystery, is to pluck out the very heart of the living body of truth which constitutes the Christian Gospel. To succeed in reducing this transcendent and fundamental event to the non-miraculous and the ordinary, is to dethrone the living and reigning Christ, and to undo His whole redemptive work.

For all these reasons, therefore, as well as others unmentioned, it is submitted that we must not only pause before accepting what is termed the "spiritual resurrection," but after pausing must put it aside as really, though not intentionally, subversive of the true Gospel of Jesus Christ.

By way of conclusion, it may not be amiss to give in brief, the findings of three modern Christian writers who have earned a right to be heard respectfully.

In his article on "Jesus Christ" in the new *Bible Dictionary* (edited by Dr. Hastings, p. 641), Dr. Sanday says: "This is the least that must be asserted. A belief that has had such incalculably momentous results, must have had an adequate cause. No apparition, no mere hallucination of the senses, ever yet moved the world. But we may doubt whether the theory of visions, even as Keim presents it, is either adequate or really called for. It belongs to the process of so trimming down the elements that we call supernatural in the Gospel narratives, as to bring them within the limits of everyday experience. But that process we must needs think has failed. The facts are too obstinate, the evidence for them is too strong, and the measures which we apply are too narrow and bounded. It is better to keep substantially the form which a sound tradition has handed down to us, even though its contents in some degree pass our comprehension."

Again, Dr. Bruce in his *Apologetics* (p. 397) thus concludes his examination: "The result of the foregoing inquiry is that all naturalistic attempts to explain away the resurrection, up to this date, have turned out failures. The physical resurrection remains, it need not be added, a great mystery. Much that relates to this august event is enveloped in mystery; not to speak of the discrepancy in the narratives, or the angelic agency, there is the fact that the resurrection body of Jesus appears even in the evangelic accounts a pneumatic body, and the further fact that according to the teaching of Paul as well as the suggestions of reason, flesh and blood, a gross corruptible body, can have no place in the kingdom of God or in the eternal world. In the resurrection of Jesus two processes seem to have been combined into one ; the revivification of the crucified body, and its transformation into a spiritual body endowed with an eternal form of existence ; the first process being merely a means to an end, the actual, if not the indispensable, condition of the second."

And Dr. Clarke of New York, in his recent and most valuable work upon *Christian Theology*,[1] sums up the whole in these weighty words: "No one can claim thoroughly to understand the resurrection of Jesus, for the whole event partakes in the mystery that hangs over the world of spirits. With what body He rose has been much discussed, and without much profit, for the materials for a clear answer do not exist. If we define the resurrection of Jesus according to the data that the Gospels give us, we shall not call it a return to bodily life in the old condition, but rather a rising from death into glorious spiritual life, with power to manifest Himself at will to men in this world. According to these data, He was alive, the same Jesus as before, and showed Himself in recognisable presence and spiritual identity to those who knew Him. That death had not destroyed Him, but that He lived unchanged, and with new glory, and appeared among His friends to prove it, this is the testimony of the gospel concerning His resurrection."

---

[1] P. 273—a volume which should be carefully studied by all modern inquirers.

Note to p. 123.

The estimate given in the former edition may be considered extreme, although it was taken from definite published authority. The precise number is irrelevant to the argument, but Gibbon's estimate of 15,000 as a total is certainly far too small. For a valid refutation of his famous "five causes," as well as for a vivid yet sober representation of the dire sufferings and marvellous fortitude of the early Christians, see Dr. J. H. Newman's *Grammar of Assent*, pp. 456–486 ; Storrs' *Divine Origin of Christianity*, pp. 275, 591–595, 613, 4 ; Dr. G. P. Fisher's *History of the Christian Church*, p. 50 ; Pressensé's *Martyrs and Apologists*, passim.

VI

THE REALM OF PSYCHOLOGY

"From the time of the appearance of Jesus Christ in human flesh, a regenerating power has been at work in the world altogether out of proportion to any other that has ever influenced mankind. It is therefore eminently reasonable, eminently scientific even, to contend that the supernatural forces demonstrably overruling the forces of the natural world, received their highest embodiment in the supernatural life and work of Jesus Christ."—Rev. Chancellor Lias, *Vict. Inst. Trans.*, No. 116, p. 269.

"The man who accepts the consummation of Christianity in the Resurrection of Jesus, and the supernatural doctrines connected with it (such as the abiding presence of the Spirit and the forgiveness of sins through the death of Christ), may reasonably presume that the miraculous manifestations were not limited to that one supreme moment. He is therefore prepared to accept a preliminary miraculous history which has a 'reasonable' amount of direct evidence supporting it, and which is not manifestly incongruous with the system. As already remarked, the general congruity of the Christian system and the remarkable restraint under which the miraculous narratives have been written, form a large part of the evidence compelling us to accept the Bible as true history."—Dr. G. F. Wright, *Scientific Aspects of Christian Evidences*, p. 190.

"I do not know why, two months ago, I took it into my head to read the New Testament, before my studies had advanced to the age in which it was written. I had not read it for many years, and was prejudiced against it before I took it in hand. I have read no book on this subject, but hitherto in all my study of the ancient times, I have always felt the want of something, and it was not until I knew our Lord that all was clear to me; with Him there is nothing which I am not able to solve. If this religion is not Divine, I understand nothing at all."—Johann von Müller, the Swiss historian, 1782, *Werke*, 15, 315, etc.

"What was the turning-point of Paul's life? The Acts and the Epistles agree in declaring that it was a supernatural revelation of Christ to him. This was to him a most certain reality. He classes it along with the appearances of the risen Jesus to His disciples on earth as an objective fact. The Apostle believed that a miraculous disclosure of Christ's heavenly glory formed the crisis of his life, and he had the best opportunity of knowing. No explanation tallies with all the facts which are known to us except that which Paul himself gives."—Dr. G. B. Stevens, *Theology of the New Testament*, p. 329 (International Theological Library).

VI

THE REALM OF PSYCHOLOGY

MENTAL phenomena have to do not only with history but psychology. The former is concerned with the past, the latter with the present. To ordinary readers the technical term " psychology " may perhaps be unfamiliar, but nothing can be more common or more easily apprehended than the realities to which it refers. For it simply signifies our assured knowledge of human nature through daily observation and experience. Facts of mind are just as real, and as open to examination, as those of light or sound. Relative to our subject there are at least two well-known Christian phenomena which, under this head, here call for earnest attention. These are, the conversion of St. Paul, and the nature and origin of the New Testament.

I. THE CONVERSION OF ST. PAUL

For those who would do justice to this remarkable event, there can scarcely be, even now, a better statement of the case than that of Lord Lyttleton.[1] It was issued,

---

[1] Published in neat and cheap form by the Religious Tract Society, together with a valuable introductory essay by the late Professor Henry Rogers.

indeed, many years ago, at the request of his friend Gilbert West, who from being a Deist had become a Christian, and published his still valuable *Observations on the Resurrection of Jesus Christ*. But it has never been definitely answered, and the positions maintained in it have not been in the least degree weakened by any of the intervening investigations of the modern critical school. "I thought," says Lord Lyttleton, that "the conversion and apostleship of St. Paul alone, duly considered, was of itself a demonstration sufficient to prove Christianity to be a Divine revelation." And, adds Mr. Rogers, "Lord Lyttleton was, in several respects, especially well qualified to treat this subject, and his judgement ought to have weight with the reader. He had been a sceptic, he became a Christian after deliberate examination. Being a layman, he had no professional bias in favour of his conclusion. His studies being honest, ended in conviction."

The narratives given in Acts ix., xxii., xxvi. are too familiar to need detailed quotation here. But two remarks are definitely in place. First, that the authentic character of this record known as the "Acts of the Apostles" has been confirmed rather than otherwise, by the keen scrutiny of modern Biblical criticism. It is easy to say with McGiffert[1] that "the supposition" that it is "from the pen of one of Paul's companions" is "beset with serious difficulties." Far more serious difficulties attend his own suggestion, that it emanated from the pen of some anonymous

[1] *History of Christianity in the Apostolic Age*, p. 237.

author in the time of Domitian.[1] However, discussion of the date and genuineness of the Acts does not come here within our scope. It is enough to remark that, as the author just quoted himself acknowledges, Paul's conversion, according to reliable records, "was one of the most remarkable transformations in history."

Secondly, that whilst we are by no means compelled to relinquish our hold of any of Paul's writings at the behest of modern destructive criticism, there are at least four of his Epistles, the genuineness of which may now be said to be established beyond controversy. These are, as is well known, Romans, 1st and 2nd Corinthians, and Galatians. These are abundantly sufficient as data for our present summary. To put the whole into a word, there can be no doubt whatever as to the supernaturalness of Paul's conversion, if we accept his own account of it. This narration, as set forth directly in the Acts, and indirectly supported in his letters, gives us at once clear and adequate cause for the marvellous change from Saul of Tarsus, the learned young Rabbi, the abettor in Stephen's murder, and fiery persecutor of Christians generally, to Paul the prisoner of Jesus Christ, the founder of Christian Churches, the foremost Apostle of the Gentiles, the aged martyr for the truth. At the same time it yields complete and irrefragable testimony to the Divineness of the nature and mission of Christ Himself. Doubtless it is the perception of this latter inference, with its manifest inclusion of the miraculous, which has led not a few to call in question the reliability of the whole account.

[1] Cf. *The Apostolic Age*, by Prof. Vernon Bartlet, pp. x., 1, 509,—a brief but valuable note.

Meanwhile Lord Lyttleton's treatise waits, apparently in vain, for specific answer. It is most in accord with our present purpose to point out that those who deny the New Testament narrative of an event thus alike wonderful and undeniable, are themselves bound to furnish a reasonable account of it without the supernatural.

For all such, three, and only three, avenues of explanation are open, as Lord Lyttleton also pointed out. His words are worth repeating—

"The person asserting these things of himself, and of whom they are recorded in so authentic a manner, was either (i.) an impostor, who said what he knew to be false with an intent to deceive; or (ii.) an enthusiast, who, by the force of an overheated imagination, imposed on himself; or (iii.) he was deceived by the fraud of others, and all that he said must be imputed to the power of that deceit; or else what he declared to be the course of his conversion, and to have happened in consequence of it, did all really happen, and therefore the Christian religion is a Divine revelation."[1]

Now the equal incredibility of each of these three suppositions requires only a few moments' consideration to make it manifest. Or, to express it more in accordance with the tenor of our present examination, whichever of these three suggestions be adopted, greater difficulties inevitably arise than those of the original account which they are intended to displace. The attempt to eliminate the supernatural, issues in contradictions so grossly unnatural, that they are seen to be more glaring violations of natural law than the ordinary Christian account. In Professor McGiffert's phrase, the

---

[1] *Conversion and Apostleship of St. Paul*, by Lord Lyttleton (Religious Tract Society), p. 82.

event becomes, in each of these three cases alike, "psychologically inconceivable."

For (1) shall we say that Paul was a wilful and deliberate deceiver? Then he himself is a standing miracle of contradiction and perversity, to an utterly unparalleled degree. For he must have acted not only without any of the motives which all our experience and observation show to be quite indispensable in such a case, but also in utter defiance of every conceivable inducement to the contrary. In addition to which, he so succeeded in carrying through his deception, that Greek and Jew, Roman and barbarian, equally without motive and against inducement, became his confederates, and together spread throughout the world what they well knew to be false. The absurdity of all this is self-manifest. To quote from the late Professor Henry Rogers—

"The world has renounced this hypothesis. It refuses to believe in the possibility of a hypocrite, whose writings inculcate, and whose conduct exemplifies, the highest order of moral excellence; it refuses to believe in a benevolent, self-denying, modest, magnanimous liar, in whom falsehood speaks with the very tongue, looks through the very eyes, and personates the very gestures and tones of truth; it refuses to believe that a man with no earthly motive for it, and every earthly motive against it, spent thirty years in cheating men into truth and virtue, which he himself had utterly renounced."[1]

(2) Was he, then, deceived by others? Let us see what such a supposition involves. He was a Jew; a devout, devoted Pharisee, a cultured, clever Rabbi. Are such so easily befooled? Especially, are they easily deceived in the direction of Christianity? Let any modern missionary

[1] *Op. cit.* p. 57.

to the Jews reply. What, then, did these poor unlettered early Christians do—these untaught fishermen of Galilee? They singled out the most cultured, most able, most energetic, most determined of their persecutors, in the very heat of his intensest fury against themselves and their Lord, and entirely succeeded in persuading him that the false was true. At one stroke they reversed all his life convictions, changed his hatred into love, and—in the very city and decade where these strange facts were alleged to have occurred—converted the zealous Rabbi into a weak-minded and credulous believer of whatever they chose to tell him. Thus, in their ignorant or fraudulent simplicity, with no help whatever from any source—there being by the supposition no supernatural, no risen Christ at all, in fact nothing to act upon learned Jewish fanaticism save the same temperament unlearned—they transformed the strong-minded, tireless, virulent persecutor into Paul the Apostle of the Gentiles, the author of the Epistles, who of all men did most to establish Christian Churches everywhere, and finally laid down his life for the crucified Christ! Is there any need whatever to inquire into their "arrangement" of the phenomena on the road to Damascus? Is it not rather overwhelmingly manifest that the absurdity of this whole supposition sufficiently confutes itself?[1]

(3) There remains, then, only the possibility that Paul may have been an enthusiast who, somehow or other,

[1] The deliberate judgement of Keim is perhaps here worth recording by reason of his manifest freedom from orthodox bias. He says (*Jesu von Nazara*, i. p. 52): "It would be even easy to show

was carried away by heated imagination into self-deception. By way of helping out this manifestly flimsy suggestion, modern pseudo-scientific doubt has also called in pathology, and sought to represent him as an epileptic, who probably experienced a sunstroke *en route* for Damascus. Does this, however, really assist the case for unbelief at all? Let us see. Two things have to be borne in mind. First of all, we are fairly well acquainted, from constant observation as well as history, with the natural elements of fanatic enthusiasm. Secondly, we do also know, from his unquestioned labours and writings, what were the leading features of the apostle's character. Fair juxtaposition will suffice to decide whether the latter can have naturally proceeded from the former.

What, then, are the marks of the genuinely fanatic temperament? Of these we stand no more in doubt than of the distinctive reactions of a chemical compound. They include great excitability, extravagance, credulity, vanity, narrowness of mind, unpracticalness, imprudence amounting to recklessness, and these all associated more or less with morbid fancies and melancholy moods, often also with a general disregard for the plain elements of morality, and utter disregard for the sacredness of human life. The history of fanaticism through ages past, marks out these traits of character as unmistakably as the study

that Paul was compelled to satisfy his own mind, historically and critically. His conversion had to struggle into existence through doubt and denial, and his mental character was pre-eminently logical; he was never happy until his ideas were firmly established, until he had arrived at positive conclusions, and had anticipated all objections."

of geology makes plain the various strata of the earth's crust.[1]

Now the task of the unbelief which rejects the supernatural is, given such a temperament, and a murdered teacher of strange doctrines who before his death had only succeeded in impressing a few unlettered folk, whilst he had aroused to passionate heat against himself the religious prejudice of the Jew, the haughty hate of Rome, and the contemptuous malice of scribes and Pharisees, to produce—in the midst of most hostile surroundings, and within not more than five-and-twenty years—a character and a life such as that of Paul, with his gospel of purity, and peace, and truth, and love. Surely those who can believe this to have been possible, ought not to be staggered by miracle anywhere.

But even if we assume the credibility of the incredible, and allow for a moment the possibility of the impossible, under the pretext that sheer fanaticism may bring about unexpected results, is it shown that Paul truly was such an enthusiast? The answer must be that from all that we know reliably concerning him, one and only one of all these characteristics can honestly be acknowledged as true, namely, warmth of temperament. But if this constitutes valid ground for an accusation of fanaticism, what shall we say of half the best known and noblest of mankind! Such a man as Paul may, confessedly, be the slave of his strongest impulses. But there is no proof whatever that he did so lack self-control. Whilst as to

[1] Tragic illustration is afforded, whilst these sheets are passing through the press, by the fearful ravages of the "Boxers" in China, and the ghastly murder of the King of Italy.

the other indubitable marks of the true fanatic, his whole character exhibits continual proof of traits the very opposite. To sum up, therefore, under this head of enthusiasm, the only way of so accounting for the actual facts of the case, is to attribute to the apostle a character which he certainly never possessed, and then endow that character with utterly incredible potentialities. And this by way of getting rid of difficulties! From such a tangle of incredibilities it is refreshing to turn once again to the judgement of Keim [1]—

"We are thus led to two important conclusions. In the first place, the apostle's faith must have rested, not upon the meagre notices of the person of Jesus which we find in his writings, but upon a knowledge of His life sufficiently comprehensive to justify all the results of his reasoning, and to present to his mind, either on the ground of his own observation or that of others, the picture of a character without spot and full of nobility. And, in the second place, this knowledge is not the fruit of a blind acceptance of unexamined Christian tradition picked up here and there, but, as the case of the inquiry into the evidence of the resurrection shows, was arrived at by means of a lucid, keen, searching, sceptical observation, comparison, collection and collation of such materials as were accessible to him."

Finally, even if we should waive all the difficulties of unbelief which are associated with Paul's actual conversion and following career, we have yet to give rational account of his letters. Let these be honestly examined, and their ethics compared with those of any other of the world's best known teachers. Are these writings the work of a fool, or a knave, or a sunstruck epileptic, or a crack-brained enthusiast? Is such a result from such a cause "psychologically conceivable"?

[1] *Jesu von Nazara*, i. p. 52.

This at least, must in the end be unhesitatingly affirmed, that if the conversion, character, career, and writings of the Apostle Paul did so originate, then all objection to the miraculous should cease. For in such a case a far greater and grosser contradiction to nature is before us, than all the Christian miracles together can supply. The supernaturalness of such a miracle of unbelief would only be equalled by its unnaturalness, or surpassed by its anti-naturalness.

II. Nature and Origin of the New Testament

Under the same head of psychological contradiction we pass to consider the case of the New Testament generally. It is confessedly too vast a theme to treat here with the detailed attention that it merits. Happily, however, the literature of the subject has during recent years so been cleared of fog and rendered accessible, that we may honestly assume much, and leave the rest open to the careful scrutiny of every person of intelligence and sincerity who is disposed to examine for himself.

The New Testament, with all its remarkable characteristics, is manifestly before us, and we are driven to ask both what it is and whence it comes. We will, therefore, first summarise the plain facts, and then briefly estimate them, in order that we may clearly see whether of the two is the more difficult—or indeed the more miraculous—the account of their origin given by Christian belief, or that suggested by unbelief.

Here, then, in our hands, is a collection of writings upon subjects most of all difficult to handle, and in regard to which, between all other authors upon earth, the greatest conceivable confusion and contradiction prevail. These Christian writings comprise twenty-seven different portions, acknowledged to have been written at different times, by not less than eight or nine distinct persons, perhaps more. They are addressed to entirely different communities called Churches, situated in various localities distant from each other. Besides the difficulties which are inseparable from an admixture of matters historical, ethical, and religious, these writings introduce events and opinions emphatically peculiar to themselves, and involving considerations in which above all others "many men" were likely to have "many minds." Such themes are the conception of Christ's person and work, together with His Crucifixion and Resurrection, and all those ensuing results which are connoted in the New Testament term "salvation."

Eight distinct classes of facts at least, merit attention.

1. Every reader of the Acts of the Apostles, in which Paul's conversion is recorded, sees that there is presupposed—and indeed in the opening verses distinctly asserted—the existence of just such another narrative of great events connected with the Christ, as we find in the Gospel of Luke. But we possess besides this, three other similar records, making together a unique quadruple biography. Now at whatever time these Gospels themselves were written, the events which they record manifestly preceded those related in the Acts. This being the case, we are most of all concerned to know whether we may rely upon this fourfold account as true, whenever and by whomsoever written. Certainly they give us a full and sufficient narrative of such things as

must be presupposed necessary, both to Paul's conversion and that of all others mentioned in the Acts. Were it not for the supernatural element involved in them, probably no one would question their authenticity. When, however, this is impugned, it becomes the task of critical unbelief to account for these narratives as they have come down to us, and to show cause for regarding as more reliable some other record of what undoubtedly happened.

Meanwhile, these our Gospels not only exist, but are better known in the modern world than any other ancient writings whatever. If, therefore, the general Christian view respecting their origin be rejected, then all those features which go to make them absolutely unique in the world's literature, must be explained upon purely natural principles and according to the acknowledged laws of psychology.

Much has been said elsewhere, well and deservedly, concerning their style, both in the form in which English readers know it, and yet more emphatically as to the original Greek. Their simplicity has also been justly admired, in that they give so marvellous a history with such naturalness and such marked repression of both the personal characteristics and comments of the writers. The conception of such a figure as that of the Christ, moving through them with traits of character quite unprecedented and utterly foreign to the ideals alike of Judaism and Paganism, has been freely acknowledged to be sublime. The wonderful harmony of four such witnesses, who, to say the very least, have been shown to be distinct in person and to have written at different times, has been conceded. Whilst no less remarkable are the numerous differences which no conceivable forgery would have allowed to pass. For all this adequate cause must be found.

But there is a great deal more to be accounted for. Difficult beyond measure as the biographical subject manifestly is, no honest mind can deny the real unity of the fourfold portrait. The wonder and beauty of the character thus displayed has been not only revered by believers, but warmly appreciated by the noblest amongst unbelievers. Of this attitude the well-known words of John Stuart Mill may be taken as typical—

"Whatever else may be taken away from us by rational criticism, Christ is still left—a unique figure, not more unlike all His precursors than all His followers, even those who had the direct benefit of His personal teaching. It is of no use to say that Christ as exhibited in the Gospels is not historical, and that we know not how much of what is admirable has been superadded by the tradition of His followers. Who among his disciples or among their proselytes was capable of inventing the sayings ascribed to Jesus, or of imagining the life and character revealed in the Gospels ? Certainly not the fishermen of Galilee, still less the early Christian writers." [1]

It is quite certain, moreover, from all the scrutiny of criticism, that the wondrous unity in the portraiture of the Gospels was not the result of any collusion between the writers. The many so-called "discrepancies" between these records, especially between the Synoptics—Matthew, Mark, and Luke — and the Fourth Gospel, suffice to establish this. None of these, indeed, at all avail to destroy the real unity of the general conception, but it is quite "psychologically inconceivable" that accounts so

[1] *Essays on Nature, the Utility of Religion and Theism*, pp. 253-255.

apparently differing, should be given by writers working together for purposes of deception.

2. Yet it is not merely of the Gospels and their idiosyncrasies that unbelief is bound to furnish adequate account. The three-and-twenty other distinct writings which are included in the rest of the New Testament, demand none the less to be taken into careful regard. The Christian view of the origin of these also is simple and sufficient, whilst the difficulties of unbelief thicken into a hopeless tangle. For here we are called upon to consider a great deal more than merely special features of style and subject. To read, even superficially, the letters which form so large a portion of the Christian Scriptures, and believe that such candour, simplicity, and ethical dignity, can be the work of either clever forgers or deluded enthusiasts, bespeaks much more credulity than can ever be attributed to believers.

But it is only when we come to examine all these writings with calm and critical comparison, that the magnitude of the task which scepticism sets itself becomes apparent. Here are twenty-three writings, longer or shorter, all dealing with a subject most of all difficult to delineate, viz. a new religion, resting upon the words and works of a once crucified but afterwards risen Saviour, a theme which had never before entered into the human mind; all assuming the happening of events and the existence of facts so strange, that the uttermost precautions could never have ensured substantial agreement amongst narrators, had the facts been other than as represented; all, moreover, written at different times, and to a great extent by different authors, and sent, without explanation, to widely differing communities. Yet all these, despite the difficulty of their purpose and the diversity of their standpoints, so agree, that they were not merely soon gathered into one volume and regarded as inspired, but they have defied all scrutiny, of friends and foes alike, from that time to this, to find any contradiction between them serious enough to imperil for a moment the reliability of the whole.[1]

3. Between the Acts of the Apostles and the Epistles, indeed, there exists a special relation which must not be overlooked. A modern judge, giving his opinion as to what kind of evidence most deserved credence, expressed himself to the effect that it is "not that of hardy and direct assertion, but that which receives incidental confirmation from the putting together of incidental circumstances; "in short," he said, "the sort of coincidences in Paley's *Horæ Paulinæ*." This was not spoken with any reference to theology, but simply as indicating a certain kind of evidence. We cannot here give large quotations from Paley's work, but it is easily accessible, and worthy of careful study, especially from the vast number of modern readers who ignore it as antiquated. Nothing that modern

[1] In so saying one does not forget that such works as *Supernatural Religion* have appeared—nor need we discourteously ignore them. But seeing that it is manifestly impossible here to break off and attempt to hold the balances between such works and the categoric replies which have been issued by competent Christian scholars, the only course left is to give, not without examination, a deliberate judgement, and leave those who question it to the results of their own investigation. Reference may also be made to the list of books at the end.

criticism has established, avails in the least to diminish the evidential value of the marvellous network of undesigned coincidences to which Paley directs attention. The correlations in minute detail between the Acts and Epistles, are in truth such as to extract from F. W. Newman the acknowledgment that "the very complete establishment which this work gives to the narrative concerning Paul in the latter half of the Acts, appears to me to reflect critical honour on the whole New Testament." But the honour of the whole New Testament — and especially of those four Epistles to Rome, Corinth, and Galatia, which the most destructive modern criticism accepts as genuine — is undeniably pledged to the actual truth of the Supernatural in general, and the Resurrection of Christ in particular. Nor can it be too plainly pointed out, that if modern unbelief could succeed in showing that all this intricate labyrinth of mutually confirming references is but the result of foolish fanaticism or guilty deceit, it would then have demonstrated a psychological miracle which, for transgression of natural law, would far exceed anything recorded in the Gospels.

4. Still more to be considered is the substantial unanimity existing between *all* the various parts of the New Testament. Our general familiarity with these Christian writings, in their conventional juxtaposition and arrangement within the covers of one volume, blinds the eyes of the vast majority of ordinary readers to the actual marvel—on any other supposition than their truthfulness—of their consensus in regard to the most strange and, in some sense, contradictory series of

events that the world has ever known. In no other history whatever would mutual falsification between different writers have been so easy, or, one may say, so inevitable. Yet when the utmost deference has been paid to the sincerity and ability of the modern critic, it is unquestionable that the various representations of the person of Christ, the series of great events, the doctrinal and ethical consequences of Christ's mysterious death and actual resurrection, are substantially and unmistakably one. But that such a unity should issue, by the mere hap of the case, from a conglomeration of delusion, fanaticism, and deceit, is an improbability beyond mathematical expression. The improbability of the Christian miracles is small indeed by comparison.

5. Again, the historical fidelity of these writings is as marvellous as it is indirect. The references which can be directly compared with accredited history, occur, naturally, in some parts of the New Testament more than in others. But the fact that they are always and only incidental, greatly enhances their value.[1] They admit of being variously classified, but it must suffice here to point out that in their unequivocal allusions to contemporary Jewish rulers and Roman authorities, as also to the political and religious condition of the Jewish nation, with passing references to persons and events in the surrounding Gentile world, the New

[1] See No. 41 of the admirable series of "Present-Day Tracts" issued by the Religious Tract Society, in which Dr. Maclear sets forth the case with forceful succinctness. This, as well as all the other members of the series, deserves the earnest study of every person of ordinary intelligence throughout the land.

Testament writers ingenuously lay themselves open to criticism or confutation in numberless instances. The comparative meagreness of the reference to the new faith made by the non-Christian writers of the period, is capable of easy and adequate explanation. But the points of contact between the Christian narrative and the civil or political environment, are neither too few nor too many to be natural. They are free alike from evasion and from ostentation. And with such trifling exceptions as only concern those who are pledged to the untenable theory of "verbal" inspiration, the accuracy of these references is established now beyond dispute.[1] How, then, we ask, is such historical fidelity to be accounted for, on such a theme, amongst so many and so different contributors, writing at varying times, and distinctly separated from each other by distance and by circumstance? There can be but one valid psychological explanation, namely, that they spoke and wrote the truth. Any other supposition makes greater demands upon our powers of belief than all the miraculous elements of the events recorded.

6. We have yet, however, to take some notice of that selection of some Christian writings from others, and collection of them into a universally recognised whole, which is summarised under the term "Canonicity." On this theme the works of Drs. Westcott and Charteris will be appreciated only by students. Yet it is not for students so much as for all ordinary people, that

---

[1] See, especially, "Discoveries illustrating the Acts of the Apostles," on pp. 291–302 of Dr. Lightfoot's *Essays on Supernatural Religion.*

Mrs. Besant and others have issued manuals in which special attention is directed to the number of so-called "Apocryphal" Christian writings, in the course of the first and second centuries. The intention of such enumeration is, avowedly, to damage the received authority of our New Testament. The actual effect is exactly the contrary.

Mr. J. S. Mill might well say — in answer to the question, "Who wrote the Gospels?" — "Certainly not the fishermen of Galilee, still less the early Christian writers." For the comparison of those writings which, as being included in the New Testament, are called "canonical," with the productions generally comprised in the Christian Apocrypha, as well as the writings of the early "Fathers," is happily possible to-day to anyone who chooses to make it. It is simply impossible to conceive of any person of intelligence and honesty who would not endorse the verdict of Mr. B. H. Cowper, the accomplished translator of the best of these pseudo-Gospels and Epistles, when he says—

"Before I undertook this task, I never realised so completely as I do now, the impassable character of the gulf which separates the genuine Gospels from these."[1]

How is this gulf to be accounted for? It cannot be denied. It can scarcely be measured. That mere chance or blind credulity should first create such a distinction, and then cause it to crystallise permanently out of the tossing sea of differing opinions, bitter conflicts, and energetic heresies which, we know, so soon

[1] *The Apocryphal Gospels*, by B. H. Cowper (Norgate). Preface.

characterised the early Church, is indeed "psychologically inconceivable." How came it to pass that the writings which, whether we think of them as comprising the New Testament or not, are acknowledged to be incomparably superior to any other Christian productions, ancient or modern, were really though gradually separated from all others, and with such emphasis that, equally then and now, a man might as well set himself the task of creating a world as either to increase or diminish their number? For such attempted alteration of the Canon, we know that the heretical acumen of a Marcion, the rude strength of a Luther, and the critical determination of a Baur, proved alike futile.

To assign all this ultimately to the Spirit of God, working out a definite purpose towards humanity by means of the truth and its influence on the minds of men, is at least an adequate and reasonable cause. But to ascribe such an event, utterly without parallel as it is in the world of literature, to the mere accident of religious party conflict, inspired only by hysteria or fanaticism, is a psychological monstrosity, compared with which the "ghost theory" of Mr. Spencer and Mr. Clodd, as recently shown up by Mr. Andrew Lang, scarcely deserves mention.

7. This, however, is by no means all. A whole volume might be written upon another phase of the question which can here receive only passing notice, namely, the wonderful preservation and unquenchable vitality of these writings. Such a theme would, of course, include also the whole Bible. But even if, for the time being, we

should allow the reverence or jealousy of Jew and Samaritan to have been sufficient cause for the preservation of the Old Testament, much more remains to be considered.[1]

The New Testament has had more vigorous friends and enemies than any other known collection of human writings. These, however, have not so much cancelled each other's influence as they have together tended to injure the proper understanding, the honest reading, the sheer existence of the whole Bible. What other writings amongst men have been subject to such contrary extremes as bigoted Bibliolatry on the one hand, and fierce hatred, like that of heathenism or the Romish Inquisition, upon the other? Neither the Koran nor any of the writings of the East has passed through such vicissitudes of storm and stress as have repeatedly spent themselves upon the Bible. Vain attempts to destroy it have been accompanied by compensating prophecies that it would soon be blotted out, and it has been the shrewd habit of a certain section to refer to it again and again as passing into oblivion. But all has been in vain. It not only still exists, but is to-day more widely diffused and more influential than ever.

Meanwhile the very fact of the difference, and in some manifest aspects the contradiction, between the Old and New Covenants, emphasises the marvel, oft underrated and forgotten, that these two so long have been, and

[1] See Professor Henry Rogers, *Superhuman Origin of the Bible*. An able and convenient summary of the case will also be found, for ordinary readers, in No. 23 of the series of "Present-Day Tracts" (Religious Tract Society), by Rev. Dr. Blaikie.

henceforth are, bound together in one volume as an indissoluble whole.

Again, the acknowledged loss of the original autographs, alike as regards the Hebrew and Christian Scriptures, contrasts notably with the double fact that their translations—made from admittedly better "texts" than the ancient classics—are more widely known throughout the world than any other, and rest to-day upon a firmer critical basis than at any time since the days of the Apostles.

On the whole, it is not too much to say that there is in these days just as much room to question the best known events of history, as the reliability of the Hebrew and Greek texts, in regard to all those great facts which they adduce as demonstrating the reality of the supernatural in the spiritual evolution of mankind. Nor is there any risk in the affirmation that gravitation will cease to be a force in this earth's physics, as surely and as soon as the Bible and its influence will be cast out of the heart of humanity. If, therefore, the root of this manifestly indestructible tree be but pure delusion, if the source of this mighty and resistless stream be only an accidental confluence of the deceiving and the deceived, truly it is not enough to say with Tennyson—

> "There's something in this world amiss
> Shall be unriddled by and by";

for all is chaos and confusion in the world of mind, whatever we may think we see in surrounding physical creation.

At least it must be affirmed that there is no parallel in history to this peaceful but irresistible dissemination throughout the world, of writings which are unique alike in their doctrine of God and man, which admit of neither rival nor partner in their claims, which pander to nothing in human nature that is unworthy, but, on the contrary, set up a standard of conduct that most men find quite unattainable.

In regard to the New Testament especially, to suggest that a band of a dozen men, mostly unlettered, should succeed in concocting a story which they all knew to be false, and not only force it upon Jew and Gentile of their own day, but so embalm it in records and letters as literally to fill the world with their doctrine after an interval of nineteen centuries, until it were as vain to attempt to destroy all human knowledge, and substitute savagery for civilisation, as to blot out this doctrine from human affairs, is surely to ask credence for a greater as well as darker miracle than any of the supernatural events recorded in the Gospels, Acts, or Epistles.

8. There is yet another consideration which certainly must not be left out of account, namely, the nature of the influence which is thus confessedly indestructible. This opens the door, it must be owned, for an estimate of the whole value of religion in the development of human nature and civilisation. But we need not enter it in order to do justice to our present theme. It were alike discourteous and vain to ignore, or treat as trifles, the strongly expressed convictions of unbelievers who have been sometimes as distinguished for intellectual ability as for moral probity. The true Christian has neither need nor desire to cast scorn upon the writings of such men as Strauss, Renan, Büchner, Haeckel, John Stuart Mill,

Herbert Spencer, H. T. Buckle, Charles Bradlaugh, Prof. Clifford, the author of *Supernatural Religion*, Carl Pearson, and the like; nor again of such women as Marian Evans ("George Eliot"), Annie Besant, and Mrs. Humphry Ward. At the same time, the personal disavowal of Christianity on the part of these prominent writers by no means avails to settle the question as to the influence of the Bible, and especially of the New Testament, in the mental and moral history of humanity.

For, in the first place, if personal testimonies are to count, according to the acknowledged intellectual power, manifest sincerity, social influence, world-wide prominence, of well-known writers and leaders of thought, there cannot be a moment's hesitation as to which side would show to greatest advantage. It is not sufficient to aver that in every realm of civilised life, in literature, science, art, and politics, no less than in philosophy and morals, the names of eminent believers would amply suffice as a set-off against those of unbelievers. The fact is that they would be in an overwhelming majority. It is not seldom forgotten, especially by the younger or popular advocates of scepticism, that the common appeal to the authority of Huxley, and Tyndall, and Clifford, etc., as instances of unbelief, introduces a principle of decision which would tell irresistibly on behalf of Christian faith. We do not, of course, here appeal to such testimony as decisive on the general question, but when we remember that deliberate expressions of strong conviction, from men acknowledged to be among the world's greatest and best, could be multiplied indefinitely, we do at least conclude that the question as to the influence of this wondrous collection of writings which we call Holy Scripture, is by no means foreclosed by a few notable instances of sceptic disparagement. Its perpetual re-statement is, rather, as desirable as permissible.

The appeal is always twofold, to principle and to fact. We have to ask both what is likely to be, and what has been. The logical and legitimate consequences of principles demand estimate, equally with the actual events of history. By far the greater part of the common objections raised by Secularists and others against Christianity, consists of reminders and accusations in regard to conduct which the Bible itself condemns far more emphatically than its opponents do. Of these we need take no notice. If so-called Christians have carried fire and sword, opium and alcohol, greed and treachery, throughout the world, or if, even at home, "envy, hatred and malice, and all uncharitableness" do sometimes characterise their behaviour, the New Testament is its own witness that the condemnation of faith concerning such things is far more severe than the censure of unfaith. The Gospels and Epistles are no more responsible for these occasional evil doings of Christian nations or individuals, than the laws of England are for the greed of gamblers or the vile deeds of every criminal.

But, on the other hand, what a change for the better would necessarily come over our cities, our nation, the whole of Europe and the world, if only such fundamental Christian principles as are set forth in the Sermon on the Mount, or Rom. xii., or Col. iii., or Eph. iv., etc., were actually enshrined in all human hearts, and embodied in the daily conduct of humanity, every honest mind must be called upon to judge for itself.

Meanwhile we are able to estimate that which actually has been. We may inquire frankly as to the effect of Scripture upon national character, upon family life, upon civic behaviour, and indeed upon human development in general. It is also quite right that we should take into account the efforts and results of modern Foreign Missions. Nor is there any sound reason why we should refuse to listen to well-substantiated personal testimony.

To do all this in detail would, of necessity, occupy volumes rather than pages. The following deliberate expressions of opinion, therefore, may be taken as convenient summaries, representative not only of many more, but of the preponderating judgement of the human mind, when all due subtraction has been made for the opposing attitude of unbelievers. It may be avowed without hesitation that every one of the eminent men whose words are here given, is no less distinguished for intellectual eminence than raised above suspicion for probity and truthfulness. Nearly a century ago Fichte wrote thus—

"It remains certain that we with our whole age and with all our philosophic inquiries, are established on and have proceeded from Christianity; that this Christianity has entered into our whole culture in the most varied forms, and that, on the whole, we might have been nothing of all that we are, had not this mighty principle gone before us in time." [1]

Lord Macaulay, again, expresses himself thus—

"How vast the difference between Christianity and heathenism! I altogether abstain from alluding to topics which belong to

---

[1] *Doctrine of Religion*, Lect. vi. p. 473, Smith's edition.

divines. I speak merely as a politician, anxious for the morality and the temporal well-being of society. And so speaking I say that to discountenance that religion which has done so much to promote justice, and mercy, and freedom, and arts, and science, and good government, and domestic happiness, which has struck off the chains of the slave, which has mitigated the horrors of war, which has raised women from servants and playthings into companions and friends, is to commit high treason against humanity and civilisation."[1]

Professor Huxley's words, above-quoted, merit repetition:—

"By the study of what other book could children be so much humanised and made to feel that each figure in the vast historical procession fills, like themselves, but a momentary space between two eternities; and earns the blessings or curses of all time, according to its effort to do good and hate evil, even as they are also earning their payment for their work?" "I do not say that even the highest Biblical ideal is exclusive of others or needs no supplement. But I do believe that the human race is not yet, possibly may never be, in a position to dispense with it."[2]

Sir Andrew Clark has left his deliberate judgement to this effect—

"No one can doubt who has had adequate opportunities of observation and powers of reflection, that there is one remedy, and one alone, for all this spiritual disease, and that is to be found in the person and work of Jesus Christ."[3]

So, too, Sir Risdon Bennett, late P.R.C.S.—

"How can we look round the world and fail to see proof of the power of Christianity wherever the gospel is known, among all races of mankind, all classes of society, all ranks of intellect! What is there comparable to Christianity in promoting the happiness and welfare of mankind?"[4]

The Right Hon. W. E. Gladstone, whose life was

[1] Speeches—*The Gates of Somnauth.*
[2] *Essays on Controverted Questions*, pp. 51–53.
[3] *Report of Christian Evidence Society*, p. 33.
[4] *Ibid.* p. 41.

sufficient witness to the reality of his convictions, has left behind him abundant testimonies which are well summarised in these his words—

"Christianity, even in its sadly imperfect development, is, as matter of fact, at the head of the world. As the first existing power, it rules the world; and of all the more or less noisy pretenders who, as if it were an Ottoman despotism, are prematurely disputing for the succession, there is not one which has given evidence either of being capable, or of being accepted, for the place it has so long held."[1] "For the last fifteen hundred years Christianity has always marched in the van of human improvement and civilisation, and it has harnessed to its car all that is great and glorious in humanity."[2]

Such testimonies as these could easily be multiplied and confirmed. They may suffice here, as fair specimens of the best thought of some of the ablest judges of the true welfare of society.[3]

It would, however, be an injustice to the truth to omit all reference to the equally significant witness afforded by the work of modern Christian Missions in foreign countries. Strange ignorance prevails, accompanied by an amazing underestimate, both within and without the Churches, as to the wonderfulness and the value of the results of such effort. The following expressions of the judgement of representative men, may again be taken as truly typical of a general consensus

---

[1] Rectorial Address, Glasgow, p. 26.   [2] Private letter.

[3] Reference to other works upon this theme, to be inclusive only of the best, would resemble the catalogue of a large library, but the following may be singled out from a host as being worthy of special study. *The Influence of Jesus*, Bohlen Lectures, by the late Dr. Phillips Brooks; *Gesta Christi*, by the late G. Loring Brace; *Christian Sociology*, by Dr. Stuckenberg; and *Practical Christian Sociology*, by Dr. Crafts.

which is simply overwhelming in its testimony to the worth of such Christian work.

A more impartial witness it would be difficult to find than the late Mr. Charles Darwin. When he touched at New Zealand in 1835, we find him recording his impressions thus—

> "I believe we were all glad to leave New Zealand—the greater part of the English are the very refuse of society. I look back to but one bright spot, and that is Waimate, with its native Christian inhabitants."

Again, referring to the attacks made upon the missionaries by critics at home, he says—

> "They forget, or will not remember, that human sacrifices and the power of an idolatrous priesthood—a system of profligacy unparalleled in any other part of the world—infanticide a consequence of that system—bloody wars where the conquerors spared neither women nor children—that all these have been abolished, and that dishonesty, intemperance, and licentiousness have been greatly reduced by the introduction of Christianity. In a voyager to forget these things is base ingratitude; for should he chance to be at the point of shipwreck on some unknown coast, he will most devoutly pray that the lesson of the missionary may have reached thus far.'
> ... "The lesson of the missionary is the enchanter's wand. The house had been built, the windows framed, the fields and even the trees grafted by the New Zealander. When I looked at the whole scene I thought it admirable. The march of improvement consequent on the introduction of Christianity, throughout the South Sea, probably stands by itself in the records of history."[1]

Another equally unbiassed authority, the *Standard* newspaper,[2] in regard to the formerly savage "Society Islands," writes as follows:—

> "Up to 1820 they resisted vigorously any attempts to impose upon them the new faith. Even the lives of the missionaries were in

---

[1] *Journal of Researches*, 2nd edition, pp. 414, 425, 428, 505.
[2] For October 26, 1887.

danger. Now all this is changed. With few exceptions the natives have abandoned their idolatry, and even send missionaries to other islands. Churches and schools have been erected, and in other respects they might set an example to the world nearer home."

Miss Gordon Cumming, writing of Fiji,[1] says—

"It is only forty years since the missionaries landed, and already they have won over to the new religion of peace and love, upwards of a hundred thousand ferocious cannibals."

When Protestant missions were first projected in regard to the island of Madagascar, the French governor of the island of Bourbon declared—

"You make the Malagasy Christians! Impossible! They are mere brutes, and have no more sense than irrational cattle."

Now there are hundreds of Protestant Churches, and that in spite of a bloody persecution, in which vast numbers bore themselves as nobly as any other martyrs of history. Whilst in connection with the London Missionary Society alone, there are nearly 1000 native pastors, and 100,000 children in the schools.

If we turn our thoughts for a moment to India, with its immense numbers and ancient history, the testimony is the same. Mr. Hutton has reminded us not so long since that up to 1837, about 150 human sacrifices were annually offered in Goomsur alone, that in Kattiawar and Kutch alone about 3000 female infants were annually exposed, that in four months, in 1824, no less than 115 widows were burnt alive near Calcutta. What has been done in face of such evils may best be summarised in

[1] See the whole of *At Home in Fiji*, by the Authoress.

the "Report of the Secretary of State and Council of India." [1]

"The Government of India cannot but acknowledge the great obligation under which it is laid by the benevolent exertions made by the missionaries, whose blameless example and self-denying labours are infusing new vigour into the stereotyped life of the great populations placed under English rule, and are preparing them to be in every way better men and better citizens of the great empire in which they dwell."

Babu Keshub Chunder Sen, the well-known leader of the Bramo Somaj in Calcutta, said [2]—

"The spirit of Christianity has already pervaded the whole atmosphere of Indian society, and we breathe, think, feel, and move in a Christian atmosphere. Native society is being roused, enlightened, and reformed under the influence of Christian education."

In 1880 the Maharajah of Travancore said [3]—

"Long before the State undertook the humanising task of educating the subject population, the Christian missionaries had raised the beacon of knowledge in this land. One cannot be sufficiently thankful for the introduction of this civilising element and its happily steady development. Your labours have been increasing year by year the number of a loyal, law-abiding, and civilised population—the very foundation of good government."

Sir Bartle Frere, formerly Governor of Bombay, declared [4]—

"Whatever you may be told to the contrary, the teaching of Christianity among 160 millions of civilised, industrious Hindoos

---

[1] On the progress of India for 1871–72, ordered to be printed by the House of Commons, April 28, 1873.

[2] *Lectures*, Bramo Tract Society, Calcutta, 1883, pp. 2, 6, 15, 281, etc.

[3] Replying to an address from the missionaries at Cottayam.

[4] Lecture before the Christian Evidence Society, July 9, 1872.

and Mohammedans in India, is effecting changes, moral, social, and political, which, for extent and rapidity of effect, are far more extraordinary than anything you or your fathers have witnessed in modern Europe."

And the late Lord Lawrence, who was Governor-General of India, and probably knew India better than any other man of his day, declared that—

"Notwithstanding all that the English people have done to benefit India, the missionaries have done more than all other agencies combined."

Whilst these pages are passing through the press the strained attention of Europe is being drawn towards China in its terrible convulsions, brought about by the savage fury of "Boxers" against the "foreign devil," which Li Hung Chang and others ascribe to the influence of missionaries. How far this is from the actual truth does not come within our sphere of discussion; but the following is only one out of numberless testimonies which might be quoted from experts in Chinese matters.

In a recent interview Dr. John Dudgeon says [1]—

"The missionary question in China is the question of the century! When you ask me if missionary enterprise in China has made for good on the whole, I answer,—Unquestionably, without any reservation—not only almost an unmixed good, but almost the only good. As to whether the Chinese will ultimately become a Christian people—I believe it. The civilisation that half the

---

[1] From *Great Thoughts*. Dr. Dudgeon is a M.D. and C.M. of Glasgow, thirty years resident in China, head of the Imperial College, Pekin, Physician and Surgeon to the British Legation and the Japanese Legation in that city: author of *To Yeng-Chi-Kwan; The Land Question, or Peasant Proprietorship in China; Diet, Dwellings, and Dress of the Chinese*, etc. etc.

Powers would introduce is the civilisation of selfishness. Railways are not everything, and will not take the place of mental and moral training. We are upsetting the ideas of the Chinese, and not giving them anything in their place. The only influence that can counteract the evil effects of a breaking away from old restraints and abandonment of old beliefs, is the civilisation that springs from Christianity. It is the only hope for China."

Only space is required to adduce evidence in regard to other countries. If we pass from China to South Africa, or from North America to the isles of the Pacific, similar testimonies to the degree in which the influence of the Bible, and more especially of the Christianity of the New Testament, upon the character and destinies of humanity has been equally beneficent and irresistible.

Nor is there any sufficient reason why the personal experience of Christians at home should be ignored. For it is as scientifically valid as other testimony, and could be adduced, with all the modesty of truthfulness, from all conditions of life and all classes of the community. It is quite as rational to consider the highest as it is to note the lowest estimate of Christianity. At least it must be owned that in these Christian writings which we are considering, men of intelligence and sincerity have found, in cases without number, a comfort and an inspiration, as well as solemn warning and clear guidance, which have made life altogether a new thing, filling hearts with joy and homes with gladness, regenerating society with elevating influences, and, when all that is human fades away, providing a worthy hope that transforms death itself into a benediction. Such, in very deed, has been, and yet is, the influence of that gospel which through the Christian Scriptures has permeated the world.

The facts, in a word, are such that, with all that we can gather concerning the history and influence of other religions, it must be owned that these Scriptures have affected the progress of the world, and that for good, more than any other records known to humanity. Here then, once more, is a vast congeries of fact for which adequate cause must be discovered if either our religion or irreligion is to be rational.

The eight distinct lines of thought thus summarised have been sufficiently elaborated in other volumes; what we have here to do is to sum them up in one clear view, and find for the whole, as for each, an adequate cause. It is an entirely true, but by no means sufficient, avowal, that there is no parallel to this whole case in human history. For the uniqueness of the records and the unparalleled influence for good of the Christian Scriptures, become more and more manifest in proportion to the thoroughness with which they are investigated.

Now the explanation of this total complex phenomenon, according to Christian faith, is confessedly as adequate as manifest. The actuality of the fundamental events recorded, the reality of the co-operating Divine influence, the energy of human nature working upon well-known lines, supply together reasonable and sufficient cause for all the phenomena in question. But to remove any one of these three forces, is to wreck the whole, as infallibly as the swift progress of a locomotive would be prevented if we take away the fire, or the water, or the mechanism, by the conjoint means of which it works.

Dr. Wace has therefore well said, that

"The whole case of the Christian reasoner is that the records of the New Testament defy any attempt to explain them by natural causes. The German critics Hase, Strauss, Baur, Hausrath, Keim, all have made the attempt, and each, in the opinion of the others, and finally of Pfleiderer, has offered an insufficient solution of the problem. The case of the Christian is not that the evidence ought not to be explained naturally, and translated into everyday experience, but that it cannot be."

In other words, it is simply "psychologically inconceivable" that this vast and marvellous structure can have had fraud, or folly, for its foundation, and fanaticism or delusion for the plan of its development. Could it be demonstrated that such was the case, the reality of the miraculous element would not merely remain, but would be as manifestly increased in quantity as subverted in quality, by its transference from the side of faith to that of unfaith. The miracles of unbelief would be immeasurably more "difficult," in all respects, than those of belief.

One final feature of the case merits separate mention. It has become increasingly the fashion of late years to insist upon the foolishness, and ignorance, and superstition, of the men of the primitive Christian age, in order to make it easy to understand how they could believe in miracles, and be led away into accepting the Christian story generally. Now this would be all very well if they had only left behind them such religious Munchausen tales as the Apocryphal writings; or if the practical results of their associated folly had been equally mischievous and shortlived. This, however, we know to be the exact opposite of the truth. Whilst, therefore, the honesty and reliability of these Christian Scriptures are becoming more clear the more closely they are examined, and the world is gradually but surely learning so to distinguish Christianity from ecclesiasticism as to recognise in the true mind of Christ the greatest blessing and noblest hope of our race, correspondingly more serious grows evermore the problem for unbelief. For the more weak and foolish these early Christian disciples and advocates were, according to the naturalistic hypothesis, the more impossible it becomes to explain how, from such an origin, there can have sprung the Christian writings, with their wonderful representations, their indestructible vitality, their elevating and ennobling influence.

It would indeed be a stupendous problem to explain how the world's highest ideal of truth could have originated in falsehood; how the severest standard of purity and honour could have arisen out of fable, fraud, and fanaticism; how writings which are unique in simple excellence of style, and sustain the strictest investigasion into their mutual relations, could yet be utterly unreliable as to the main facts which they assert and upon which they wholly depend. If "men do not gather grapes of thorns or figs from thistles," it is worse than fatuous to talk of the credulity of certain fanatic Jews of the first century, as the sufficient cause of the New Testament record of facts and system of doctrine. It is simply preposterous to avow that a mere handful of tares can be the source of untold acres of wholesome wheat.

The problem of accounting, therefore, for the Bible,

and more especially the New Testament, without the substantial accuracy of the alleged events, and without the reality of the supernatural influences which are asserted as having interworked with human energies, is a veritable Sisyphus task, recoiling evermore upon him who attempts it. To treat such a problem as either of small account or easy to solve, is a feat of mental jugglery which has been reserved for modern anti-supernatural philosophy. Nor are there any better words with which we may close this section, than those of J. J. Rousseau, who may fairly be regarded as an impartial witness, and whose question, now a century old, has in the interval gathered additional weight for the men of this generation—

"Can a book, at once so sublime and so simple, be the work of men? Can the Person, whose history it relates, be Himself but a mere man? Should we suppose the gospel was a story, invented to please? It is not in this manner that we forge tales, for the actions of Socrates, of which no person has the least doubt, are less satisfactorily attested than those of Jesus Christ. Such a supposition, in fact, only shifts the difficulty without removing it. It is more inconceivable that a number of persons should agree to write such a history, than that one only should furnish the subject of it." [1]

---

[1] *Emilius and Sophia*, vol. iii. bk. iv. p. 136, English edition, 1769.

VII

THE MORAL REALM

"In ordinary cases the presumption against the occurrence of a miracle is so great, that it would be extremely difficult to accumulate sufficient proof to make it credible. The course of nature is so well known in certain respects and so fixed, that only the most important reasons could suffice for a miraculous interference with it. But to the student of Christian evidences such a reason is clearly present in the field. Man is great. His wants are profound. The remedial agencies of the gospel are of such transcendent value, and their adaptation to human necessities so perfect, that they clearly constitute a sufficient reason for such an inauguration as shall make them effective. So complete is this adaptation that the antecedent presumption against its miraculous inauguration is more than overcome in the minds of those who most fully understand the condition of things. The presumption is not that the gospel is 'too beautiful to be true,' but that it is 'too beautiful not to be true.'—
—Dr. G. F. Wright, *Scientific Aspects of Christian Evidences*, p. 189.

"No religion ever appeared in the world whose natural tendency was so much directed to promote the peace and happiness of mankind as Christianity. The system of religion which Christ published and his evangelists recorded, is a complete system for the purposes of religion, natural and revealed. Christianity as it stands in the Gospels is not only a complete but a very plain system of religion. The Gospel is, in all cases, one continued lesson of the strictest morality, of justice, of benevolence, and of universal charity."—
Viscount Bolingbroke—Deist—Works published in 1754 by Mallet.

"Miracles have sometimes been used too exclusively as testimonies to a supernatural mission; but the value, even in this respect, is immensely enhanced when they are further regarded as the unique testimony of experience to the moral fact, that the highest Might has never been seen on earth apart from Right, and that unlimited mastery over the whole forces of evil has only been exercised by perfect holiness. Miracles are indeed revelations of power, but the power is that of a righteous will."—Dr. Wace, *Boyle Lectures* 1874, pp. 305, 306.

VII

THE MORAL REALM

From the intellectual realm we pass, by the next higher stage of transition, to the moral. That man is a moral being may be assumed without apology. All that may be said or thought as to primeval savages, or the aborigines of Africa, etc., is irrelevant; for our inquiry is concerned with the highest, not the lowest. If evolution, uncreated, unguided, unhelped, is to account for anything, it must account for everything. As regards the physical universe, we have seen that all Agnosticism can do is to postulate matter, assume the necessary and convenient potentialities, take motion for granted, add chance, and then claim to have fully accounted for the boundless mystery of good within and around us, "without the supernatural"! We have also seen that the preposterousness of such a claim is manifested by the unnatural monstrosities which it necessitates. In their attempt to eliminate the miracles of Theism, Atheism and Agnosticism are "compelled to posit" far greater miracles of their own.

When, however, we turn from the physical facts which plunge unbelief into mental difficulties, and confine our attention, be it ever so briefly, to morals, the problems become as much more complicated as refined. The moral element in our nature is as much higher than the mental, as the mental is above the physical. Consequently, as mental problems require more careful handling than physical, if we would in their case sift out the truth, so do matters involving moral questions demand proportionately greater delicacy of treatment. At the same time, far from weakening the importance of the latter, this really exalts it to a very high degree. Modern science shows emphatically how the problems which deal with minutest quantities, and therefore require the most tender handling by means of the most delicate instruments, are of the very first importance, and are indeed laden with issues of health or sickness, life or death, to the whole human race.

1. The first item of moral difficulty for the anti-supernaturalist may seem to be elementary, but that does not lessen its significance. The universal idea of God, and the cultivation of religion, in some form or other, amongst all mankind, have often been referred to by Christian apologists, but no adequate account of them has ever been given by those who reject the idea of revelation. Many efforts, indeed, have been made to diminish the force of this consideration. But it would here again be easy to collect testimonies from those best qualified to speak, showing that the term "universal," in this application, may be truly taken within such a hair's-breadth of literalness, as to justify the neglect of two or three alleged exceptions. The few savage tribes, moreover, which have come nearest to exemplifying the absence of the idea of God, have not only been the

very lowest representatives of humanity, but have in almost all instances shown signs of degeneration from a better past.

It belongs, therefore, to the unbeliever to account for this inherent and indestructible human instinct, which has confessedly played such an important part in history. It is no reply to characterise it all as a delusion. If it be such, to explain its origin and persistence becomes an even harder task. A better index to the felt desperateness of the situation can scarcely be found than in the serious suggestion of an eminent modern scientist, that the moral sense which emphasises the distinction 'twixt right and wrong, and culminates in the most reverent and sublime conception of God, originated far back in the brain of some prehistoric anthropoid ape who was "pining with hunger or crossed in love"!

Meanwhile the words of Cicero deserve to be reiterated, for they receive confirmation rather than confutation from our later and wider knowledge—

"There never was any nation so barbarous, nor any people in the world so savage, as to be without some notion of gods; many have wrong notions, for that is the nature or ordinary consequence of bad customs, yet all allow that there is a certain Divine nature or energy. Nor does this proceed from the conversation of men or the agreement of philosophers; it is not an opinion established by institutions or by laws; but no doubt in every case the consent of all nations is to be looked on as a law of nature."

How hideously "wrong," as Cicero hints, may be the notions of God cherished by some men, we know, not only from the reports of travellers and missionaries, but even from the history of theology. Yet the very prevalence of fetish-worship and theological error is only a proof, as

Ruskin reminds us, of the distorting influence of the human mirror which reflects the Divine Presence. It may be surprising and even revolting to view a fair face twisted into a monstrosity in a concave or untrue mirror, but we are well aware that all such distortion can be explained by the laws of optics. That which has, however, in this case to be explained, is the appearance of any face at all, if there be nothing in front of the mirror from which it can, even distortedly, be reflected. Such a phenomenon science does not regard as even conceivable. Yet this, and no less, is the task of the unbelief which "posits" the rise and development of this world-wide human instinct out of nothing but chance and the primitive nebulosity. If, however, such a task should be accomplished, all objection to the supernatural must forthwith cease. For cause will then be no longer necessary to effect, and "laws of nature" will have been shown to be mere figments of the imagination.

2. But we have here to do not with the lowest so much as the highest thought of good and of God which has entered into human hearts and lives. For this, it is no exaggeration to say, the world is learning, and to a large extent has learnt, to look to the New Testament. The yearning of Plato—"We will wait for one, be it a God or a God-inspired man, to teach us our religious duties, and to take away the darkness from our eyes"—has found its fulfilment in the mission of the Christ of whom His least sympathising contemporaries said, "Never man spake like this man." Such an estimate concerning Christ's revelation of God, with its inseparable corollaries concerning human morals, is undoubtedly well warranted.

Our appeal here must be, for brevity's sake, to testimony rather than to discussion. The convictions of the best Christian teachers in every age, are sufficiently attested by their lives and writings. If we abstain from quoting their words, it is by no means an acknowledgment that their testimony should be ruled out of court. There is not a vestige of reason for suggesting that, in intellectual apprehension or in honesty, the standard of faith is lower than that of unbelief.

But there are certain names well known in the world of letters which here must have all the more weight as impartial, seeing that their recorded convictions did not, for reasons inexplicable to us, issue in their becoming definitely Christians. They represent, therefore, the least that the best minds free from bias can say, in regard to the lofty excellence of the New Testament scheme of faith and morals. Thus the great German philosopher and poet Goethe, in his conversations with Eckerman, is reported to have said—

"Let mental culture go on advancing, let the natural sciences progress in ever greater extent and depth, and the human mind widen itself as much as it desires, beyond the elevation and moral culture of Christianity as it shines forth in the Gospels, it will not go."[1]

In 1835 there appeared on the Continent a book which was reported to be the deathblow of Christianity. It was Strauss' *Leben Jesu*. But in the very midst of its reasons for scepticism we find this avowal[2]—

"Amongst the personages to whom mankind is indebted for the perfecting of its moral consciousness, Jesus occupies, at anyrate, the

---

[1] For original, with comment by Prof. A. Harnack, *vide* p. 278.
[2] *Life of Jesus*, People's edition, 1864, p. 625 ff.

highest place. He introduced into our ideal of goodness some features in which it was deficient before he appeared,—by the religious direction which he impressed upon morality, he gave it a higher consecration, and by incarnating goodness in his own person, he imparted to it a living warmth. With reference to all that bears upon the love of God and of our neighbour, upon purity of heart and upon the individual life, nothing can be added to the moral intuition which Jesus Christ has left us."

Such an estimate as this is confirmed, beyond expression, by comparison with the facts which relate to the only two other world teachers who here merit notice, namely, Buddha and Mohammed.[1]

The former tendency of Christian advocates to scorn comparative religion has in our day happily ceased. In its place, however, we sometimes find the opposite extreme. The excellences of Mohammed, and the goodness of the "Light of Asia," have been extolled to an unprecedented degree. But a fair comparison of the New Testament with the Koran is amply sufficient for any ordinary mind. Whilst as to Buddha and the sacred writings of the East, all Christians owe a deep debt of gratitude to Professor Max Müller for his prolonged labours in putting these before English readers, so that any person of fair intelligence can form his own conclusions. With these in our hands, we can appreciate the estimate of Strauss and Goethe and others, as never before. Without entering upon the technicalities of Christian theology, we cannot but see, by emphatic contrast, how much we owe to the Christ of the Gospels for setting before us God not only as the infinite Spirit,

[1] See hereupon a thoughtful little volume by Dr. Marcus Dods, entitled *Mohammed, Buddha, and Christ.*

but the Eternal Father, whose "tender mercies are over all His works" more fully and intensely than even the Psalmist thought. To Christ alone humanity owes the threefold assurance, "God is Spirit," "God is light," "God is love," which invests religion with unprecedented meaning and inspiration for all men, and makes the Christian life to be both richest in comfort now, and fullest of hope in face of coming eternity.

It is this highest, purest, noblest conception of God and goodness, of faith and duty, which has to be traced to its fount and explained by adequate cause.

3. But along with this purest and sublimest conception of the Divine nature, comes at once the highest and lowest estimate of the human. That conviction of sin which has haunted mankind from the beginning, finds in the doctrine of Jesus its broadest scope and deepest intensity. But how did it originate at all? The horrors associated with this sense of wrong in barbaric ages and amid savage tribes, put gruesome emphasis indeed upon it, but show it nevertheless in all cases to have been derived and not spontaneous. In civilised communities and modern times the conviction is no less strongly manifest, even where Christianity is disowned. It proves itself to be equally ineradicable with the thought of God and the tendency to worship. Now, that all this, with all that it connotes, should have evolved itself out of the ante-primeval nebular mist, is certainly more miraculous than anything related in the Bible concerning the creation and higher education of man.

4. Let us, however, inquire more closely into the doctrine and influence of Christianity as regards this

moral sense in men. It is beyond dispute that the ordinary expression of the feeling of guiltiness, even from the earliest times, has been the practice of animal sacrifices. In some extreme cases we know that even human victims were deemed necessary by way of atonement or propitiation. The advanced civilisations of Greece and Rome put no stop to this. On the contrary, such slaughter of animals was looked upon as the fittest and most necessary part of religion, to be insisted upon authoritatively and continually.

Nor was this view of the case by any means confined to these nations. Whatever else may be said concerning the Old Testament, its main outlines of Jewish history are unquestionably true, as also is the fact that in the Hebrew Scriptures we have the record of the intensest feelings of the most religious nation in all history. In perfect accord with the foregoing, we find its system of sacrifices most of all elaborate in detail and exacting in requirement. So far as the circumstances of the Jews permitted it, this their feeling and practice continued right down to the time of Christ.

But from His time living sacrifices have gradually but surely ceased. This is a great fact which calls for valid explanation. Considerable influence may no doubt be attributed to the destruction of Jerusalem as the chief centre of Jewish worship. But it is plain enough that no other such change has come over the national idiosyncrasies. Except in this one matter of sacrifices, the characteristics of the Jews are as patent to-day as they were when so vividly described in Deuteronomy and the prophetic writings. It is to be noted, moreover, that not only within the pale of Judaism has this cessation of sacrifices come to pass, but throughout the world, wherever the influence of Christianity has penetrated. Only seventy years after Christ's crucifixion, it was the complaint of the Roman governor that in his province the sacrificial victims remained unsold. The fact has proved itself so typical, that the lament of the ancient Pagan is echoed in the cry of modern cannibals from distant islands of the sea.

Now it is acknowledged freely, even by unbelievers, that of all human ideas and habits, those pertaining to religion are the most obstinate and least liable to alteration. How, then, is this vast change to be accounted for? The supernatural events recorded in the New Testament, with their attached doctrines, give us the adequate explanation we require; but if these be rejected, a pyramid is left to poise itself upon its apex. Even as regards the destruction of the Holy City and the cessation of the Temple worship, all this had happened before, and more than once. The preceding oppression of Antiochus had been far more religiously bitter, as is well known, than that of the Romans. The latter, indeed, made it a principle of their conquests not to interfere with the religions of their dependencies. It was unquestionably due to the spread of Christian influence rather than to Roman might, that Jewish and heathen sacrifices gradually became a thing of the past. So that if the supernatural elements of the gospel preaching were mere delusion or deception, upon one or the other of these two, it matters little which, must be founded the most marked and important change in the general features of religion which has occurred in the world's history. Science had nothing to do with it, for science was not yet born. Philosophy had flourished for generations before, and had made no difference whatever. Inexpressible probabilities are against our regarding such a change as a mere fortuitous development. That it should proceed from nothing, or worse than nothing, is indeed " psychologically inconceivable."

5. But this is by no means the whole case. It will doubtless be remembered that there is one well-known religious system besides Christianity, which appears to ignore the practice of sacrifice. But Buddhism rejects, along with sacrifice, the notion that past sin is any real obstacle to man's being at peace with God. Now, if there be, as would certainly seem, a definite natural connection between these two, the sense of sin and the offering of sacrifice, then the cessation of the latter throughout Christendom ought also to be accompanied by a corresponding approach to Buddhism in lessening the importance of sin. That intensity of the conviction of moral ill which is connoted in the suffering and death of animals, ought to wane away until it becomes a vanishing point. But is it so in fact? Has Christianity driven out all painful sense of personal shortcoming as if it were but a mocking fiend? The very opposite, we know, is what has really come to pass. One writer has well remarked that " there has never been a time when the conviction of sin was more and more intensified, amongst the most cultivated nations, than during the last eighteen hundred years." So manifestly true is this estimate, that it has become a fairly common thing amongst modern rationalists to follow the example of

Emerson, and inveigh against the word "sin" in its Christian usage, as being a pessimistic exaggeration, and a moral bugbear because of its gathered extent and intensity. And the attitude of the modern press, echoed continually by the man in the street, is much to the same effect.

This remarkable phenomenon, then, awaits the explanation of unbelief. Sacrifice, as the ancient and widespread symbol of guiltiness, has ceased; but with that cessation there has come upon the human heart a deeper conviction than ever of the sinfulness of sin. A sufficient explanation is indeed forthcoming, if we accept the truth of the words of Christ which are at once suggested: "And when He the Spirit of truth is come, He shall convict the world of sin." But if this be treated as a pious fiction, if the most transcendent elements in the gospel be rejected because they involve the supernatural, if Christ Himself be thus necessarily reduced to a deluded seer, or a mistaken if not hypocritical teacher, then the explanation of the above paradox may truly be said to be a task in morals akin to a demand in physics to account for the motion of our earth in its orbit without the sun.

By way of confirmation, let us call to mind the eloquent words of the late Professor Seeley, an author whose ability and freedom from bias are alike unquestionable [1]—

"Compare the ancient with the modern world: look on this picture and on that. One broad distinction forces itself into prominence. Among all the men of the ancient heathen world,

---

[1] *Ecce Homo*, small edition, p. 161.

there were scarcely one or two to whom we might venture to apply the epithet holy. In other words, there were not more than one or two, if any, who, besides being virtuous in their actions, were possessed with an unaffected enthusiasm of goodness, and besides abstaining from vice, regarded even a vicious thought with horror. Probably no one will deny that in Christian countries this higher-toned goodness which we call holiness has existed. Few will maintain that it has been exceedingly rare."

Compare with this the confession of Mr. Bradlaugh, in his well-known Socratic debate with Dr. Baylee, that the term "holiness" was to him, as an unbeliever, without meaning or recognition.

Here are at least three facts which ought to pass unchallenged, as beyond controversy. (1) Neither in the natural mind nor under the Jewish dispensation, do we find such a conception of moral purity as is implied in the Christian term "holiness." (2) The origin of this highest ideal is directly traceable to the life and character, the teaching and working, the death and resurrection, of Jesus Christ. (3) Since the Christian era it has spread with blessed contagion, as an ideal, over all the world, and through the intervening ages, until to-day its existence and import are more fully recognised than ever.

Yet according to the thesis of unbelief, the germ of all this most actual and potent influence for human elevation came into being by sheer accident; in an ignorant and superstitious age, it was born of credulity and guile, and only prolonged its life by the weakness of mind or falsity of heart of those who cherished it. Is this psychologically conceivable?

6. Concerning the general morality of the New

Testament, so much has been said that it is only necessary here to touch upon it lightly. One would think that no unbiassed mind could for a moment question its marked superiority, whether as compared with the Old Testament, or with the disquisitions of pagan philosophy. It would suffice for our present purpose, if we took only the stand of Thomas Paine, to the effect that [1]—

"Jesus Christ was a virtuous and amiable man. The morality which he preached was of the most benevolent kind—it has not been exceeded by any."

But we have quite as good reason for regarding with acceptance the estimate of Dr. Wace, in his well-known Boyle Lectures. No short quotation can do justice to their sustained argument. But a deliberate conviction so reached, ought to command at least respectful regard—

"It is, alas! scarcely possible for us adequately to realise the immeasurable and overpowering glory of this revelation, but we may form some estimate of it by the effect which has been produced by those means of those four reflections of it which have been preserved to us in the Gospels. Those outlines—for they cannot, however admirable, be called more—of the Lord's life and character have sufficed to command the homage not merely of the Church, but of the world; and their reflected rays have, in every age and country, acted like the sunlight of the moral sphere, awakening in the soul of man a new life and beauty. Conceive all that influence infinitely multiplied, and brought to bear upon pure and true souls, and you may then form some distant conception of the supreme influence which led them, through love, to the profoundest adoration which can be offered by the human heart." [2]

Nor is there any rational ground whatever for refusing to be influenced by such deliberate and cultured findings

[1] *Age of Reason*, 1794, p. 3.
[2] Boyle Lectures, *Christianity and Morality*, 3rd edition, p. 247.

as those of Professor A. S. Wilkins, who, in his most valuable little volume, *The Light of the World*, writes [1]—

"I have tried in the following pages to give my reasons for believing that the Christian ethics so far transcend the ethics of any or all the pagan systems, in method, in purity, and in power, as to compel us to assume for them an origin, differing *in kind* from the origin of any purely human system."

"Not only because the system of Christian ethics transcends all others in purity, but because this perfect purity is reached by a scientific method of development, is based on a sure foundation, and has shown itself by far the most powerful help that the world has known for its regeneration, do we claim for it an origin directly and immediately Divine."

"It was much that Christianity based morality no longer on the shifting sands of speculation, but on the revealed condition and destiny of man, and spoke with authority on his end of life. It was much that it embraced the whole nature of man within the compass of its moral laws, and taught him to present his whole being, body, soul, and spirit, a living sacrifice, which was but his reasonable service. But it was more, far more than all the rest, that it made the mainspring of all right action to consist in an enthusiasm that all might feel, that the laws of its kingdom might be known and obeyed by the meanest and humblest of its subjects."

When, however, such an estimate is confirmed by words like the following, from an author of the acumen and character of Thomas Carlyle [2]—

"Look on our divinest Symbol: on Jesus of Nazareth and his life and his biography and what followed therefrom. Higher has the human thought not yet reached: this is Christianity and Christendom, a symbol of quite perennial, infinite character: whose significance will ever demand to be anew inquired into and anew made manifest"—

the high estimate of Christian morality usually assumed, may be considered as established beyond cavil. Truly, apart altogether from the appreciation of believers,

[1] *Hulsean Prize Essay*, 1869, pp. viii, 146, 147, 148.
[2] *Sartor Resartus*. Bk. iii. chap. iii.

the purity and loftiness of New Testament ethics is abundantly confirmed from the testimonies of unbelief. Whilst even those dark pages of history which tell of Christian corruption, bear witness by contrast to the nobility of the ideal which they knowingly ignored. Mr. Mill unquestionably voiced the total conviction of the nineteenth century when he wrote [1]—

"Nor even now would it be easy, even for an unbeliever, to find a better translation of the rule of virtue from the abstract into the concrete, than to endeavour so to live that Christ would approve our life."

But besides being the inaugurator of a spiritually lofty ideal of personal goodness which has availed to make modern civilisation a thing wholly different from ancient, Christian morality has operated upon a wider social and political scale. In these days, indeed, we have become quite accustomed to hear of Christianity as the deliverer of Western-world civilisation from the triple curse of corruption, slavery, and cruelty. Such a claim may, of course, be called in question. But the onus of detailed discussion belongs to those who challenge it, although all the points raised have been fairly met by Christian apologists. It might surely be considered sufficient to appeal to such writers and thinkers as are well known to be far removed from orthodoxy. From the recorded judgements—assuredly unbiassed—of Montesquieu, Mill, Comte, Lecky, and others of similar calibre, we may learn how real, equally beyond ancient cruel calumny and modern carping

[1] *Essays on Nature, the Utility of Religion, and Theism*, pp. 253-255.

criticism, is the regenerating power which awoke for human society at the fiat of Jesus Christ.[1]

Almost all that can be adduced by way of serious reply, is found in such superficial reminders as that the Buddhists of India still outnumber the followers of Christ, and that Christianity, as a whole, has not yet obtained " even the nominal adhesion of more than a third of the human race." But to treat this as an argument against the divineness of the Christian revelation, is to perpetrate many fallacies in one. Not only is the avowed conclusion far wider than the premisses, but there is a measurable underrating of great facts. The attitude is indeed substantially the same as if one should declaim against the poverty of some individual, on the ground that he only possessed a few paper notes whilst his neighbour's pockets were full of copper coins. Not that there is, indeed, from the standpoint of Christianity, any " copper " humanity. The very imperfection of the simile testifies to the superhumanness of Christian morals. Horace, truly voicing the feeling of earth's " great ones," might cry

"Odi profanum vulgus"—

but no Christian poet has ever echoed his contempt. One of the very first lessons impressed with especial emphasis upon the first disciples, was that they should " not call any man common or unclean." The Christianity of Christ has never forgotten this, as even the darkest of the dark ages could clearly testify.

[1] Those who wish for a fuller statement of this position will find it in Mr. G. L. Brace's *Gesta Christi*, and Storrs' *Divine Origin of Christianity*. See also Appendix.

Yet without despising the teeming millions of Asia, or casting any scorn upon the followers of Sakya-Mouni, or of Confucius and Mencius, it is none the less true that the nations which have been formed under Christianity and are still more or less ruled by its sanctions, are the foremost nations of the world. In all that tends to the possession of power, the exercise of influence, and the promise of progress, the "third," referred to above with such contemptuousness, far outweighs in the scale of humanity all the rest put together. Nor can it be doubted, even by those who make lightest of Scripture prophecies, that this "third" is growing more and more, with the manifest prospect of overrunning and overruling the world. Whilst in those farthest nations which have hitherto known little or nothing of the gospel, Christianity is now obtaining such hold that missionary zeal and success can no longer be smiled at as the fancy of religious fanaticism, but have to be taken into serious account by Governments as well as Churches, in considering the programme of the future.[1]

Here then we have a world-wide influence sufficiently real, potent, and beneficent, to warrant our insisting upon the discovery of an adequate cause for it. If the supernatural origin of Christian morality be denied, then it and all its influences must be accounted for upon purely natural principles. We know at what time it first appeared, we know under what circumstances, we know

[1] The lamentable outbreak of fanatic fury in China, which is working such sad havoc whilst these pages are passing through the press, is, at least in part, the protest of the ignorant native mind against the degree in which Christian missions are succeeding, in spite of all opposition, throughout that vast empire.

amidst what men and in what conditions of society. The great question then is, do these data in themselves, absolutely without any help *ab extra*, suffice to explain the conception and promulgation of the purest and loftiest system of morality which has impressed itself upon human consciences?

We shall perhaps be reminded again of Gibbon's famous chapter, — which calmly begs the whole question, in assuming the very thing to be proved,—and we have the self-evident fallacy of Hume's argument buttressed by Professor Huxley.[1] But eyes which are not previously blinded by the *odium anti-supernaturale*, cannot help seeing that these are as ineffective for their alleged purpose, as are the little muddy brooklets that struggle down to the seashore, to account for the depth and fulness of the ocean. At least, if these do account for Christian morality, we are face to face with a miracle which all that we know of morality and psychology pronounces to be far more strange, more difficult, more unaccountable, than anything recorded in the New Testament. So that if in this matter belief had to be decided by the measure of the difficulties upon an opposite side, for very easiness' sake we could not but be Christian.

7. Nor is explanation required only for these and other features of the New Testament morality or ethics, which are actually present, but with well-nigh equal force its omissions press also for recognition. It must be borne in mind that no compromise whatever can be

[1] The logical worth of this attempt to rehabilitate a position long acknowledged to be untenable, may be seen in Lord Grimthorpe's *Huxley and Hume on Miracles*, published by the S.P.C.K.

effected between the account which the gospel gives of its great facts and any other. The Apostles and Evangelists were either dealing with supernatural realities, and received supernatural help, or not. If not, then everything must be accounted for upon those plain principles of human nature with which, by observation and experience, we are perfectly familiar. And we must keep well in memory the characteristics of the age in which the events in question took place. He, therefore, who rejects the New Testament narratives, has not only to find natural cause for the existence of the Gospels and Epistles, but also for the rise and development of Christian morality with all its idiosyncrasies. He has to produce what Renan and Mill said could not be found, the men of that age who were capable of originating a system of faith and morals rendered thus doubly unique, first by what these Christian records (on which it is based) contain, and then by the not less remarkable absence of other elements that could not but be naturally expected in genuine human productions of such a period.

How often, for instance, has it not been alleged against the New Testament morality that it does not prohibit slavery, that it passes social problems by unheeded, that it takes no notice of political economy, that it does not deal with international relations, nor insist upon patriotism, nor even inculcate what now is known as "public spirit"? These very objections are of value as showing to what men are inclined when dealing naturally with great matters of human welfare. We have, moreover, the treatises of Plato and Aristotle, of Cicero and Seneca, in addition to all the later writings of moralists and political economists upon similar themes. From these we can judge with fairness and certainty what might have been expected from a band of uninstructed zealots, who, in the time of Tiberius and Herod, set themselves to re-create the world of morals.

If, indeed, we rule out the supernatural, our first inquiry should surely be as to the reason of their ever thinking of such a thing. Is there any parallel on earth to such an event as a company of men banding themselves together for such a purpose, with no hope of reward beyond opposition, shame, and suffering? Even if, however, we pass over this, it could scarcely be denied that the men who were capable of conceiving such a notion, under all the known circumstances, must be fanatics. And there need be little hesitation as to the kind of programme that pure fanaticism would draw up. We have had fair specimens of such in more recent times. To say nothing of the wild schemes of the French Revolution, or of Russian Nihilism, or of Irish Fenianism, or Continental Anarchism, the propaganda of modern Socialism supplies us with sufficient illustration. Had this same natural spirit prevailed in the first century under the Christian name, there can be no reasonable doubt that the New Testament would have been pledged to the absolute and immediate prohibition of slavery, and quite possibly might have advocated universal revolt, the results of which tenets would doubtless have been similar to those associated with Rome's Servile Wars. Such fanatics would also, in all human probability, have chosen some rigid and extreme political ideal, and in binding themselves fast to it, have effectually prevented the adoption of Christianity by other nations, or its adaptation to the immensely varied circumstances of our modern world.

How far the Christian Scriptures actually are from the fatal rigidity of this pseudo-comprehensiveness, we are our own witnesses. The significant omissions of the New Testament have been often noticed by Christian apologists, but the true state of the case has not been made as clear as it might be. For it stands thus. Whereas these alleged deficiencies are brought forward in proof that the Gospels and Epistles are merely natural productions, it is really far more difficult to account for such omissions upon purely natural principles, than it is if we allow the presence of the supernatural element claimed for them.

All this is emphasised beyond measure, if we compare the New Testament with the so-called Apocryphal Gospels, or the writings of the Fathers, or the Koran of later date, as well as with subsequent attempts of moral teachers and reformers who have abjured Christianity.

That it should be possible for a few ordinary and ignorant men in the age of Tiberius, or a mere handful of Jewish fanatics in the days of Herod, to enunciate a system of faith and morals which, quite as much by what it did not teach as by what it did, should prove itself equally adapted to the first century and the nineteenth, to ancient Rome and to modern England,[1] and should thus work out results of elevation and benevo-

[1] See an able lecture by Sir Bartle Frere on "Christianity adapted to all forms of civilisation," *Faith and Freethought*, Christian Evidence Society Lectures.

lence beyond any other system ever promulgated, is a fact that waits for explanation, as being utterly without a parallel in the history of the world, and without a clue in all that we know of human nature's capabilities or proclivities.

Here again, therefore, we see that to reject the Christian account of these psychological and ethical realities, because of the difficulty involved in the conception of the supernatural, is only to bring ourselves once more face to face with far greater difficulties in attempting to explain the actual phenomena upon natural principles.

8. Before we close this section, one other matter should not escape notice. There is no doubt whatever that the early Christians did genuinely believe in the great miraculous events recorded in the Gospels and the Acts of the Apostles. In order to discount the value of this fact, regarded as evidence for their actual occurrence, recent scepticism has put forth strenuous efforts to show that the men and women of those times were so sunk in ignorance and superstition, and withal so utterly devoid of any critical faculty of investigation, that they could easily be persuaded to believe anything. Thus their testimony would count for comparatively nothing. Such a suggestion, however, surely illustrates rather the wish than the thought of unbelief. For even if this contention were allowed—though there can be no reasonable doubt that it is a gross exaggeration— it brings more difficulties than it removes. It was pointed out above (cf. p. 211) under the head of Psychology, that this process of belittling the early Christians and besmirching them with ridicule, only

serves to make any rational account of the idiosyncrasies of the New Testament impossible. It is even more so when we view the moral aspect of the case. For whatever seems thereby to be taken off the task of naturalism in explaining the physical miracles, becomes so much added incubus to the mental and moral miracle which must ensue, if from out the uninspired bosom of men most ignorant and superstitious, there should spring a system of morality so sublime as to elicit in after ages the profoundest admiration of the greatest minds, and wring out of noblest hearts the confession that it was above their highest aspirations after goodness. The words of Rousseau a century since[1] come back to us with redoubled force—

"Whence could Jesus have derived among his countrymen this elevated and pure morality of which he alone has given the precept and example? From the bosom of the most furious bigotry, the most exalted wisdom is heard, and the simplicity of the most heroic virtues honours the vilest of the people."

If the moral sphere be allowed to be higher than the physical,—and this much we here assume,—then that which is contrary to all experience and observation in the former, must involve even greater difficulty of conception than in the latter. Hence the instantaneous healing of disease, the feeding of five thousand with a few loaves, or even the resurrection of the dead, pale into smallness of import beside the stupendous contradictions hinted at by Rousseau and Mill, namely, that ethical wisdom should be spontaneously generated by folly, that a faith equally sober and sublime should

[1] *Emile*, IV. vol. ii. pp. 110, 111.

spring from mere credulity, and earth's highest-toned morality arise suddenly out of sheer fanaticism.

Thus it becomes manifest that, the facts being as they are, the withdrawal of the supernatural as an explanation of the origin and development of Christian morality, serves only to intensify the miracle. That the purest and loftiest and most comprehensive moral ideal known to men should spring forth out of the dregs of popular superstition, Rabbinic narrowness, and Pharisaic pride, demands an inspiration of some sort, in very deed. But that such inspiration, leading from the lowest and least spiritual[1] to the highest and holiest, should arise from nowhere, or from below, is and must ever be far more miraculous than that it should come from God.

On the other hand, if the unwarranted depreciation of the early Christian times be withdrawn, the case for unbelief is scarcely any easier. Of the three nations which were concerned in the New Testament records of events, we have fairly full knowledge. Although the Roman power has disappeared, we have its history and its codes of law. The wisdom of the Greek has never lacked appreciation in modern times, certainly not to-day. The Jews, everywhere present, always distinct, continually persecuted, generally despised, are their own witnesses as to character. The Old Testament, with its doctrines and precepts, is in our hands. The Jewish commentaries, both Talmud and Targums, upon which the scribes and Pharisees relied, are accessible to our scholars. The task, then, of unbelief is, out of these sources to formulate New Testament ethics, and construct

[1] Cf. Matt. xxiii. *passim.*

the moral teaching of Christ. Evolution of any kind is here out of the question. A single century covered the whole of the time occupied by the data of the problem. Such limitation entirely cuts off the forlorn hope of accounting for the facts upon the principles of unaided human nature's gradual amelioration.

9. To sum up. We have seen how from the very critics and opponents of Christian faith comes the concession that we have in Christianity a system of morals whose lofty purity justifies our unbounded respect and admiration. This high ideal, with its accompanying motive force and potent source of obligation, has proved itself the greatest " power not ourselves that makes for righteousness " ever operating in the world, and has established its claim to universal adoption, by the wonders of elevation and ennoblement which it has caused to spring forth from modern quarters as little likely to foster it as ancient Palestine was to create it.

An influence at once so gracious and so potent assuredly demands adequate cause. This the New Testament account confessedly supplies. The supernatural events alleged, together with the actuality of the sublime character and mighty works of the supernatural Person portrayed, afford a simple yet sufficient reason for all that accompanies them in doctrine and effect. But if these all are rejected as incredible, what necessarily follows? Let us fairly face the general conclusions which in such case are simply inevitable. We are, then, called upon to believe—always assuming, of course, that there is no supernatural, nor anything at all beyond what we know as natural—

(1) That the purest and sublimest conceptions of God sprang spontaneously from the heart of the narrowest religious fanaticism.

(2) That from amidst the most mechanical pietism and self-complacent religious superficiality, there arose a moral revolution which has issued in the immeasurable deepening of the world's conviction of sin, coincidently with the cessation of those animal sacrifices which have always been the keenest acknowledgment of human guiltiness.

(3) That the world's loftiest standard of morality generated itself out of the conceits of shallow-minded rustics and hysterical women, who were themselves deceivers, or deceived, or both.

(4) That those remarkable omissions in the original programme of Christian Ethics, by means of which Christianity became an embodiment of eternal principles rather than of temporary details, that is, a universal faith instead of a mere local enthusiasm, happened by pure accident, in emphatic contradiction to all human probability.

(5) That the most exalted ideal of self-sacrificing love, as embodied in that "higher toned goodness which we call holiness,"[1] suddenly evolved itself out of the very midst of an environment of gross and sordid self-seeking.

(6) That the broadest as well as most exalted and benevolent code of Ethics known to men, was devised, for no special purpose but at fearful cost, by weak-minded and credulous fisher folk, aided and abetted afterwards by a bigoted Jewish Rabbi.

[1] *Ecce Homo*, small edition, p. 161. Cf. 1 Cor. xiii. etc.

THE MORAL REALM 243

(7) That, finally, the brightest hopes of blessed immortality after death, in a condition and a service worthy of the Christ of whom (to say the least) Rousseau and Strauss, Renan and Mill, have spoken in such high terms, were created out of the helpless murder of a reformer who failed to keep his word, by men whose whole expectations and longings were limited to local Jewish deliverance, personal prosperity, and present-life triumph in Palestine.

The alternative comprised in the sum-total of these paradoxes, is undoubtedly that which has to be faced by honest Agnosticism. And it is here submitted that the "difficulties" therein involved, are far greater than all those associated with the Christology of the New Testament.

For whilst the miracles of faith confessedly transcend reason, those of unbelief manifestly contradict it. Now there can be no justification of the contradiction of reason, seeing that it is, as Bishop Butler rightly said, "the candle of the Lord within us," and our chief guide to truth. But there is nothing whatever in reason against the assumption that the universe is greater than all our thought concerning it, and that there may have arisen human circumstances exceptional enough to call for Divine methods beyond our ken. Consistently with itself, the Bible alleges that this was the case in the moral history of mankind when Christ came.

To reject, therefore, that which, though transcending our knowledge of nature, is not only possible but even in fair measure probable, and then accept alternatives which flatly contradict the surest principles of reason and philosophy, no less than all experience and observation, is assuredly to leap over a precipice in order to escape a shallow ditch. It is to shudder at a shrimp-pool and make light of an ocean.

VIII

CHRIST, HIS ORIGIN AND CHARACTER

1. Introduction.
2. Estimate of Christ's Character — Testimonies of Unbelief.
3. Evolution as an Explanation.
4. Christ's Witness concerning Himself — if Good, then also True.
5. His Representation of Himself as a Worker of Miracles.
6. His Claims to be Sinless.
7. His Assumption of Divine Authority.
8. The Authenticity of the Gospel Account.
9. Summary of the Dilemmas of Unbelief concerning Him.

"It was reserved for Christianity to present to the world an ideal character, which, through all the changes of eighteen centuries, has filled the hearts of men with an impassioned love, and has shown itself capable of acting in all ages, nations, temperaments, and conditions; has not only been the highest pattern of virtue, but the highest incentive to its practice, and has exerted so deep an influence that it may be truly said that the simple record of three short years of active life has done more to regenerate and to soften mankind than all the disquisitions of philosophers, and than all the exhortations of moralists. This has, indeed, been the wellspring of whatever has been best and purest in the Christian life. Amid all the sins and failings, amid all the priestcraft, the persecution, and fanaticism which have defaced the Church, it has preserved, in the character and example of its Founder, an enduring principle of regeneration."—Mr. Lecky, *History of Morality*, vol. ii. p. 88.

"Measure the religious doctrine of Jesus by that of the time and place he lived in, or that of any time and place. Consider what a work his words and deeds have wrought in the world. Remember that the greatest minds, the richest hearts, have set no loftier aim, no truer method than his of perfect love to God and man. Shall we be told such a man never lived — the whole story is a lie! Suppose that Plato and Newton never lived. But who did their wonders, and thought their thought? It takes a Newton to forge a Newton. What man could have fabricated a Jesus? None but a Jesus."—Theodore Parker, *Life of Jesus*, p. 363.

"It was neither for his miracles, nor for the beauty of his doctrine that Christ was worshipped. It was for this, that he, whose power and greatness as shown in his miracles were overwhelming, denied himself the use of his power, treated it as a slight thing, walked among men as though he were one of them, relieved them in distress, taught them to love each other, bore with undisturbed patience a perpetual hailstorm of calumny, and when his enemies grew fiercer, continued still to endure their attacks in silence, until, petrified and bewildered with astonishment, men saw him arrested and put to death with torture, refusing steadfastly to use in his own behalf the power he conceived he held for the benefit of others. It was the combination of greatness and self-sacrifice which won their hearts, the mighty powers held under a mighty control, the unspeakable condescension, the Cross of Christ." —*Ecce Homo*, small edition, p. 46.

VIII

CHRIST, HIS ORIGIN AND CHARACTER

1. THE morality of Christianity and the origin of the New Testament, can never be fairly considered apart from Him who is the manifest centre and substance of the whole. Often has it been said, and ever truly, that "Christianity is Christ." Professing Christians are disciples indeed, only in the degree in which they resemble Him whom they avow to be their Master and Lord. By His character, therefore, not by theirs, Christianity has to be judged.

This does not, however, amount to a lessening in any degree of the arguments outlined in the preceding chapter. However lamentably Christians may have failed from their high example, Christianity still involves and contains enough of the moral mystery of good to warrant the position taken above. In this regard, it may be well to quote once more a witness, equally able and impartial. In his *Ecce Homo*,[1] the late Professor Seeley penned a most scathing indictment of conventional Christianity. By very virtue of this we are the more free to appreciate his further estimate, part of which was quoted above,[2] and to give heed to his concluding summary.

[1] Popular edition, pp. 159, 160.   [2] P. 227; *vide* also p. 262.

"On the other hand, the Christian morality, if somewhat less safe and exempt from perversion than science, is more directly and vitally beneficial to mankind. The scientific life is less noble than the Christian : it is better, so to speak, to be a citizen in the New Jerusalem than in the New Athens. . . . But the achievement of Christ in founding by his single will and power a structure so durable and so universal is like no other achievement which history records. The masterpieces of the men of action are coarse and common in comparison with it, and the masterpieces of speculation flimsy and insubstantial. When we speak of it the commonplaces of admiration fail us altogether. Shall we speak of the originality of the design, of the skill displayed in the execution? All such terms are inadequate. The creative effort which produced that against which, it is said, the gates of hell shall not prevail, cannot be analyzed. The inconceivable work was done in calmness; before the eyes of men it was noiselessly accomplished, attracting little attention. No man saw the building of the New Jerusalem—it descended out of heaven from God." . . . "And if this be so, has Christ failed or can Christianity die?"

This last question of the Professor of Modern History we may leave facts themselves to answer. The matter in hand here, is to account adequately for the Christ of whom we read and speak. That is to say, we must first truly estimate Christ as a person and a character, and then—on the supposition that the New Testament account of His origin, nature, and mission, is rejected by reason of its dependence upon the supernatural—it remains to ask whether He can be rationally accounted for on "natural" lines.

2. As to the personality and character of Christ, of one thing we are absolutely sure, namely, that no subtlety of thought or speech can ever reduce Him to unimportant mediocrity. His character and influence are incontrovertibly extreme. Utterly unique in the history of

our world, He must be pronounced either supremely good as the noblest teacher, prophet, and, indeed, Saviour of our race, or else unapproachably bad as earth's most disappointing deceiver. Between these two, judging by the New Testament, there is no possible compromise.

Now the general estimate of Christendom is well known. But there is, in not a few quarters, a growing tendency to treat this estimate as worthless. Religious bias is supposed so to warp the judgement of believers as to render their testimony valueless. Well, however, may we ask why should this be so. Is there any department of business or of morals, of science or of art, in which, to say the very least, believers have not equalled unbelievers ? Assuredly there is none whatever. Moreover, it is universally conceded that to do justice to any human character there must be at all events some measure of sympathy and affection. Whilst of every person worth knowing at all, it is equally true that those who are most closely and tenderly attached to him, best know him. That reverent appreciation, therefore, of Christ's character which, through all ages and amidst all divisions of creeds and Church systems, has been the one great centre of agreement between all who profess and call themselves Christians, is not to be set aside as irrelevant.

So that if we now proceed to waive it, and content ourselves with the judgement of sceptic authorities, it is only for two reasons, first, that we may exercise the utmost courtesy towards unbelievers and indeed be generous rather than just, and secondly, that we may make sure of an *a fortiori* argument which cannot be set aside. For if our inferences hold good upon the lowest estimate of Christ which deserves notice, they become so much the more convincing in the light of those higher estimates of Christian faith which we find no valid reason to discard.

The lowest estimate we can truthfully take, is found in the best utterances of unbelief. By "best" is not necessarily here intended those most favourable to our purpose, but utterances of men who for culture, candour, ability, and reverence, deserve our highest esteem. Scurrilous pamphlets and the coarse buffoonery which has characterised some Secularist publications, merit only pitiful silence. Those who are so given to quotation from Thomas Paine's *Age of Reason*, would do well to remember not only his scathing invectives, but the reverence for good evidenced in his declaration, quoted above, that "nothing that is here said can apply even with the most distant disrespect to the real character of Jesus Christ."

But unbelief as well as faith has its worthy representatives. It is matter for deep Christian sorrow, yet unquestionably true, that there have been and are men in all respects able and estimable, who more or less absolutely reject the Christian faith. If, now, we accept their judgement in reference to the character of Christ, we shall at least obtain data which ought to be regarded as beyond controversy for the starting-point of our thought. When we turn to these nobler advocates of scepticism, we find an agreement amongst them which differs only in degree from that prevalent throughout Christendom. Let us take but a few, as specimens of many.

CHRIST, HIS ORIGIN AND CHARACTER 251

Spinoza [1] speaks of Christ as the symbol of Divine wisdom, and attributes to Him an immediate intuition of God.

Rousseau asks [2]—

"Can the Person whose history the Gospels relate be himself a man? What sweetness, what purity in his manners! What affecting goodness in his instructions! What sublimity in his maxims! What profound wisdom in his discourses! What presence of mind, what ingenuity of justice in his replies! Yes, if the life and death of Socrates are those of a philosopher, the life and death of Jesus Christ are those of a God."

Goethe, too, speaks thus [3]—

"I esteem the Gospels to be thoroughly genuine, for there shines forth from them the reflected splendour of a sublimity, proceeding from the person of Jesus Christ, and of as Divine a kind as was ever manifested upon earth."

Strauss accounts Him [4]—

"The highest object we can possibly imagine with respect to religion, the Being without whose presence in the mind perfect piety is impossible."

Renan's estimate is well known, and equally emphatic [5]—

"Jesus is in every respect unique, and nothing can be compared with him. Be the unlooked for phenomena of the future what they may, Jesus will not be surpassed. Noble Initiator repose now in thy glory! Thy work is finished, thy divinity established. A thousand times more living, a thousand times more loved since thy death, than during the days of thy course here below, thou shalt become the corner-stone of humanity, insomuch that to tear

---

[1] *Tractatus Theol. Polit.*   [2] *Emile*, IV. vol. ii. p. 110.
[3] *Conversations with Eckerman*, iii. 371.
[4] *Life of Jesus*, People's edition, 1864, p. 625.
[5] *Étude d'Hist. Rel.* pp. 175, 213, 214.

thy name from this world would be to shake it to its very foundations. No more shall men distinguish between thee and God."

John Stuart Mill's testimony has been quoted above, but a few more deliberate utterances of acknowledged leaders of thought merit attention. Thus Theodore Parker avows that [1]

"Christ unites in himself the sublimest principles and divinest practices, thus more than realising the dream of prophets and sages, rises free from all prejudices of his age, nation, or sect, and pours out a doctrine beautiful as the light, sublime as heaven, and true as God. Eighteen centuries have passed since the sun of humanity rose so high in Jesus. What man, what sect has mastered his thought, comprehended his method, and fully applied it to life?"

Miss F. P. Cobbe considers that

"The originator of the Christian movement must have been the greatest soul of his time, as indeed of all time."

Dr. Channing's whole estimate may be expressed in one sentence of his—

"I know not what can be added to heighten the wonder, reverence, and love which are due to Jesus." [2]

Mr. W. R. Greg affirms that [3]

"Jesus had one of those gifted natures rarely met with, never in equal perfection, the purity and absolute harmony of whose mental and moral elements confer a clearness of vision which almost rises to the quality of prophecy."

Hausrath thinks that

"There is no other noble life known to human record encumbered with so little that is earthy, transitory, local; no other that can be put to purposes so high and universal."

---

[1] *Discourses on Religion*, pp. 294, 303.   [2] *Works*, vol. ii. p. 61.
[3] *Miscellaneous Essays*, p. 247.

CHRIST, HIS ORIGIN AND CHARACTER

Dr. Congreve, speaking for Positivism, says [1]—

"The more truly you serve Christ, the more thoroughly you mould yourselves into his image, the more keen will be our sympathy and admiration."

So, too, the author of *Supernatural Religion* wrote concerning Christ [2]—

"A man of unparalleled purity and elevation of character, surpassing in his sublime earnestness the moral grandeur of Chakya-Mouni, and putting to the blush the sometimes sullied, though generally admirable teachings of Socrates and Plato and the whole round of Greek philosophers."

Professor Seeley, in his well known *Ecce Homo*, writes—

"Of this human race Christ himself was a member, and to this day is it not the best answer to all blasphemers of the species, the best consolation when our sense of its degradation is keenest, that a human brain was behind his forehead and a human heart beating in his breast, and that within the whole creation of God nothing more elevated or more attractive has yet been found than he?"[3]

Mr. Lecky's oft quoted words are so true that they merit repetition here by way of emphasis [4]—

"The simple record of three short years of (Christ's) active life, has done more to regenerate and soften mankind than all the disquisitions of philosophers, and than all the exhortations of moralists. This has indeed been the well-spring of whatever has been best and purest in the Christian life."

These witnesses may suffice, though it were an easy task to multiply them. Taken together with the reverent judgement of Christian thinkers, they do at least show that we are here dealing with a real person, whose character was one of unique and transcendent

---

[1] *Essays*, p. 298.
[2] Vol. ii. p. 487, 2nd edition.
[3] Popular edition, p. 155.
[4] *History of Morality*, vol. ii. p. 88.

goodness. According to this united testimony, no other answer can truthfully be given to the question, "What think ye of Christ?"

But His own query immediately following upon this, demands equal attention. "Whose son is He?" was not only rightfully put to the cynical Pharisees, but waits for answer also from the modern unbeliever. With this wonderful portraiture before us, the further inquiry is inevitable, "Whence came He?" Was He born naturally or supernaturally? Is He merely Son of man, or, also and supremely, Son of God? We know that those around Him were early driven to ask—

"Whence hath this man this wisdom and these mighty works? Is not this the carpenter's son? Is not his mother called Mary? And his brethren, James and Joseph and Simon and Judas? And his sisters, are they not all with us? Whence then hath this man all these things?"[1]

3. The modern reply to all such questions is supposed to be, in one word, Evolution. No other answer, indeed, is possible for those who reject the supernatural and therefore deny alike the miraculous conception and Divine incarnation. In this case Christ could only be the natural product of heredity plus environment. He must be just as really and entirely the outcome of His parentage and circumstances as any other man of genius or notable character, such as Luther, Washington, Napoleon,[2] Wesley, Gladstone.

[1] Matt. xiii. 54.
[2] Napoleon, indeed, flatly contradicted such a notion. In plain words, the genuineness of which is well established (see Liddon's *Bampton Lectures* for 1866, p. 148), he affirmed: "I think I under-

Now, whilst such an assertion may be made as easily as any other impossible suggestion, it really proves nothing. Its assumptions must be subjected to twofold scrutiny. First, we are bound to ask whether the principle of evolution finds here any valid application at all? And secondly, what necessarily follows if the Christ of the Gospels be so derived?

We say advisedly "the Christ of the Gospels," because all the searching criticism of the last century has unquestionably tended, in the main, to establish rather than weaken alike the early date, the genuineness, and the authenticity of these Christian records.[1] Whence it follows that if they are sufficiently reliable to warrant the eulogies from unbelievers above quoted, they are also for the distinctly Christian estimate. If their accounts of Christ's environment may be trusted, so too may their representations of His works and words. It is sometimes assumed that the mere presence of the supernatural element is sufficient proof of unreliability, but besides the fact that such assumption is alike unreasonable and unwarranted, the most ordinary reader can see that the

stand something of human nature, and I tell you all these were men and I am a man; none else is like Him, Jesus Christ was more than man. . . . This phenomenon is unaccountable, it is altogether beyond the scope of man's creative powers. This it is which proves to me convincingly the divinity of Jesus Christ." It is easy to sneer at this testimony as an "improvised Christology," but that neither disproves the genuineness nor lessens the significance of such an utterance.

[1] It is, of course, impossible here to branch off into a detailed proof of this statement. But it is not too strong. Abundant justification of it will be found in the list of works given in the Appendix, under the heading "Biblical."

character and personal history of Christ are inseparably bound up with His whole environment.

Professor Henslow has summed up in a sentence the true answer to the first of the inquiries just indicated [1]—

"When evidence for a natural evolution of Christ as He is portrayed to us in the Gospels is looked for, none is forthcoming."

For we do know, without doubt, what were the "environmental conditions of Jesus Christ" at the time of His birth and life in Palestine. Politically, we need scarcely consider it, seeing that Christ did not teach politics, though even then one might well ask how He came so to transcend narrow local conceptions. As regards Greek philosophy, it is perfectly manifest that to it Christ Himself owes nothing. The operative environment, therefore, must be limited to the religious atmosphere and the national spirit. The latter would be represented in His parentage and surroundings, mostly at Nazareth, though also in greater degree afterwards at Jerusalem. The former is exhibited in the three sects, with their tenets, which at that time divided Judea between them, namely, the Pharisees, the Sadducees, and the Essenes. Of these, the first two are manifestly and at once ruled out of consideration. That Christ could be the natural product of Pharisaism or of Sadduceism, is mere fatuity even to suggest. Some few attempts, however, have been made to derive Jesus from the Essenes. But His emphatic contradiction of their best known and most

---

[1] *Christ no Product of Evolution.* Published by G. Stoneman, Warwick Lane. This little volume, from the pen of a pronounced Evolutionist, is well worthy of close attention.

cherished principles is quite sufficient, apart from other considerations,[1] to show how utterly impossible it is to credit these monkish ascetics with being the soil out of which the Jesus of the evangelists spontaneously sprang.

The more closely and impartially we acquaint ourselves with all the facts as to Christ's religious environment, the more emphatically true appears the remark of Renan, that His special and intense sense of communion with God as His Father "was His grand act of originality, there was nothing here in common with His race." Even if we do utmost justice to the highest and best of the Old Testament heroes and saints, honest consideration cannot but bring out the truth of Mr. Mill's remark that Christ is "a unique figure, not more unlike all His predecessors than all His followers."

But other undeniable facts have to be borne in mind. There is no room for controversy touching the actual condition of Judaism when Christ appeared. The High Priests with their jealousies, the Rabbis with their traditions, the unspiritual conceits of the Pharisees, the immoral hair-splittings of the Talmud, the hypocrisies of the Elders and Scribes, all contributed to an environment out of which the evolution of Jesus by mere natural processes is quite as unthinkable as the

[1] For which see Lightfoot on *Colossians*, pp. 148-179: "It has become a common practice with a certain class of writers to call Essenism to their aid in accounting for any distinctive features of Christianity which they are unable to explain in any other way. I purpose testing these strong assertions by an appeal to facts." The thirty pages which follow do not admit of condensation here, but to an unprejudiced mind they certainly amount to a demonstration that "we may dismiss the statement as mere hypothesis, unsupported by evidence and improbable in itself."

production of grapes from thorns, or figs from thistles. His whole character, teaching, works, promises, were indeed an unequivocal reversal and contradiction of what men in general, and His own countrymen in particular, held for the best, the most sacred, the most necessary. So that if Christ's character actually justifies but half what the above-quoted estimates affirm, then evolution, as a merely natural method of progression, by means of infinitesimal variations with no breach of continuity, can only account for Him by flatly contradicting itself.

So let us come to the second half of the inevitable scrutiny suggested above. If it be insisted that the Jesus of the evangelists *must*, after all, have been naturally evolved from His age and environment and parentage, the conclusion immediately and necessarily follows that, in such case, evolution is no longer what we have so often been assured, nor does it work as is continually alleged. For here, in the person, the character, the doctrine, the influence of Christ, as compared with His ancestors and contemporaries, is a sudden and immeasurable leap instead of continuity; here is reversal not development, here is contradiction rather than modification. If these results be in accordance with the natural working of evolution, then certainly it can no longer, on the lines of modern science, account for the world of nature around us, still less for the vast universe of which we form such a tiny part. In a word, evolution, *per se*, can only account for Christ by destroying itself.

4. Meanwhile another equally pertinent reflection must be fairly faced. The testimonies to the character

of Christ quoted above, may fairly be taken, apart from any other views of their respective authors, as affording an unbiassed estimate of Him from the standpoint of intelligent criticism. Beyond controversy they are all in one respect emphatically agreed, namely, that He was supremely good. Now goodness cannot possibly be divorced from truthfulness, any more than moral sublimity can be attached to self-delusion. It becomes, therefore, of the very first importance to ascertain what the truthfulness of Christ involves. If He was so good and so sublime as has been acknowledged, He must also have been true, both in regard to His representations concerning Himself, and the doctrines which He put forth for the benefit of mankind. The same applies also to His "mighty works." It is utterly impossible to conceive of a good man and true pretending to do miracles of healing, or indeed signs of any kind, knowing them all the time to be mere impositions. It is equally inconceivable that in matters of greatest moment Christ should be a self-deceived enthusiast, and at the same time—to quote Strauss— "the highest personage to whom mankind is indebted for the perfecting of its moral consciousness."

Let us ask then, what really did Jesus do and teach? The answer, for our present purpose, may be summed up in few words. As regards Himself, He unequivocally insisted upon a supernatural origin and pre-existence, to be followed by a voluntary death, which should issue in a miraculous resurrection and ascension. In reference to His works and doctrine, He claimed that His whole mission was the revelation of the reality and nearness of the supernatural, both in the constant presence of His Father and in the special co-operation of the Holy Spirit who was to be afterwards more fully manifested. To which He added unmistakably, the promise of a future life perfectly in accord with these supernatural premisses. It has been reserved for the hardihood of modern Agnosticism to treat all this as a trifle or an "illusion," whilst yet professing to regard Christ as humanity's highest type of goodness. But the naturalism which denies the reality of miracle, and finds in Christ only an elevated human element throughout the whole history of His origin and influence, is bound to show how He can be at once supremely good and utterly false. One is driven to ask in the words of James, "Doth the fountain send forth from the same opening sweet water and bitter?" Does not such goodness necessarily involve corresponding truthfulness? In the case of a supremely lofty character, exercising proportionate influence towards human regeneration, is it reasonable to allege utter self-deception as coexistent with transcendent nobility?

The simple truth of the case is, that the moral and spiritual phenomena of Christ's character are such as to occasion far greater difficulties without the supernatural than with it. It were a much greater and more staggering miracle that the Christ of the Gospels should be either a deceiver or deceived, than that He should be a worker of real miracles and a teacher of eternal truth. In a word, if He be false in His doctrine, then He is no longer supremely good in His example. If the mighty works to which He Himself appealed were only delusions, then His own chosen credentials of character are unreliable.¹ If, however, He be as true as good, then the supernatural element in His whole nature and mission is no longer a matter of question.

It is particularly to be observed, and for this cause it may be reiterated, that the dilemma of unbelief herein is hopeless. That Jesus professed to work miracles, and that His contemporaries believed Him actually to do so, may be assumed as not open to question.² These avowed miracles were either real or false. If real, our main contention is settled. If false, they must have been so either consciously or unconsciously upon His part. For the requirements of unbelief, one supposition is as helpless as the other. In the one case we get ignorant superstition, in the other wilful deception, as the method and accompaniment of the sublimest character ever recorded in history, and the foundation of the purest and most powerful system of ethics known to men. "Which is absurd," as Euclid says.

6. But there is yet another special feature of Christ's character which must by no means be lost sight of, if we would do justice to the whole truth. To view it aright we must revert once more to His own declarations concerning Himself. When the

[1] Cf. John x. 37, 38 ; Acts ii. 22, etc.

[2] Cf. the statement of Professor Seeley quoted on p. 44 from *Ecce Homo*. Also the following (*E. H.* p. 41): "Now, if the character depicted in the Gospels is in the main real and historical, they must be generally trustworthy, and, if so, the responsibility of miracles is fixed on Christ. In this case the reality of the miracles themselves depends in a great degree on the opinion we form of Christ's veracity, and this opinion must arise gradually from the careful examination of his whole life."

acknowledgment is wrung from unbelief that He is unique as a human character, it is generally quite overlooked that He represents Himself, and is portrayed by all the New Testament writers, as sinless. If we accept as it stands the whole account given of Him in the Gospels, it cannot be doubted that this assumption, which would concerning any ordinary individual be pronounced intolerable, in His case perfectly harmonises with all else that is related concerning Him. Is there, however, on record any other case of a truly good man thus posing as utterly exempt from moral ill? Has it not rather been ever true that the nobler the individual the more sensitive, or even hypersensitive, has he been to moral wrong, within as well as without? Certainly in all Christian ages and countries, as has been pointed out above, the conviction of sin has so deepened that the universal verdict of conscience has been that

"—they who fain would serve Thee best
Are conscious most of wrong within."

Professor Seeley has, indeed, good reason for saying[1] that

"Perhaps the truth is that there has scarcely been a town in any Christian country since the time of Christ where a century has passed without exhibiting a character of such elevation that his mere presence has shamed the bad and made the good better, and has been felt at times like the presence of God Himself."

But has any one of those who have unquestionably illustrated this "higher toned goodness which we call holiness," ever given a hint to his fellows that he regarded himself as sinless? Full well we know that it has always been exactly the reverse. It is in accord

[1] Cf. also the quotation on p. 228.

with the clearest principles of high morality, that the sense of wrong should always be in proportion to the appreciation of right. Yet Christ Himself, from whom, on the acknowledgment of the most cultured unbelief, we get our highest and most delicate perceptions of right, makes no confession of sin and has apparently no consciousness of wrong! Nay, on the contrary, He not only challenges His enemies to convict Him of any visible moral failure, and in presence of His keenest and most bitter foes exclaims — "Which of you convinceth Me of sin?"—but avowedly, speaking from the most secret depths of His own consciousness, represents His inner life as perfectly pure, and utterly in harmony with that supremely holy will Divine which He came to make vivid for all men.

Now it is for the deniers of the supernatural to reconcile this unmitigated self-assertion on the one hand with Christ's moral sanity, and on the other with that high degree of moral excellence which we have seen above accorded to Him by cultured and impartial criticism. It is also for unbelief to explain how, on the hypothesis that He was only naturally man, it came to pass that, surrounded by malignant foes whose Jewish keenness was sharpened against Him to its finest point by hate, he could defy them to find any real moral blemish in His life or character. And yet again, how it was that such a Roman as Pilate, and such a Roman matron as Pilate's wife, and such a man of blood and iron as the centurion by the Cross, were all alike compelled to echo the acknowledgment of His innocence which was wrung out of His very murderers. Last, though not least, it must be explained how it happens that all the very few attempts to convict Him of sin, have recoiled and still recoil upon those that make them; how it comes about that this very claim of sinlessness, which would be at once pronounced intolerable presumption on the part of any other man, however noble, has been in His case almost universally allowed. Also how, above all, He, being at once a mere man and a good man, could so represent Himself. But that this transcendent claim was endorsed to the uttermost by those who first believed on Him, the whole New Testament testifies. Hence, as we survey all this, the only conclusion to which we can possibly come, after the lapse of nineteen centuries, is that the difficulties in the way of regarding Him as merely Son of man, are far greater than those which give us pause before we can accept Him as the Son of God.

7. For still our contemplation is unfinished. The problem intensifies itself as we proceed. The claim of Christ is not only to sinlessness, but to Divine royalty. He proclaimed Himself a king. The "good confession"—to quote the Apostle Paul[1]—which Christ witnessed before Pilate, was uttered when that astute and haughty Roman "said unto Him, Art thou a king then? Jesus answered, Thou sayest it, I am a king."[2] When He said "My kingdom" manifestly Pilate winced, but when He added that His regal sphere was the truth, we can catch the sigh of relief mingling with the sneer of Pilate's rejoinder. He had no more perception of the reality and vastness of that royal realm, than the infant has of the ubiquity and potency of electricity.

[1] 1 Tim. vi. 13.   [2] John xviii. 36-38.

Yet Miss Cobbe is assuredly right when she says—

"Let us obtain the measure of the change introduced into the world by Christianity, and we shall at the same time obtain the best measure of the greatness of Christ."

No test can be fairer. Nor can the result of such a scrutiny be better expressed than in the words of one who had striven for and obtained such sway over his fellows as few monarchs on earth have equalled. The estimate of Napoleon[1] merits attention most of all because it is according to facts—

"Christ alone has succeeded in so raising the mind of man towards the unseen that it becomes insensible to the barriers of time and space. Across the chasm of eighteen hundred years Jesus Christ makes a demand which is beyond all others difficult to satisfy. He asks for that which a philosopher may often seek in vain at the hands of his friends, or a father of his children, or a bride of her spouse, or a man of his brother. He asks for the human heart ; He will have it entirely to Himself ; He demands it unconditionally, and forthwith His demand is granted. Its powers and faculties become an annexation to the empire of Christ. All who sincerely believe in Him experience that supernatural love towards Him. This phenomenon is unaccountable, it is altogether beyond the scope of man's creative powers. Time, the great destroyer, can neither exhaust its strength nor put a limit to its range."

All this has been proved true in innumerable cases, and is so still, concerning greater numbers than ever. No honest man can deny that to-day Christ rules millions of hearts and lives, the wide world over. It is, moreover, plain as the light of day, that amongst these have been and yet are included some, if not most, of the noblest men and women who have lived since the Christian era. And they would be the first to avow, with the emphasis of their

[1] See note on p. 254.

whole soul, that this love of Christ had been to them what Mr. Lecky has said, " the well-spring of all that was purest and noblest " in their nature or conduct. It is no exaggeration to affirm that the list of names which might easily be drawn up, of those who have rejoiced to avow this, would, for purity and loftiness of character, be at once the longest and the noblest that earth could furnish from its whole history. Yet if the supernatural be false, these all have been, and all their living representatives still are, merely the pitiful victims of a delusion and the misguided followers of an impostor. Which would, again, be a greater contradiction to nature than any miracle recorded in the New Testament.

But if the claim of sinlessness, even on the part of the best of men, would amount to moral presumption and falsity, the demand and expectation to rule as king in the hearts and consciences of men could be accounted nothing less than blasphemy. Moses of old was condemned for putting himself on a level with the Divine at a critical but unthinking moment. Of how much greater blasphemy must any mere man be guilty, who should deliberately and emphatically insist that he and God were so one, that for all time the true and sufficient test of loyalty to the Divine should be this—" If ye love Me, keep My commandments." The pretensions of Mohammed, the precepts of Buddha, the maxims of Confucius, pale into feebleness by the side of this. Yet according to the anti-supernaturalist, all the time Jesus was nothing more than the illegitimate[1] son of a Jewish carpenter, equally deceiving and deceived! Truly such

[1] See note on p. 39.

a suggestion does indeed require for its acceptance more credulity than all the Christian miracles together.

8. Now there is one way, and only one, by which the overwhelming force of the preceding difficulties for unbelief can be avoided. And it reminds one of what often happens in some bewildering labyrinth, in which the wanderer, after having tried in vain every apparent way of escape, suddenly lights upon a previously overlooked outlet which promises to lead at last into freedom. What then is his dismay when, after following it up thoroughly, he finds himself in the end brought back once more to his original position! Such is unquestionably the case of unbelief when it seeks escape from the difficulties of its own creation by the short and easy method of denying altogether the credibility of the Gospels. It would seem that the knot which cannot be untied must be cut. The supernatural being — *ex hypothesi*—necessarily false, all that involves it must be somehow or other untrue. This is but a fair representation of the bias which modern scepticism seeks to make axiomatic in the study of Christian origins. In the case before us, the shortest apparent way of evading the dilemmas of doubt, is to refuse to accept the reliability of the quadruple history of Christ and His work which we know as the four Gospels.

Now it is manifestly impossible to deny that we possess these ancient records, and that, as they stand, they involve the supernatural Christ. But this fourfold testimony is put into the crucible of "destructive criticism," and after much tossing to and fro, we are presented with—no one knows what. It is difficult, almost to impossibility, to represent fairly in few words the conclusions of the extreme school of modern Rationalism in regard to our Gospels. But allowing for all detailed disharmony between the conflicting theories and their following inferences, the position may be generally summarised in a few leading points. The *a priori* assumption is that there can be no supernatural. Hence the Gospels in their present form cannot be authentic. This leads on to the suspicion that they may not be genuine. Further scrutiny results in dismissing the Gospel of John altogether from our credence, and in making the first three Gospels—the "Synoptics"—to be of wholly unknown authorship, and of such late date that the historical Christ, who, to start with, was only a Jewish peasant of originality and promise, is transformed by myths and floating fancies from the non-miracle-working, natural teacher of the "Triple Tradition," into the mighty worker of miracles, the supernatural Christ, and the risen Lord.

The unsophisticated reader will be ready to ask with Nicodemus, "How can these things be?" And well he may. For if by this process what some deem the great ghost of the supernatural is supposed to be laid, the very air becomes immediately thick with spectral questions clamouring for attention and answer. The simplest way to a succinct summary is to inquire whence in this case come such estimates as those of Strauss, Renan, etc., already quoted? The reply can only be, from our Gospels. But our Gospels certainly involve the supernatural. Then those portions which thus insist upon supernatural facts and doctrines must be omitted. But upon whose authority? Upon that of the subjective faculty of the particular critic! In plain English— which is perfectly warranted by prolonged study of the latest Continental school of criticism with its nearer echoes—what the critic "feels" to be genuine and reliable may be accepted, but what he "feels" to be obliged to reject, must be dismissed at once and finally as incredible!

Now much might be said concerning the vastly differing opinions of the leaders in these critical processes. Scarcely any two of them agree in the published results of their investigations. Such differences necessarily follow from the carrying out of the subjective method. It is significant that the hushing of the "still small voice" from on high, only results in a discordant Babel of human opinions all around. Great stress is not seldom laid upon the differences of doctrine which exist amongst Christians. It is confessedly a fact which admits of being used with some effect against the reality of a Divine revelation. But if unanimity be the valid test of truth, things will go much more hardly with unbelief than faith. It may generally be kept out of sight, but it is emphatically true, that the camp of anti-supernaturalism is split up into sections far more mutually contradictory than those which constitute the ordinary Christian Churches. For in regard to the subject before us, namely, the reality or unreality of the supernatural in the New Testament, all sections in Christendom — except perhaps a few "Broad Churchmen" or "advanced" Nonconformists or "extreme" Unitarians—are entirely one. Whereas on the other side, save only as to the simple denial of the supernatural, there are as many strongly differing attitudes as there are varieties of opinion amongst politicians.

Meanwhile, is there no plain answer to all this mingling of assumption and assertion? There is. There is such answer as makes us see yet more clearly that the onus of explanation which was shown above to rest upon unbelief, cannot possibly be shifted by this last desperate resort. We have a fifth Gospel, of unimpeachable genuineness, and allowed to be of earliest date, even by most extreme "destructive" critics. This consists of the "four" above-mentioned "great Epistles" of Paul to the Romans, Corinthians, Galatians. These, therefore, demand notice once more, at this juncture.

Now it is abundantly manifest to every careful reader, that the Christ of Paul in these his acknowledged letters, is no other than the supernatural Christ of the Gospels. All the main features of the description of His person, character, doctrine, works, passion, and resurrection, which appear in the Gospels, are clearly affirmed and directly insisted upon by Paul, in writing to these various Churches. Thus we have much more than the testimony of Paul. For it is evident that he could not write in this style to Churches which knew nothing of the subjects referred to. His method of indirect allusion unquestionably supposes these entirely distinct and distant Churches, to be all intimately acquainted with just such a series of facts as is recounted in the four Gospels. But we have to remember that the earliest of these letters was certainly written within thirty years of Christ's crucifixion. And we cannot

CHRIST, HIS ORIGIN AND CHARACTER

but see that it contains a taken-for-granted portrayal of Christ, similar in all important features to that of the Evangelists. Hence appears the utter futility of the appeal to myth, as an explanation of the supernatural element in the Gospel narrative. The keenest criticism cannot deny that years before the earliest date allowed by the Tübingen school for the first written Gospel, there was thoroughly spread abroad amongst the whole body of Christians, precisely such a conception of and belief in the supernatural Christ as the Gospels themselves warrant. So far, therefore, from these records being the creation of a gradually developing mythical tendency, they did but record what was already unanimously received by the whole of the then Christian world.

All that is accomplished, indeed, by the last extreme effort of sceptic criticism under this head, is the narrowing and therefore the aggravating of difficulties for the anti-supernaturalist. There is no valid ground for doubting what is now generally accepted, that the Epistles of Paul to the Thessalonians, to the Corinthians, to the Galatians, to the Romans, were all written, probably in this order, before the year A.D. 60; that is, within about thirty years of the Crucifixion. Between these letters there is no sign whatever of any sinister connexion. The substance, therefore, of what is assumed all through each of them to be well known and accepted by those to whom they are addressed, is of the very highest character as testimony, and is of the very earliest date. Now we are surrounded on all hands, every day, by men who can easily go back over thirty years of recollection. To all such the appeal may be made as to what likelihood, or rather what possibility, there was that in such a time, a mere man who had been put to death as a malefactor, amidst almost universal execration, should be received and worshipped as risen and Divine, without any further cause, by men and women of all grades and nations, who were almost His contemporaries.

We might, indeed, be content to contemplate a much longer period than thirty years in the case of one who, like Jesus of Nazareth, drew upon Himself the notice of vast multitudes. Take a modern instance by way of analogy. Is it possible for any devoted admirer of the character and career of Napoleon Buonaparte to weave around his memory at this distance from his death, a wreath of wild imaginings contrary to acknowledged facts? Archbishop Whately has well shown in his little book — *Historic Doubts concerning Buonaparte* — what may result from the thorough application of that subjective method which has become the soul of modern criticism. He thereby perfectly demonstrates that Napoleon never existed. At which conclusion, of course, we smile. But it must plainly be affirmed that there is only one way of escape from the questions and reasonings put forth, and that is, appeal to the experience and testimony of those who were connected with him and were influenced by his career, precisely in the same way as were the great bulk of early Christians by the life and works, the death and resurrection of Jesus Christ.

The final stand, therefore, of the anti-supernatural critic is of no avail. It must be observed that only as a matter of courtesy have we even temporarily adopted his attitude of "extreme" criticism. It is by no means made out that the time-honoured credentials of our evangelists are wholly unworthy of credit. Every year's additional sifting does but tend, slowly maybe but really, to show that their reliability is rather less than more to be called in question.[1]

There is, therefore, no reason why we should withdraw, or even modify, our general statement of the difficulties of unbelief in regard to the person, and work, and character of Christ. We have such reliable records of the doings and sayings of Jesus as give us sure ground for not only pronouncing Him supremely good, but also for relying upon His own emphatic claim to supernatural origin and powers. This claim

[1] Thus in regard to Luke's Gospel, Dr. McGiffert, almost the latest critical writer upon the Apostolic age, says: "It is therefore safe to conclude that it was written before the close of the first century, very likely a decade or two before." Again, in regard to the vexed questions as to the authorship and date of the Fourth Gospel, he gives his judgement that "there are traces in the literature of the second century both of the Gospel itself and the first Epistle, which compel us to push them back at least as far as the early years of that century." And again: "The Gospel of John alone reveals the secret of Christ's marvellous power in his profound God-consciousness, and it is this that gives it its permanent historic as well as religious value." Moreover, one of the latest issues of the *Life of Christ*, in German, from the able and fearless pen of Dr. Weiss, strongly insists that this Gospel of John is the most reliable of all. True, he underrates to some extent the value of the Synoptics, but the point to be here noted is that this modern scholar, with all the results of other critical labours before him, and after unbiassed scrutiny, flatly contradicts what not a few were beginning to claim as settled, and gives us full permission to build our estimate of Christ upon those facts and discourses which by his predecessors have been loudly proclaimed to be forbidden ground.

is such that if the goodness of Christ be conceded, His truthfulness of necessity follows, and the supernatural is placed beyond question. If Christ be not true He is not good, and destructive criticism must eat its own words. The only valid method of attack upon the supernatural is by destruction of the character of Christ.[1] Jesus Himself must be crucified again, and put to a worse shame than has ever yet been attempted, before the supernatural message of love and truth and hope which He pronounced " finished," can be tortured into a delusion or twisted into a fraud.

9. Let us then sum up the miracles of unbelief as they appear in regard to Christ Himself. We start, be it remembered, with Palestine during the time of Augustus, and especially with Jerusalem under the government of Pontius Pilate. On the principles of unbelief we may postulate no *Deus ex machina*, no supernatural help whatever, no spiritual instincts, but simply Jewish history and temperament environed by Roman civilisation, and national pride smarting under the foreign yoke, together with the pronounced leaven of the scribes and Pharisees. From this total has to be evolved naturally, *i.e.* without any of those powers and influences which are included in the "supernatural" of ordinary Christian parlance, the Christ of the Gospels, with the whole of His doctrine and its effects, as exhibited in the Christianity of the New Testament, and perpetuated on the larger scale in all Christian history to this hour.

If, then, we lay aside, for the sake of sureness and

[1] See Note A, p. 276.

generosity in discussion, all prevailing Christian estimates of Christ and the ethics of His gospel, and accept only those of unbelief, as above outlined in quotation, what necessarily follows upon naturalistic lines? Manifestly nothing less than the following:—

(1) That the purest, sweetest, noblest, character in all human history [1] was at the same time either a conscious liar or a deluded fanatic, judged by His own accepted words.

(2) That the world's acknowledged sublimest teacher was, of all mankind, most emphatically either deceiving or deceived.

(3) That the most marked and mighty impulse of the past towards all that is purest, worthiest, loftiest, in the evolution of human nature, emanated spontaneously from the untutored, peasant-bred son of an adulteress.[2]

(4) That the most elevated, and indeed "perfect" system of morals known to philosophy, the "moral intuition to which nothing can be added," the rule of life which "even an unbeliever cannot do better than follow," has for its changeless centre one whose whole career was at best infatuated self-deception, or at worst conscious falsehood.

These concluding dilemmas of doubt are inevitable. The premisses upon which they are based are those conceded by men of equal ability and impartiality. The sequence of thought is clear and valid. The miracles of unbelief which emerge speak for themselves. Thus it is manifest once more, that to reject the principles of

---

[1] Note especially the testimonies of Strauss, Renan, Mill, Seeley, Lecky, etc., given above.

[2] Cf. note, p. 39.

Christian faith and accept those of unfaith, is in very deed to reject the lesser and accept the greater difficulty. In a word, the more thoroughly the facts are contemplated, the more assured becomes the final certainty that the miracle involved in the creation of the Christian Church through the life and works, the death and resurrection of the supernatural Christ, is as nothing by the side of that which is absolutely necessary, in order to the creation of the Christ of the Gospels by the Church of the first century. The former is at least possible and conceivable. The latter is alike unthinkable and impossible.

NOTE A.—That this is the case is apparently realised by some of the advocates of the lower grade of scepticism referred to on p. 3. Thus a pamphlet was published recently by Mr. G. W. Foote, based on the *Jesus and the Gospels* of M. Joules Soury, in which, with no sense of shame, the author asks, as a title, *Was Jesus Insane?* and after a dozen pages of coarse misrepresentation and contumely, comes to the conclusion : " We can, indeed, only excuse the wanton actions of Jesus, and sympathise with him in his bitter fate, by reflecting that he was incurably insane." Such ribaldry may, of course, be left to answer itself. But when it is remembered that publications of this character are circulated to-day by the thousand amongst the artisan population of all our great cities, it ceases to be a wonder that so many of them, who read nothing better than the newspapers, and hear nothing higher than the talk of the streets, should become as indifferent to as ignorant of the actual truths upon which Christian faith rests. Surely the growing need for careful teaching, as well as "preaching," could receive no weightier emphasis.

IX

THE SPIRITUAL REALM

"It is incomparably more free from difficulties to believe in an all-embracing mind, endowed with goodness, than to deny it. Granted such a mind, it is really no step in advance at all, but only a necessary unfolding of what is implied already, to call it personal. A personality so vast may indeed be to us unpicturable, but it does not follow that it is inconceivable. On the other hand, when we approach the question through the open door of resemblances—a door opened wider to us by the doctrine of evolution than by any other view of things that was ever current among men—we find that the personality of God is easier to believe in than to set aside."—Dr. W. N. Clarke, *Can we believe in God the Father?* p. 113.

"'Mag die geistige Kultur nur immer fortschreiten, der menschliche Geist sich erweitern, wie er will; über die Hoheit und sittliche Kultur des Christentums, wie es in den Evangelien schimmert und leuchtet, wird er nicht hinauskommen.' In diesen Worten hat Goethe nach vielen Versuchen und in unermüdlicher Arbeit an sich selbst das Ergebnis seiner sittlichen und geschichtlichen Einsicht zusammengefasst. Spräche auch der eigene Wunsch in uns nicht, so wird es sich doch schon um der Zeugnisses dieses Mannes willen lohnen, dem ein ernstes Nachdenken zu widmen, was ihm als so wertvoll aufgegangen ist."—Adolf Harnach, *Das Wesen des Christentums*, p. 3.

"The last place in the world to which I should go for information about a state of things, in which thought and feeling can exist in the absence of a cerebrum, would be cerebral physiology. The materialistic assumption that there is no such state of things, and that the life of the soul accordingly ends with the life of the body, is perhaps the most colossal instance of baseless assumption that is known to the history of philosophy. For my own part, therefore, I believe in the immortality of the soul, not in the sense in which I accept the demonstrable truths of science, but as a supreme act of faith in the reasonableness of God's work."—J. Fiske, *Man's Destiny*, p. 109.

IX

THE SPIRITUAL REALM

Two things, Kant avowed, overwhelmed him with awe, namely, "the starry heavens above and the moral law within." His conviction is shared by almost all who make any claim to be accounted thoughtful. We have seen in the foregoing pages how, in regard to the former of these, it is worse than foolishness to attribute the awful grandeur of the physical universe, so far as we can apprehend it, to the blind hap of mindless evolution. It remains to be shown that it is equal fatuity to ascribe to the same source those elements of human nature which, always in some degree and sometimes with unmeasured emphasis, convince us of its marvellous capacities and unmatched dignity.

Amidst the complex features which so markedly distinguish humanity from the surrounding brute creation, two instincts stand out above the rest in universality and indestructibility. These are, the tendency to worship, and the yearning for immortality. The numberless volumes which have been written upon these themes, have neither exhausted the material nor diminished its interest. We are concerned now, however, only with some few salient points. Whilst fully acknowledging the variations in kind and degree which have often veiled these instincts in obscurity, we are here entirely warranted in taking them at their highest and best, and as such seeking an adequate explanation of their origin and development.

I. Concerning ourselves first with the instinct to worship, one cannot fail to see that two distinct subjects open out at once for consideration. Worship always necessarily implies both an object and an influence. The kind of worship adopted is ever contingent upon the assumed nature of the God or gods adored; whilst there must always ensue some definite effect upon the worshippers, in proportion as any particular belief, with its accompanying rites and ceremonies, is elevating or degrading. Now we may dismiss as quite irrelevant the modern attempts to prove that a portion of the human family has been without religion altogether. Our concern, as already hinted above, is with the immense majority, not with the minority; with the highest and best, not with the lowest and worst. If there be no supernatural, then everything has to be accounted for by natural evolution. And that which most manifestly demands adequate explanation, is not the vice but the virtue of humanity. What we have to discover is the true source not so much of the low, coarse, sensual desires and practices, which may well enough be associated with an animal nature, but of the high and noble and unselfish aspirations which confessedly form so large a part of the best forms of religious devotion.

First, then, as to the object of worship and the methods adopted in the service of the accepted deity. The task before us is to examine and decide upon two things, namely, which form of religion deserves to rank as highest and best, and, when this is settled, to account for it upon the naturalistic hypothesis. Mr. Herbert Spencer has not said one whit too strongly that

"An unbiassed consideration forces us to conclude that religion, everywhere present as a weft running through the warp of human history, expresses some eternal fact."

But as surely as the vegetable world yields fruits that vary by all the difference between wholesome cereals and deadly poisons, so does the world of human religiousness produce its higher and lower conceptions of the deity demanding adoration and service. If we accept, indeed, the criterion of the late Professor Clifford, that "belief in God is a source of refined and elevated pleasure to those who can hold it," we shall neither be yielding to Christian bias, nor have any need whatever to consider those forms of religion whose god has been a fetish or a monster. The God whose worship is to yield us "refined and elevated pleasure" must Himself be manifestly elevated and refined. This conveniently and truthfully narrows the area of our thought. In fact there are, on such terms, but three forms of religion which can for a moment come into comparison with Christianity, namely, Buddhism, Mohammedanism, and Positivism.

As regards the last of these, we may surely save ourselves the labour of a protracted comparison, by quoting the words of two critics of ability who are acknowledged as controversial experts, and who are manifestly free from any undue disposition to favour the Christian ideal.

Thus in regard to Positivism and the worship inaugurated by Comte, Professor Huxley says—

"Great was my perplexity, not to say disappointment, as I followed the progress of this mighty son of earth in his work of reconstruction. Undoubtedly God disappeared, but the New, the Supreme great Being, a gigantic fetish, turned out brand new by M. Comte's own hands, reigned in his stead."

Whilst Sir James F. Stephen, referring to Mr. Spencer's "Unknowable," in comparison with the deified Humanity of Comte, remarks that

"Humanity with a capital H, is neither better nor worse fitted to be a god than the unknowable with a capital U. Each is a barren abstraction."

The trenchant words of Mr. Wm. Arthur are thus not without justification, as regards the definition of the "Humanity" whom we are called upon by Positivism to worship—

"We began with an unknown, the sum of past, present, and future men; from this we were told to subtract an unknown, the sum of the useless men; to the remainder, the third unknown, we were told to add a fourth unknown, the sum of helpful animals. Four unknowns do not make one known. The first sum-total was an abstraction, the sum deducted was an abstraction, the sum added was an abstraction; the result is an unknown fraction of an unknowable abstraction. This is the New Supreme Being of M. Comte's tumid abortions, and of Mr. Frederic Harrison's crackling audacity. This it is which men claiming above all things to be thinkers, can with a serious air offer to our soul, to our trust and hope, instead of our Maker, Preserver, Redeemer, and Judge."

Again, as regards Buddhism, we are not here concerned with the vast number of its adherents, nor the moral attractiveness of the life of Gautama, nor yet with the desperate attempts made by modern teachers, from Max Müller downwards, to derive Christian history from Buddhist legend. We are estimating the nature and object of worship as a universal human instinct.[1] In this respect, when we inquire concerning Buddhism, we find that it is well-nigh impossible to characterise its tenets. For whilst it is true, as Dr. Reynolds has remarked, that

"Buddhism on a stupendous scale has occupied the thoughts, stimulated the speculations, and to some extent satisfied the cravings of mankind,"

it is equally the fact that besides its "pessimistic cosmology and ethical fatality, with its ghastly Nirvana and the hopelessness of its *summum bonum*," the supreme object of its devotion is but confusion and contradiction. Essentially Buddhism is agnostic, inasmuch as originally it insists that "a vast cycle of events, and not a will or a cause, have produced the universe."[2] However unbounded the eulogy bestowed by Buddhist writings upon Gautama himself, he is never really invested with the attributes of Deity. "The Buddhist theory of the universe," well says Dr. Reynolds, "is that it forms one vast lazar house, through which the flame of all devouring desire and boundless illusion is ever rushing." Southern Buddhism has adhered to this

[1] Although Buddhism and Mohammedanism were mentioned above (p. 222) in connexion with the Christian basis of morality, it is necessary to renew the comparison briefly from the distinctly spiritual standpoint of worship with its influence upon the worshippers.

[2] The Yasomitra, quoted by Burnouf.

dismal conception, but in Nepal, Tibet, China, Japan, and Mongolia, there have been marked changes in the direction of living deities, taking indeed the form of a definite Trinity. In regard to the earliest of these, Vajrapani, Manjusri, Avalokitesvara, Mr. Rhys Davids says—

"These beings and one or two less conspicuous Bodhisatwas had become practical gods; and it need not be pointed out how utterly contrary their worship was to the original teaching of Gautama, which knew nothing of God, taught that Arahats, holy men, were better than gods, and acknowledged no form of prayer. The name Avalokitesvara, which means 'the Lord who looks down from on high,' is a purely metaphysical invention."

No comment is required to emphasise the difference between this conception of the origin and order of the universe, and the Christian doctrine of God. The simple yet sublime conception that "God is Spirit," "God is light," "God is love," is as far removed from the original agnosticism and later god-inventions of Buddhism, as it is exalted both spiritually and intellectually above the ridiculous inconsistencies of Positivism.

As regards Mohammedanism, the case is somewhat different. Here Sir William Muir's words are to the point—

"There can be no question but that with its pure monotheism and a code founded in the main on justice and humanity, Islam succeeds in raising to a higher level races sunk in idolatry and fetishism, like those of Central Africa, and that in some respects, notably in that of temperance, it materially improves the morality of such peoples."

But its doctrine of God, as the supreme object of worship, whilst undeniably superior to Positivist

Humanity, and Buddhist metaphysical abstract Trinities, falls immeasurably short of the doctrine of Christ. Rightly again says Sir William Muir—

"While the Coran represents God as Creator, Ruler, and Preserver, the Rewarder of good and evil, and the Hearer of prayer, it nowhere recognises Him as a Father, much less the Father of our Lord Jesus Christ"

The best and highest conception of the Moslem in regard to God, is that of an overruling Power, sometimes benevolent, always terrible. Such a sentiment as that so often and emphatically expressed by Christ, "The Father Himself loveth you"—"He that hath seen Me hath seen the Father"—"God so loved the world, that He gave His only-begotten Son, that whosoever believeth on Him should not perish, but have eternal life"—is as far beyond and above the stern and unbending monotheism of Islam, as the character of Jesus Himself is in every respect superior to that of the Arabian prophet. Indeed as regards the character of Mohammed, none too strongly does Mr. T. P. Hughes say [1]—

"We follow the would-be prophet in his self-asserted mission, from the cave of Hira to the closing scene when he dies in the midst of the lamentations of his harem, and the contentions of his friends. Then it is that the Divine and holy character of Jesus rises to our view, and the inquiring mind sickens at the thought of the beloved, the pure, the lowly Jesus, giving place to that of the ambitious, the sensual, the time-serving hero of Arabia."

It is unnecessary here to pursue this comparison further. Enough has been set forth, even if succinctly, to warrant the assertion that of all earth's forms of

[1] In his *Notes on Muhammadanism*, p. 7.

religion, the purest and loftiest object of worship has unquestionably been set before mankind by the teaching of Christ and His apostles, as exhibited in the New Testament. The thought of God, as not only Creator of all but also the Eternal Father, the Infinite Spirit Who is also light and love, is at once the worthiest, sublimest, and most inspiring that has ever exercised the mind or moved the heart of humanity.

But it is manifestly impossible to separate the cult of any religion from its effect upon the character and lives of its devotees. What ideals of conduct are enforced? What are the actual results of such ideals? These are the questions which must ever be asked and answered, if we would estimate the comparative worth of human forms of faith. In these respects Christianity has from its very commencement challenged comparison with all other religions.

As to its ideal of life and character, the testimonies of unbelievers quoted above might well suffice. But the New Testament is after all its own best witness. For it is not merely true, as J. S. Mill remarked, that "some precepts of Christ as exhibited in the Gospels, carry some kinds of moral goodness to a greater height than had ever been attained before," but that the whole Christian ideal admits of being summed up in a word, namely, communion with God, the God whom Christ revealed in response to Philip's representative cry, "Lord, show us the Father, and it sufficeth us." Christ's answer we know was, "I and My Father are one"—"Abide in Me, and I in you." And that this most pure and lofty conception of spiritual life is indissolubly joined with practical behaviour, all His own words, no less than those of the Apostles, bear overwhelming testimony. The world of morals may safely be challenged to produce a parallel to such ethical programmes as appear in the twelfth chapter of Romans, or the fourth of Ephesians, or the third of Colossians, or the whole of John's first Epistle.

Again, when it is asked whether facts correspond with ideals, there need be no hesitation as to the reply. The inconsistencies of Christian believers have indeed been neither few nor small. But ample justice has been done them, both as regards individuals and nations, by ancient and modern cynics and sceptics. The fact is generally overlooked that the more inconsistent they are shown to be, the more it redounds to the honour of the ideal they have failed to reach. The blacker the shadow, the brighter ever is the light that casts it. The whole truth —to quote once more from *Ecce Homo*—can scarcely be better expressed, as a fact corroborated times without number, than in the following words:[1]—

"As love provokes love, many have found it possible to conceive for Christ an attachment the closeness of which no words can describe, a veneration so possessing and absorbing the man within them, that they have said, 'I live no more, but Christ lives in me.' Now such a feeling carries with it of necessity the feeling of love for all human beings. It matters no longer what quality men may exhibit; amiable or unamiable, as the brothers of Christ, as belonging to his sacred and consecrated kind, as the objects of his love in life and death, they must be dear to all to whom he is dear."

For emphasis' sake the assertion made above[2] may be repeated here, that if we could but have a fairly complete list of those who, for sheer purity and nobility of

[1] Small edition, p. 157.   [2] P. 266.

character have stood out conspicuous in the history of the past nineteen centuries, or even during the last century have wielded mightiest influence for the highest welfare of mankind, the vast majority of names, in every sphere of human life, would be definitely Christian. And of all the rest, could there be found one who was truly under no obligation to the work and influence of Christ? Moreover, though it may be assailed as a prejudiced statement, it is probably quite true, that to-day, amidst all the turmoil and fight of our advanced civilisation, the actual "salt of the earth" and "light of the world" are those who, in every grade of life, are ceaselessly endeavouring to shape their whole character and conduct as in the sight of the living "God and Father of our Lord Jesus Christ."

The effect upon society in general and the nations at large, demands also to be taken into full consideration. It is too vast a theme, of course, for exhaustive treatment here. But a glance, though general, may be careful and reliable. This at least is possible. Voltaire said that "not to believe in any God would be an error incompatible with wise government." But no country has more tragically illustrated than his own, the Nemesis that follows upon belief in a false god who is worse than no god. French history during the last hundred years has been a vivid comment upon Mr. Frederic Harrison's avowal not so long since,[1] that

"Those who teach that the future can be built upon science and civilisation, are attempting to build a pyramid of bricks without straw."

---

[1] *Nineteenth Century*, April 1877.

Nor has anything been more pitifully as well as amply proved, in the past history of society, than that "human nature is not a thing so docile and intellectual that it can be tamed by fine thoughts, nor is society amenable to pure ideas." But besides mere ideas—

"Morals are not adequate to direct human life until they are transfused into that sense of resignation, adoration, and communion with an overruling providence which is the true mark of religion."

Where, however, has this actually taken place outside of Christianity or Christian influence? For it must be borne well in mind that, as Professor Seeley says [1]—

"The atmosphere of Europe has been saturated for some fifteen centuries with Christian principles, Christian influences are in the air, our very conception of virtue is Christian; the tone, the habits of sentiment and language, in short all the associations of virtue, have been furnished by the discipline of the Christian Church."

Let another equally unbiassed witness answer our question. Says Professor Goldwin Smith—

"Progress is conterminous with Christendom. Outside the pale of Christendom all is stationary. Japan, to whatever she may be destined to come, has kindled her new civilisation with a coal from the Christian hearth."

This judgement is corroborated, as regards Islam,—which is sometimes spoken of as the great rival religion to Christianity,—by the weighty words of such experts in that subject as Sir Wm. Muir and Mr. T. P. Hughes. Says the former—

"But having raised them (*i.e.* peoples sunk in barbarism) to a certain point, it leaves them there. Whether in things secular or things spiritual, there is no advance."

---

[1] Preface to *Ecce Homo*.

And the latter confirms such a judgement—

"Notwithstanding its fair show of outward observance, and its severe legal enactments, there is something in Islam which strikes at the very root of morals, poisons domestic life, and in its truest sense disorganises society. Freedom of judgment is crushed, and a barrier has been raised not merely against the advance of Christianity, but against the progress of civilisation itself. For everything in religion, in law, in life, and in thought, has been measured for all time. Mohammedanism admits of no progress in morals, law, or commerce. It fails to regenerate the man, and it is equally powerless in regenerating the nation."

It is confessedly strong language to aver that "however far the rebellion against the Church may have spread, it may still be called the Moral University of the world—not merely the greatest, but the only great School of Virtue existing."[1] But Professor Seeley was by no means a champion for orthodoxy, and gave good reasons for his assertions. His avowal that "the scientific life is less noble than the Christian; it is better, so to speak, to be a citizen in the New Jerusalem than in the New Athens,"[2] may be especially hard for this generation to realise, but such a judgement, from such a source at least, cannot be accused of Evangelical bias. Without, therefore, enlarging further upon the spiritual superiority of the Christian faith, enough has been established, especially when taken in conjunction with a former chapter,[3] to call for very definite explanation as to its origination and development. Let us take but one more quotation, by way of final summary, from a source which should be unimpeachable. The author of *A candid Examination of Theism*, apart from his eminence in

---

[1] Preface to *Ecce Homo*, small edition, p. xvii.
[2] Cf. p. 248.   [3] Cf. Chapter VII.

science, gave sufficient pledges of ability and impartiality. But his final finding is thus expressed [1]—

"It is on all sides worth considering (blatant ignorance or base vulgarity alone excepted) that the revolution effected by Christianity in human life, is immeasurable, and unparalleled by any other movement in history. This whole system of religion is so immeasurably in advance of all others, that it may fairly be said that if it had not been for the Jews, the human race would not have had any religion worth our serious attention as such. But not only is Christianity thus so immeasurably in advance of all other religions, it is no less so of every other system of thought that has ever been promulgated, in regard to all that is moral and spiritual. Whether it be true or false, it is certain that neither philosophy, science, nor poetry has ever produced results in thought, conduct, or beauty, in any degree to be compared with it. Only to a man wholly destitute of spiritual perception can it be that Christianity should fail to appear the greatest exhibition of the beautiful, the sublime, and of all else that appeals to our spiritual nature, which has ever been known upon earth."

Whence then, it is time to ask, comes this system of doctrine which lifts men's thoughts most utterly above themselves, from the lowest to the highest, this ideal of conduct which tends more to make our earth a heaven than any other human philosophy? [2] No plainer or truer answer can ever be given than that of the Apostle Paul:—"For me to live is Christ." So utterly is the whole Christian scheme of thought and life centred in Jesus Christ, that it is scarcely a figure of speech, but rather a vivid truth, to say that Christianity is Christ. To this the whole New Testament bears unmistakable witness. Even if we accept the estimate of the eminent unbelievers above quoted, concerning the person and

[1] Romanes, *Thoughts on Religion*, p. 159.
[2] Cf. estimate by G. J. Romanes, facing Chapter V. p. 108.

character of Christ, the acknowledgment is inevitable that this Jesus, whom they cannot help admiring and revering, has Himself insisted upon being so intensely and entirely the emulation of His followers, that His relation to them can only be expressed in His own words, "Abide in Me, and I in you." These are among His last utterances, thrown up into more solemn and tender relief than usual by the near approach of that hour of darkness to which He had all along looked forward. The hidden prophecy of this exhortation is elsewhere plainly expressed : "And I, if I be lifted up from the earth, will draw all men unto Me." This is what has really come to pass through the ages. There can be no manner of doubt that the Cross of Christ, lit up by the light of the Resurrection morn, was "the power of God unto salvation" which the apostles themselves felt, and upon which they relied for the production of similar effects upon others, wherever they preached throughout the world. That those effects did follow, is simple matter of history. And over against the trite reminder of the failures and follies of Christians, may be set the indubitable fact that myriads upon myriads of human souls, whose goodness has found no earthly chronicler, have thus loved and served Him as their Saviour and Master, and have been miniature Christs to their surrounding generation.

Well, then, may we ask with the earliest sceptics, "Whence hath this man this wisdom and these mighty works?" How comes it to pass that—if the supernatural be ruled out as inadmissible—the purest, sublimest, most spiritual conception of God known to men, together with a moral and spiritual impulse unparalleled in the world's history, should arise from the lips of an uncultured Jewish artisan, of sinister birth, brought up in rustic ignorance, and surrounded by superstition and bigotry? How has it happened that the highest ethical philosophy which has ever moved mankind, the mightiest "power not ourselves that makes for righteousness" in our latest civilisation, sprang spontaneously, some nineteen centuries ago, from the most narrow-minded religionists, at a period of their most pronounced spiritual degeneracy, and when even their best thoughts were utterly localised in an obscure corner of an empire that has long since passed away? If this has all indeed been so, then Christianity, with all its past history and its present-day influence, is verily a much more stupendous miracle than has ever yet been acknowledged. For it is a case in which the old maxim *e nihilo nihil fit* must have been set aside for *e nihilo omnia fiunt*. Nothing has, in such case, given birth to everything, the best has been naturally born of the worst, and evolution has contradicted itself for ever.

II. There is, however, yet another consideration, which merits more attention than it often receives. One of the strongest apostolic utterances is to the effect that "if in this life only we have hoped in Christ, we are of all men most pitiable." The well-known words which follow, in Paul's letter to the Corinthians, embody the best statement of the relation of Christian doctrine to the great question of human immortality. Upon this vast theme a whole literature has accumulated, from earliest human records to the present day. The worth of this must be estimated elsewhere. We are here concerned to acknowledge and account for two great facts, namely, humanity's yearning for immortality, and the Christian answer to it. Each of these is worthy of our best thought.

1. The reality and strength of the longing for and belief in a continuance of being after death, have been abundantly manifest in human nature from time immemorial. The attempts to minimise or deny this are really not worth controverting. Dr. Tylor is well warranted in his remark, that

> "Looking at the religion of the lower races as a whole, we shall at least not be ill advised in taking as one of its general and principal elements, the doctrine of the soul's future life."

It was from out the heart of Roman civilisation that Cicero declared—

> "It is by the unanimous opinion of all nations that we hold the doctrine of the permanent existence of the soul."

But as regards some few primitive races which are generally quoted to the contrary, the authority of such experts as M. Renouf and Mr. Alger should suffice. Says the former—

> "A belief in the persistence of life after death, and the observance of religious practices founded upon the belief, may be discovered in every part of the world, in every age, and among men representing every degree and variety of culture."

And the latter—

> "The belief of mankind that a soul or ghost survives the body, has been so nearly universal as to appear like the spontaneous result of an instinct."

In the records of Accadians, Egyptians, Babylonians, Assyrians, Persians, etc., to say nothing of the nations of the far East, there is plenty of proof of the general accuracy of these statements. The witness of Jewish history is equally real though indefinite, and culminates in the more pronounced faith of the Apocrypha. The testimony of the Greeks is too well known to call for reference. Coming down to the present, the varied voices of our own nation may well be taken as true to the rest of humanity. Nor were Dr. Liddon's glowing words exaggerated—as all will know who have mingled much with the working classes—when he said [1]—

"Explain to these, the suffering classes, that you have disposed of immortality on the authority of this anatomist or of that physician, and you will encounter a conviction of which you suspect neither the strength nor the majesty. That mass of unintelligible suffering will look around it at the many who 'come into no misfortune like other folk, neither are plagued like other men,' yet without doing or being anything that could merit such exemption; it will look up to that heaven in which God reigns, hidden, indeed, by the clouds of His impenetrable providence, but in Himself eternally and unchangeably just; and, finally, after a moment of terrible suspense, it will look you in the face to tell you that your disbelief in immortality is inhuman: it will tell you that there must be an eternity, even though it should be too honest and too humble at once to add, with the Psalmist, 'My flesh and my heart faileth: but God is the strength of my heart, and my portion for ever.'"

This inarticulate but quenchless faith has been acknowledged and emphasised by the most able and fearless thinkers, of whom Dr. Momerie may be taken as type—

"But if this world be a system complete in itself, if this life is not to be followed by another, if hopes are born only to be blighted,

---

[1] *University Sermons.*

yearnings roused only to be crushed, beings created only to be destroyed—then the Author of nature is either very wicked or very weak. God and immortality stand or fall together."

And all the world knows how tenderly, yet strongly and constantly, poetry has given utterance to the same ineradicable instinct. In words almost too familiar to quote, the two great poets of this century have expressed the feeling of their fellows. In every healthy mind and honest heart, Tennyson's words [1] find an echo—

> "My own dim life should teach me this,
> That life shall live for evermore,
> Else earth is darkness at the core,
> And dust and ashes all that is."

If it be true, as according to the godless conception of Nature it must be, that

> "Man, her last work, who seem'd so fair,
> Such splendid purpose in his eyes,
> Who roll'd the psalm to wintry skies,
> And built him fanes of fruitless prayer,"

has no more exalted destiny before him than the gnat that flits for an hour in the sunshine, or the parasite that burrows in his skin, so that his utmost expectation is to be hereafter

> "Blown about the desert dust
> Or seal'd within the iron hills:"

then the agonising despair of humanity is fairly expressed in the cry—

> "No more? A monster then, a dream,
> A discord. Dragons of the prime,
> That tare each other in their slime,
> Were mellow music match'd with him."

---

[1] *In Memoriam*, xxxiv., lvi.

Whilst Browning puts it no less forcefully [1]—

> "Truly there needs another life to come!
> If this be all .   .   .
> And other life await us not—for one
> I say 'tis a poor cheat, a stupid bungle,
> A wretched failure. I, for one, protest
> Against it, and I hurl it back with scorn."

Moreover, during recent years, Science herself has awakened to a sense of the vast importance of this subject. What are called "occult phenomena" are no longer despised and left to the dreamy mystics of the East, but brought within the grasp of the cooler analysis and more rigid logic of the Western scientist. Mesmerism, Hypnotism, Spiritism, and kindred themes, which unquestionably derive their interest from the alleged revelations of another state of being, have been and are increasingly subjected to the unflinching scrutiny of students fairly represented in the Society for Psychical Research. Some are even found bold enough to claim to have set forth "A scientific demonstration of the future life." Mr. T. J. Hudson writes under this title—

"In demonstrating the fact of a future life, I have simply analysed the mental organisation of man, and shown that from the very nature of his physical, intellectual, and psychical structure and organism, any other conclusion than that he is destined to a future life is logically and scientifically untenable." [2]

Many other considerations might, of course, be added, by way of emphasising the human yearn for immortality. Our judgements and affections alike cry out against the mysteries of this life's sins and sorrows, diseases and

---

[1] *Paracelsus.* [2] Preface, p. 8.

inequalities, as a final condition of being for mortal men. But quite enough has been here suggested to warrant the inquiry, Whence comes all this? Can it have evolved, uncaused, undirected, from a primordial fire-mist? If there be, as Mr. Fiske avers,[1] "no insuperable difficulty in the notion that at some period in the evolution of humanity, this Divine spark may have acquired sufficient concentration and steadiness to survive the wreck of material forms and endure for ever," the "concentration and steadiness" are inconceivable without that Divine guidance which is avowedly supernatural. To say—

"Such a crowning wonder seems to me no more than the fit climax to a creative work that has been ineffably beautiful and marvellous in all its myriad stages"—

is to invoke a definite principle of continuity, which is simply unthinkable as proceeding from eternal chaos, without any help from the guiding hand of a supreme Mind. The very least that can be said in such a case is, that if this spiritual and quenchless yearning of the human heart, involving as it also does all that is highest and noblest in the mind of man, can have issued from nothing but the fortuitous clash of atoms with no directing influence save mindless chance, we have to accept a veritable miracle of miracles. For we are face to face once more not merely with a pyramid self-poised upon its apex, but the apex itself resting upon nothing. Assuredly this involves a "permanent intellectual confusion," far worse than follows from anything in the Bible.

[1] *Man's Destiny*, p. 117.

2. This, however, is not all. The Christian faith offers a definite and emphatic response to this human cry. And there are certain unmistakable characteristics of that response which mark it out as absolutely unique in the religious history of mankind. It is well known that there have been attempts without number to satisfy this quenchless craving of our nature. Every national faith has drawn its pictures of the life to come, and peopled the future with possibilities according to its taste. But in five respects at least, putting it succinctly, the Christian hope of immortality is distinguished from all others.

(i.) In its tone of certainty. No one questions, indeed, that the devout Moslem firmly believes that if he dies fighting for his creed, his future bliss is secure. But his faith is wholly subjective, with absolutely nothing for its warranty, save the word of the Prophet, who, even if taken at his best, died as helplessly and irrevocably as the rest of men. But the Christian certainty rests not on any mere affirmation, even of Christ Himself, but upon the confirmation of all His teaching in the actuality of His own resurrection from the dead. The final Christian standard stakes all upon this fact. "If Christ be not risen, our faith is vain." We have seen above that the negation of this fact necessarily involves greater miracles than its acceptance. In this respect, therefore, the Christian hope rests upon a firmer basis than any other.

(ii.) Again, as to its simplicity. Contrast it herein with the promised future of Islam or Buddhism, which are really the only two faiths that offer any comparison worth noticing. It is true that in the New Testament Apocalypse we find many remarkable representations of celestial things, but the whole "book" is so avowedly visionary, and manifestly figurative, that the mind of a child could scarcely be misled into taking them for literal assertions concerning the actual future. There is nothing in the whole teaching of Christ and His apostles answering to the bridge of Sirat,[1] or the eight divisions of celestial blessedness, or the seven heavenly firmaments.

As to the Buddhist doctrine of Nirvana, there is no appreciable risk in affirming that to this hour no man really knows what it is. The ablest experts in Eastern lore flatly contradict each other, some indeed asserting that " Buddha said nothing positive on the subject of an after life, because knowledge on such a subject could not advance a saint's holiness." It will assuredly be a long time before the ordinary Western mind will be able to grasp what Professor Max Müller says is the meaning of the Maitreyopanishad use of Nirvana, namely, "Absorption in the highest being, beyond which is neither being nor not-being."

(iii.) The Christian hope of immortality is no less distinguished by the intensity of the individuality which

[1] "Sirat is a bridge which all must pass over on the day of judgement. It is said to extend over the midst of hell, and to be sharper than the edge of a sword. In passing it the feet of the infidel will slip, and he will fall into hell fire, but the feet of the Muslim will be firm, and carry him safely to Paradise."—Hughes, *Notes on Muhammadanism*, p. 90. Paul's reference to the "third heaven" is manifestly a rhetorical expression, with no more doctrinal significance than when he "besought the Lord thrice," or when Peter's vision was "thrice repeated."

it postulates. Herein it agrees with the Koran, but differs alike from the dark mists of ancient Buddhism and the airy nothings of modern rationalism. How far the Buddhist doctrine of Karma includes or excludes the continuance of personal identity, must be left for specialists to discuss. But Mr. Le Gallienne, with charming frankness, leaves us in no doubt as to the faith of the modern litterateur who finds Christianity too tame [1]—

"We often hear people say that so precious is personality that the meanest creature living would not if it could change places with the highest. All I can say then is—More fool it! Such general statements are mainly fallacies. Our clinging to personal identity is an illusion. We do not really cherish it so much as we imagine. What we do cherish is living—and what matter if we live again in our present individuality or a new one. After the dip in Lethe we shall not know the difference. That we shall live somewhere in some continuation of qualities and forces is certain; so much of immortality is at least assured us."

The man who can find comfort in this vapouring farrago, must indeed both possess microscopic vision and be thankful for small mercies. Compared with this, the Christian hope is as bracing as would be the mountain air to a man who had been striving to breathe in vacuo. "So then each one of us shall give account of himself to God," conveys more weighty truth than whole tomes of such literary nebulosity

(iv.) Nor is there any more room to question the superior elevation of the Christian hope, from the standpoint of moral purity and nobility. No man acquainted with the history of Mohammed, can honestly doubt either the sensual character of his promised

[1] *Religion of a Literary Man*, pp. 48, 55.

Paradise, or its influence, as such, upon the minds of his converts and devotees. A perusal of Suras lv. lvi. lxxvi. for the former, and xlvii. for the latter, will be amply sufficient.[1]

By the side of these, the Christian conception of heaven shines forth as a clear spring day after a murky winter fog. And this not merely as regards the absence of all sensual or sensuous gratifications, which is connoted in Christ's own assertion that in the coming life "they neither marry nor are given in marriage," but in the positive anticipation of such moral purity and spiritual development as is conveyed in the apostolic assurance, "Beloved, now are we children of God, and it is not yet made manifest what we shall be. We know that if He should be manifested, we shall be like Him; for we shall see Him even as He is."[2] Whilst as to the effect of this conception upon character, the same writer truly adds, "And every one that hath this hope set on him purifieth himself, even as He is pure." It is beyond all controversy that the eschatology of the New Testament, when stripped of mediæval excrescences and fairly interpreted by itself, is the loftiest and worthiest that the mind of man has had before it to this hour.

---

[1] As regards the disposition of some writers to treat these Moslem visions of a sensuous heaven as purely figurative, Mr. T. P. Hughes has said, with the authority of an expert, "All Muslim theologians have given a literal interpretation of these sensual delights, and it is impossible for any candid mind to read the Koran, and traditions, and arrive at any other conclusion on the subject."—*Notes on Muhammadanism*, p. 93.

[2] 1 John iii. 2.

(v.) Nor is this estimate diminished, but rather enhanced, by the remarkable reserve of the Christian Scriptures upon many of the very questions which most intensely interest us. Those realistic details which constitute the essence of the fascination of Dante, the "uncanny" curiosities which keep up the spell of modern Spiritism, the intricate problems concerning material and immaterial personal identity which crowd out all other considerations for the man of science, these, strangely enough, are only conspicuous by their absence from the records which claim to be a direct revelation of the mind of the eternal God concerning the destiny of mortal men. The myriad questions which even a reverent faith eagerly desires to propose, and the darker mysteries of the present which can find relief only through some reliable utterance from behind the veil, these all equally appeal in vain to the silent reserves of Christian doctrine. This, certainly, is not the way in which false oracles make their mark or build their temples, as the history of all other religions abundantly testifies.

Whence, then, we are driven again to inquire, can have come this unique and unmistakable answer to the great human cry that refuses to be stilled by scorn or hushed by blandishment? This absolute certainty as to the general fact of continued human existence after death, this tender simplicity which comforts the heart of the peasant as surely as that of the philosopher, this unhesitating assurance that the tiny but precious individuality which sums up in itself the whole of our conscious inner world, shall not be "cast as rubbish to the void " or lost as the drop in the ocean, this unparalleled loftiness of moral and spiritual prospect, this impenetrable and dignified reserve—how can such a marvellous intertwining of golden strands in purest strength, to hold us to an eternal hope, have been all wrought out?

There is overwhelming evidence that it cannot have arisen spontaneously from unassisted human nature. We have specimens in abundance as to what can be evolved from such a source. It is not too much to say that the oft quoted reverie of Hamlet gives us at once the highest, purest, and utmost that either can be expected, or has ever yet been derived, from unhelped human thought—

> "To die,—to sleep;—
> To sleep! perchance to dream;—ay, there's the rub;
> For in that sleep of death what dreams may come,
> When we have shuffled off this mortal coil,
> Must give us pause."

Undoubtedly there speaks humanity, and in its deeper, better moods. But to put forth this sixteenth century efflorescence as fairly representing the source of the Christian hope of blessed immortality, would be less of an anachronism than a psychological impossibility. A fungus may more reasonably be expected to develop immediately into an orchid, than the thought-gropings of pre-Christian philosophy, even though directed by a Socrates, to have originated the heavenly hope which the New Testament sets with such simple but significant vividness before all men.

It is equally impossible to ascribe it to the Jew. We look in vain for any sufficient source of it in the Old Testament. The very pathos of the yearning of the Psalmists is that they had no such hope, and at their best and utmost could but anticipate the modern singer who recoiled in trembling doubt from his own highest wish [1]—

> "So runs my dream: but what am I?
> An infant crying in the night:
> An infant crying for the light:
> And with no language but a cry."

It is true that some modern writers upon Christian Eschatology, especially those who term themselves "Conditionalists," have assumed that a definite knowledge of the world to come runs through all the writings of the Old Testament. But a little honest scrutiny is sufficient, in every case, to show the fallacy of such an assumption. What Dr. Salmond has accurately said in regard to the Apocryphal "Wisdom of Jesus the Son of Sirach," applies no less truly to the canonical Jewish Scriptures: "There is nothing in it that speaks of an objective immortality, far less of the hope of the resurrection. The immortality which it looks to is the name which the departed leave behind them, and the life which they live in their children." [2]

The second Book of Maccabees is certainly said to be "eloquent on the certainties of immortality, rich in the expression of a faith in the blessedness of a future life which made men and women superior to the terrors of the most cruel martyrdom." [3] But all that is needed to differentiate this faith, and indeed all else included in the pre-Christian Apocrypha, from the Christian doctrine and hope which appear in the New Testament, is to read

---

[1] *In Memoriam*, liv. [2] *Christian Doctrine of Immortality*, p. 408.
[3] *Christian Doctrine of Immortality*, p. 410.

them side by side. The pure and sparkling mountain spring may as well be attributed to the muddy marsh around the base, as the simple but certain, lofty yet reserved, Christian confidence in a glorious hereafter, resting upon the risen Christ, to Rabbinic fancy or Maccabean frenzy. The stolidity and obtuseness of the apostles themselves herein, just before the Resurrection, is a much more truthful representation of the case as it actually stood.

It is manifestly impossible to accredit the Christian hope of immortality to science, because, as above remarked, there was no science, in the modern sense, at the time of the Christian era. Besides which, as regards this vast subject, modern science, which doubtless alone deserves the name, has scarcely now emerged from its materialistic swaddling bands. The "Proceedings" of the "Psychical Research Society" (which is the latest attempt to deal reasonably with occult phenomena) show clearly that this highly cultured body sets before itself, almost as a primary purpose, the elimination of the supernatural by natural law, and the explanation of a spiritist otherworld by reference to the present physical system. It is true that, as mentioned above, there has recently been given to the thinking world a "scientific demonstration" of the future life;[1] but even if this were now accepted as valid, it would be the grossest anachronism to posit any

[1] By T. J. Hudson (Putnam's Sons, London). "The object of this book is to outline a method of scientific inquiry concerning the powers, attributes, and destiny of the soul, and to specifically point out and classify a sufficient number of well authenticated facts of psychic science, to demonstrate the fact of a future life for mankind."—Preface.

such mental developments as the source of the Christian hope of immortality.

Meanwhile the fact remains that the world of humanity is full of the general hope and expectation of another life beyond the present. The acknowledged degrees in the quality and quantity of this expectation, do not avail to disprove the fact or lessen its significance. All that is highest and noblest within us, echoes the suggestion of our late Laureate—

> "The wish, that of the living whole
> No life may fail beyond the grave,
> Derives it not from what we have
> The likest God within the soul."

Even at its lowest and poorest, this yearning for life is something to be accounted for, as definitely as a volcanic peak that towers up suddenly out of the water in mid-ocean. No sane man or child could be persuaded that such a rock rested only upon the surface foam of the waves. Similarly, when we call to mind that no other living thing shares with man the pathos of the ceaseless cry—

> "'Tis life whereof our nerves are scant,
> O life, not death, for which we pant:
> More life and fuller, that I want"—

we are driven to ask, Can this all have evolved from nothing but nebulous matter, under the control of no guiding mind, the mere haphazard result of pure chance operating through the fortuitous clash of self-created atoms? Truly if this be so, it is a stupendous miracle, compared with which the floating of iron, or the burning of a bush that was not consumed, or the feeding of a crowd with a few loaves and fishes, are the merest trifles. On such a view, as Mr. Fiske has well said, "the riddle of the universe becomes a riddle without a meaning." Mankind becomes a veritable incarnation of contradiction.

Of all nostrums held out to suffering humanity, by way of alleviating this contradictory riddle, that of annihilation is at once the most pitiful, the most repulsive, the most degrading. In such case a man might well envy a cabbage. For whilst his marvellously superior organism affords him unparalleled capacity, both as regards suffering and enjoyment, the former becomes equally purposeless and profitless, whilst the latter is only a Will-o'-the-wisp luring him on to an ever-growing expectation which is doomed to bitterest disappointment.

Thus upon the principles of atheistic naturalism, man is, from the cradle to the grave, a gloomy enigma and a hopeless puzzle. If Mr. James Mill be correct, that "of the origin of things nothing whatever can be known," and men are not willing to be taught from above that which they cannot of themselves discover, there is nothing for it but a life of alternating delusion and depression, *en route* to a final plunge into despair. That which most seems to be, least is; that which seems as if it least ought to be, becomes finally our only resort. Annihilation is only eternal pessimism, yet to it at last the human spirit, shrinking and shuddering all the while, must turn, as the final hope! In face of this we are the more disposed to give ear to Mr. Fiske when he says [1]—

"The more thoroughly we comprehend that process of evolution by which things have come to be what they are, the more we

[1] *Man's Destiny*, p. 115.

are likely to feel that to deny the everlasting persistence of the spiritual element in man, is to rob the whole process of its meaning. It goes far towards putting us to permanent intellectual confusion, and I do not see that any one has as yet alleged, or is ever likely to allege, a sufficient reason for our accepting so dire an alternative."

If, however, we believe in the immortality of the soul "as a supreme act of faith in the reasonableness of God's work," what are we to say concerning the purest and noblest expression of that faith, as it comes from the lips of Christ and His apostles? It may not only be affirmed with general accuracy that the hope of a nobler life after death is felt most by the best men and least by the worst, but it is equally true that at this hour, the foremost nations in the world are those which are most profoundly moved, if not altogether inspired, by the Christian promise of the future.

Whence, then, comes this highest conception of the best hope of humanity, which most commends itself to the greatest of our race? Can it possibly have arisen spontaneously out of a superstitious admixture of wholesale delusion and unparalleled fraud, such as, according to the naturalistic hypothesis, must have constituted the basis of Christianity at the outset? If so, then this matchless natural miracle utterly dwarfs all those which are attributed to supernatural influence in the pages of the New Testament. Mr. Hudson avers that [1]—

"Modern psychic science reveals the same immortal destiny for man which Jesus brought to light, and prescribes the same conditions precedent to its enjoyment. It also reveals a most perfect means for conferring the rewards promised by the Christian religion for a well spent life, as well as for meting out the

---

[1] *Scientific Demonstration of a Future Life*, p. 326.

punishments for vice and crime in exact and necessary accordance with the deeds done in the body. Moreover, science ceases its revelations at the very point where Jesus paused, namely, at the portals of the tomb. He gave us an assurance of a future life, and science confirms His words. He assured us of abundant rewards in the future life for righteousness in this, and science reveals in us the capacity for the enjoyment of the promised rewards. Beyond that His lips were sealed. Beyond that science cannot penetrate."

Then if this be so, how comes to pass so remarkable a correspondence between the high and quenchless yearn of humanity and the tender yet glorious sufficiency of the hope of the gospel in Jesus Christ? Is it psychologically conceivable that such transcendent correlations should be brought about by chance? Rather, surely, viewing all the facts in their coolest aspect, and bearing in mind — with other eschatologies and philosophies before us as object-lessons — all that might most "naturally" have been expected from the times and writers of the Gospels and Epistles, there appears to be here well warranted application of the concluding words of the authors of *The Unseen Universe* [1]—

"Science so developed, instead of appearing antagonistic to the claims of Christianity, is in reality its most efficient supporter; and the burden of showing how the early Christians got hold of a constitution of the unseen universe, altogether different from any other cosmogony but similar to that which modern science proclaims, is transferred to the shoulders of the opponents of Christianity."

Finally, and as a brief summary of the results of this chapter, let us see to what we are committed on the anti-supernatural hypothesis, in the spiritual realm of human life and thought.

We have, first, the undeniable and unquenchable

[1] P. 271.

human instinct to worship. This instinct confessedly meets with its purest and noblest answer in Christianity. To repeat the strong words of the late Professor Romanes, Christian faith sets before us "the greatest exhibition of the beautiful, the sublime, and of all else that appeals to our spiritual nature, which has ever been known upon earth." This, however, on the hypothesis presented to modern thought by such writers as Mr. Edward Clodd, or the late Mr. Grant Allen, or Professor Clifford, issues wholly and solely from an inextricable tangle of ignorance, superstition, delusion (or fraud), and folly. Not only are we called upon to believe that "God is largely a manufactured article," and that "corpse worship is the protoplasm of religion," but that the Christianity which Professor Romanes, and so many others perfectly qualified to speak, declared to be "immeasurably in advance of all other religions," has created itself out of fanatic credulity embodied in baseless myths concerning an eccentric Jew whose very existence is problematic!

Yet, further, as regards the effect which Christianity, in common with all other religions, has upon its devotees. The quality of a cult may always be safely tested by its results in the lives and characters of the worshippers. The manifestly sincere author of *A candid Examination of Theism*, asserts in regard to Christianity [1]—

"That it is immeasurably in advance of every other system of thought that has ever been promulgated in regard to all that is moral and spiritual. Whether it be true or false, it is certain that neither philosophy, science, nor poetry has ever produced results in

---

[1] G. J. Romanes, *Thoughts on Religion*, p. 159.

thought, conduct, or beauty in any degree to be compared with it. What has all the science or all the philosophy of the world done for the thought of mankind, to be compared with the one doctrine, God is love?"

As to its influence on individual conduct, enough has been said above. Moreover, its ennobling power has been and is equally manifest in regard to human society and the nations at large. What we find, therefore, upon the naturalistic hypothesis amounts to this. (1) That the purest and highest conception of God the world has ever known, the simplest but sublimest ideal of communion with Him and likeness to Him, arose spontaneously in the breast of an untaught, fanatical if not fraudulent, Jew, in the midst of an environment of Pharisees and Sadducees, and at a time when these were spiritually at their lowest and worst.

(2) That the ideal of human relationship which is at once tenderest, most effective, and most comprehensive of all, namely, that of a genuine spiritual brotherhood,[1] based upon the love of an infinite Father, and thus irrespective of race or clime or nationality, is due to the illegitimate son of a Galilean carpenter, born and brought up in a despised district of the smallest, most exclusive, most

[1] Cf. Professor Knight in his valuable little volume upon *The Christian Ethic*. "The Christian religion was meant by its Founder to be both a religion and a life for all mankind, a morality for the race at large. It interwove with Jewish monotheism the further idea of the Divine Fatherhood, an idea which was first articulately taught and practically borne witness to by the Founder of the Christian religion."—"It was meant to abolish the exclusiveness of privileged orders, to overthrow their caste, to break down the barriers between alien races, and to unite men of the most diverse tendencies in one vast human brotherhood."—P. 25 ff.

bigoted of nations, whose fierce and unquenchable pride of clan was at the very time only kept within bounds by the sheer might of Roman arms.[1]

(3) That, thus, the gospel, which has for its very essence liberty, equality, fraternity, amongst all men throughout the wide, wide world, in a sense alike spiritual and practical, issued, unprompted and unprecedented, out of the midst of a community whose intense and tenacious faith had for its very basis absolute and perpetual separation from all other nations upon earth.

(4) Nor is this yet all. Similar mental monstrosities face us when we turn to the other quenchless instinct of humanity. Doubtless Mr. Grant Allen was right in estimating the belief in immortality as "the most persistent and perpetually recurring element of all religious thinking,—the core and basis of worship and of Deity." But even such writers as he must acknowledge that this indestructible faith varies in quality as well as quantity. It is equally difficult and foolish to say, with the New Testament before us, that God is nothing more than the "immortal ghost etherealised and extended." Rather is it right to ask, whence comes this sublimest and purest conception not only of Deity, but of a Heaven hereafter, equally removed from the darkling fog of Buddhist Nirvana, or the eternal harem of the Mussulman, or the wild Valhalla of our ancestral Vikings? It is quite irrelevant to allege the Purgatorial horrors of mediæval ecclesiasticism, or the well-nigh grotesque

---

[1] Cf. the details of the internecine Jewish strife during the siege of Jerusalem by Titus.

literalism of some modern "evangelical" preachers. These are but instances of the myriad mistakes of well-meaning but fallible men. The words of Christ Himself remain, as the simple but sufficient expression of the divinest hopes of blessed immortality which have ever comforted and inspired mortal men.[1] The apostle to whom we owe most of the New Testament, shrank with reverent reticence from adding anything to his Master's revelation, and the glowing imagery of the Apocalypse is at the utmost merely suggestive. Yet we are now bidden believe that this whole Christian hope of immortality, in all its tenderness and dignity, its sublimity and reserve, its purity and sufficiency, came from and is still centred in a low-born Jew, who misled his ignorant and doubting followers with high-flown and ambiguous promises which were never realised, who was at last in spite of all his assurances that he would rise again, helplessly and effectually done to death by his own fellow-countrymen and co-religionists, whilst the craven band of disciples, who at the time of his murder "all forsook him and fled," suddenly became heroes of faith, proclaiming everywhere, at the cost of shameful suffering and cruel death, a resurrection that never happened, as the all-sufficient reason for purity, love, spiritual power, and eternal hope amongst all mankind! And this faith triumphed!

There may be minds to whom all these conclusions, inevitable as they are from the naturalistic standpoint, appear easy of credence. It is not ours to judge their sincerity. But it is ours to affirm that to the average mind, working on ordinary lines of logic, there must

[1] John xiv. 1, 2, etc.

rather arise a clear and strong conviction that if these things can be, all the signs and wonders of Christian history sink into utter insignificance by comparison. These miracles of unbelief, even in the spiritual sphere alone, far surpass in strangeness, in improbability, in inconceivability, everything associated with "supernatural religion." For the Christian miracles there may at all events be urged the plea that though their rationale is beyond our present powers of perception, they do not contradict our reason. Though strange to our human experience, they are bound up with higher purposes which recommend themselves to our moral instincts. Though supernatural, they are so only in the sense of being extensions beyond our acquaintance with what is natural, not contradictions of the really universal and Divine.

But no one of these modifying considerations can be alleged on behalf of the miracles of modern naturalism. These are in essence monstrosities, flat contradictions of natural principles which are as certain as our own consciousness. They are, moreover, entirely purposeless, representing the mere hap of mindless and heartless chance, issuing only in painful deception now and in unrelieved hopelessness as to any hereafter. To welcome these latter, therefore, and reject the former, is once more in very deed to "strain out the gnat and swallow the camel." Compared with this, the acceptance of the *Arabian Nights' Entertainments* as thoroughly reliable details of veracious history, would seem to be but a light and easy matter.

X

COMPLICATION, CULMINATION, CONCLUSION

"When only eleven planets were known, De Morgan showed that the odds against their moving in one direction round the sun with a slight inclination of the planes of their orbits—had chance determined the movement—would have been 20,000,000,000 to 1. And this movement of the planets is but a single item, a tiny detail, an infinitesimal fraction, in a universe which—in spite of all arguments to the contrary—still appears to be pervaded through and through with purpose. Let every human being now alive upon the earth spend the rest of his days and nights in writing down arithmetical figures; let the enormous numbers which these figures would represent—each number forming a library in itself—be all added together; let this result be squared, cubed, multiplied by itself ten thousand times; and the final product would still fall infinitely short of expressing the probabilities against the world having been evolved by chance. Whoever believes in its accidental origin must have a singularly constituted mind. In comparison with such a supposition, the most extravagant vagaries of a theological fanatic, the wildest imaginings of a raving lunatic are calm and sober sense."— *Belief in God*, by A. W. Momerie, M.A., D.Sc. (late Fellow of St. John's College, Cambridge, and Professor of Logic and Metaphysics in King's College, London), p. 68.

"It is said that the theophilanthropist Larevellére-Lepeaux once confided to Talleyrand his disappointment at the ill-success of his attempt to bring into vogue a sort of improved Christianity, a benevolent rationalism which he had invented to meet the wants of a sceptical age. His propaganda made no way, he said. What was he to do, he asked? The ex-bishop politely condoled with him, feared it was indeed a difficult task to found a new religion—more difficult than could be imagined: so difficult that he hardly knew what to advise. 'Still'—so he went on after a moment's reflection—'there is one plan which you might at least try; I should recommend you to be crucified and to rise again the third day.' Yes, indeed! this is a lightning flash that clears the air."—*Natural Religion*, by Professor Seeley, p. 181.

X

COMPLICATION, CULMINATION, CONCLUSION

In the foregoing pages we have taken a rapid glance at the difficulties created by the rejection of the supernatural in various realms of thought and being. In each particular instance this imperfect summary might easily be expanded into a more formidable statement by detailed examination. In some few cases, indeed, this has been done. Definite monographs have been produced upon the Resurrection of Christ by authors already named, upon the conversion of Paul by Lord Lyttleton, upon the Canon of the New Testament by Dr. Westcott and others, upon the character of Christ and the influence of Christianity by numbers of the ablest writers, some of whom are mentioned at the close of this volume by way of reference. These all are open to the honest examination of every sincere student. In truth it is only by the patient and thorough scrutiny of these themes, taken one by one, that the full conception gradually dawns upon the mind of the enormity of the difficulties which inevitably arise when, after the modern fashion, the sweeping denial or the gradual elimination of the supernatural is proposed as an easy panacea for troubled intellects. Such a suggestion does but remove a mole-hill to set in motion forces which bring down an avalanche.

This, however, is far from being the whole case. Two most weighty considerations yet remain. (1) The one is the crowning difficulty exhibited in the impossibility of reconciling the complicated and mutually contradictory solutions of the problems of naturalism which have been attempted. (2) The other is the right estimate of all these distinct difficulties, considered as a complex and organic whole.

1. We have seen how each of the distinct realms of the physical, the historical, the mental, the moral, and the spiritual, presents us with facts which, even to a cursory inspection, are both real and great, and which, considered as facts, call for explanation, whilst viewed as effects they demand the finding of efficient cause. Now the idiosyncrasy of each particular class of facts must always be acknowledged. The various groups are alike only in being equally real. Questions of physical science may well be kept apart from those of history, whilst as distinct a line may be drawn between that which is purely mental, and whatever is moral or spiritual. But besides the question whether, in each case taken singly, the particular explanation offered deserves our credence, it remains unquestionably the task of the unbeliever to make all these varied explanations consistent with each other. If there is to be the formation of any valid conviction against the reality of the supernatural, it is surely necessary that there should be between all these opposing explanations at least substantial agreement. Unless, indeed, there be this, they sufficiently confute each other.

Now it requires but a very partial acquaintance with

COMPLICATION, CULMINATION, CONCLUSION 321

the literature of the subject, to show how far such agreement is from being found. It is quite a truism to point out the scarceness of such offered explanations at all. Scepticism has ever preferred the easier task of destruction, to the harder but even more necessary one of construction. Every honest thinker will own that the real test of the validity of any hypothesis, lies not in what it can pull down, but in what it can build up. It is here, in constructiveness, that unbelief has ever failed and fails still. The last efforts of Strauss, in which he for the first time really tried his hand at construction, were confessedly weakest, so much so that they satisfied neither friend nor foe. It would be, moreover, an easy task to adduce parallels to this in other well-known cases. Thus the author of *Supernatural Religion*, after his whole elaborate effort at destruction, gives us this concluding sentence as his contribution to the positive redemption, hope, and comfort of humanity—

"That mysterious Unknown or Unknowable is no cruel darkness, but simply an impenetrable distance into which we are impotent to glance, but which excludes no legitimate speculation and forbids no reasonable hope."

Which is meagre enough, in very deed, as a panacea for the sin and sorrow and despair of human hearts. Though, for that matter, it is only reasonable that a scheme of thought which "posits" as sufficient origin of our whole Kosmos a mere primeval nebulosity, should also terminate in a similarly close approximation to nothingness. If, however, that "mysterious Unknown" be "unknowable," it would be interesting to inquire how this author thus knows that it "is no cruel darkness." To most minds it must seem that to talk about a "reasonable hope" in such connection is the veriest rhodomontade, and really deserves to be pronounced the cant of unbelief.

But even if we were willing to accept as valid and sufficient the individual efforts made by well-known unbelievers, in propounding some definite hypothesis for the solution of the difficulty in any one case, there opens up at once a new and impossible task, namely, that of bringing into harmony with each other all these various attempts.

How many theories, for instance, have been promulgated in order to explain away the Gospel story of the Resurrection. The author of *Supernatural Religion* labours hard to support the vision theory of Strauss, which, as we have seen above, was rejected by Keim and contradicted by Huxley, whilst Baur ruled the whole question out of consideration. Meanwhile, Mr. W. R. Greg has well said [1]—

"Three different suppositions may be adopted, each of which has found favour in the eyes of some writers. We may either imagine that Jesus was not really and entirely dead when taken down from the Cross, a supposition which Paulus and others show to be far from destitute of probability; or we may imagine that the apparition of Jesus to his disciples, belongs to that class of appearances of departed spirits for which so much staggering and bewildering evidence is on record ; or, lastly, we may believe that the minds of the disciples, excited by the disappearance of the body, and the announcement by the women of his resurrection, mistook some passing individual for their risen Lord, and that from such an origin multiplied rumours of his reappearance arose and spread."

This is a fair example of the utmost constructive

[1] *Creed of Christendom*, p. 154, etc.

COMPLICATION, CULMINATION, CONCLUSION 323

ability of acute unbelief. Three remarks, at least, must be made hereupon.

(i.) It is certainly true that "each of these suppositions has found favour in the eyes of some writers," but it is no less true that each is utterly incompatible with the other two. Whichever of them is true, the others are necessarily false. The first duty of scepticism, therefore, in a matter of such transcendent importance, is to eliminate the false, so that what it finally considers the truth may stand alone. Manifestly there is no more likelihood of this coming to pass now than there was in the days of Celsus.

(ii.) Mr. Greg has spoken rightly of "suppositions." For they are nothing more; and even if any one of them were accepted as true, it would still leave entirely untouched the miracle of falsehood pointed out above, namely, the fact that the Christianity of Christ, with all its "sublime morality," its elevating and purifying influence in the world, originated in superficial mistake, or hysterical delusion, or deliberate fraud, or a sinister admixture of all three, which would assuredly involve quite as much the magnification as the degradation of the miraculous.

(iii.) Meanwhile there is yet another supposition, which Mr. Greg has no right whatever to omit upon *a priori* grounds, namely, that the Resurrection, as narrated in the Gospels, is true. And since it is *the only supposition which gives a rational explanation* alike of the preceding character of Him who arose, of all the attendant circumstances, and of the whole following behaviour of His disciples, it is at least entitled to be received as valid, until a better rationale of the facts is found. By that decision every Christian believer will be well content to abide.

How many mutually contradictory opinions, again, have been advanced as "natural" explanations of Paul's conversion! What we find, indeed, in regard to this remarkable event, as in regard to the Resurrection, is that one solution after another has been proposed with all imaginable confidence, each acknowledging the utter failure of its predecessor, each proclaiming itself final, but each also retaining its boast only until the next champion of unbelief saved Christian advocates the trouble of demolishing it. So far as we are able to make a composite summary of the latest findings, all that seems necessary is simply to state them. Namely, that Paul the Apostle of the Gentiles, and writer of many if not thirteen of the Epistles of the New Testament, was merely a fanatic and epileptic rabbi, who although shrewd by nature and brought up in the strictest Pharisaic school, had been converted from everything intensely anti-Christian, to devoted self-sacrificing Christian devotion by — a sunstroke! Be it so. But in such case the miracle of unbelief is enormously greater and more irrational than that of faith. The latter is confessedly remarkable, the former is utterly inconceivable.

2. It would, however, be worse than profitless to go through the whole gamut of discord which such varying answers and attempted explanations present, in regard to the facts which are undeniable in each realm of thought. But it is supremely important to point out that the only sure result which follows from the *a priori* silencing of the voice from heaven, is the outburst

of a chorus of contradictions from the lips of men. *Quot homines, tot sententiæ,* in very deed! Christianity has been more than sufficiently reminded of the differing theological sentiments which prevail amongst those who claim to have been with their Lord " in the holy mount." Difficult as those differences may be to harmonise, there is a far harder task devolving upon modern scepticism, namely, to translate the present speech of the plains of Shinar. It would seem that as in the rabid crowd which at the last hung upon the steps of Jesus, there was but one intelligible cry and that full of bitterest hate—" Crucify him, Crucify him"; so, in these later days, from the strife of tongues around His life and death and resurrection, there issues but one plain design and desire, namely, " away with the supernatural "! There are times when it may be well to reply still, as of yore, " Why, what evil hath it done?" But seeing that now, as then, such reasonable remonstrance does but serve often to increase the confusion, Christians may take refuge as their Master did, in the dignity of silence, until the facts come out which prove that the modern no less than ancient examination is prejudiced and one-sided, and that therefore to be true its judgement must be reversed.

Thus, in regard to miracles generally, it has been well remarked by one of the latest writers upon this well-worn theme, that " objectors to Christianity persist in representing the point at issue as being simply whether the Scripture accounts of miracles are worthy of credence. The real point is whether we are justified in rejecting the whole body of evidence for revealed religion, vast and varied as it is, simply on the ground that miracles are unusual, and, in all *ordinary* circumstances, incredible occurrences."[1] Dr. Lias is quite warranted in adding—

"This point in the argument requires special attention. It is invariably evaded by objectors to Christianity."

Learning from the mistakes of those who differ from him, it is rather the part of the Christian believer to press unbelief with respectful firmness, not merely for an answer to the specific questions based on fact which group themselves about the Resurrection, but for a fair, full, and rational explanation of ALL those difficulties which accumulate from the varied realms of thought, ever springing up, as they do, from the ground where with such enormous pains the supernatural has been buried as a dead delusion.

Moreover, it must be clearly borne in mind that the problems which recoil on naturalism in regard to each separate case, are in the aggregate not added together but multiplied. The rational way of unbelief is blocked, not by a mere scattered heap of suspicious circumstances, but by a solid rock of difficulty conglomerated out of the manifold ingenuities of its own advocates.

Clearly unreasonable as it is, in any one case, that the greater difficulty should be put forward as the solution of the lesser, when this is found to be the only way of escape from Christian conviction, in every realm of thought alike, the sum-total can only be a huge compacted mass of difficulty, far heavier and more intractable than can be expressed by the simple adding up of a series of contradictions.

[1] *Are Miracles Credible?* Prof. Lias, p. 13. Hodder & Stoughton.

It has been well pointed out by not a few Christian advocates,[1] that even if some lines of Christian evidence may seem to be inconclusive when taken separately, yet their perpetual convergence to one common focus, ultimately gives us grounds of conviction as conclusive as anything can possibly be to human minds. In similar fashion, though to opposite purpose, the difficulties of unbelief also have their convergence, and it is at this central core of aggregated contradictions that we most surely learn how impossible it is, out of natural law and human nature alone, to build up the vast and solid structure of the Christian faith.

It is not, of course, assumed that Christianity has no difficulties of its own—though it would seem well-nigh impossible now to find anything against it which has not already been alleged and answered. It is, however, especially worth while to point out one fundamental distinction between the difficulties which accompany Christian belief, and those which arise upon its rejection, namely, that the former bring with them assured even though distant promise of solution, whilst the latter have neither promise nor hope of any kind whatever.

Let but the reality of Christ's resurrection be granted, with all that flows from it, and although His disciples now see many things only " through a mirror in a riddle," there is well-grounded prospect of the day when " we shall see

[1] See, especially, a lecture by B. Shaw, Esq., M.A., late Fellow of Trinity College, Cambridge, in *Faith and Freethought* (Hodder & Stoughton), upon "The force imparted to the evidence of Christianity from the manner in which a number of distinct lines of proof converge in a common centre."

face to face." That love and wisdom and power Divine, which are all pledged to men in the transcendent realities of Christ's Incarnation and Resurrection and Ascension, are more than sufficient guarantee for the final and perfect solution of every problem which now may agitate the minds or trouble the hearts of sincere believers.

But it is entirely the opposite as regards the contradictions and impossibilities which spring from the rejection of the supernatural in the origination and development of Christianity. These, in the very nature of the case, can no more promise any hope of future enlightenment than afford explanation of past facts. Chaos can only issue in chaos. The acceptance of the inconceivable as the rationale of what has been, yields no reasonable grounds for hope in regard to what is yet to be.

Take but one familiar instance. It is often avowed that the most serious argument against the Christian conception of God, is based upon the terrible degree in which suffering prevails throughout the whole animal world. We have already acknowledged the reality of the problem involved. If, however, we are to deal with an honest residuum of fact, we must first "clear our minds of cant." So much has been made of this dark side of nature, that it is worth while to repeat succinctly what has already been pointed out above,[1] in connection with the argument from Design. The amount of suffering amongst the lower animals has been hugely exaggerated by means of warped philosophy and poetic sentiment. John Stuart Mill's indictment of nature under this head is well known.

[1] Cf. Chapter IV. pp. 72–76.

But his conclusion, that we are driven "to believe the animal creation to be the work of a demon," is for such a logician an astounding double fallacy. For both premisses and consequent are alike false. It was doubtless under similar misapprehensions that Sir S. Baker declared that nature was "a system of terrorism from the beginning to the end." But Prince Kropotkin is much more truly supported by facts, when they are fairly and accurately considered, in his counter assertion [1]—

"How false, therefore, is the view of those who speak of the animal world as if nothing were to be seen in it but lions and hyenas plunging their bleeding teeth into the flesh of the victims! One might as well imagine that the whole of human life is nothing but a succession of Tel-el-Kebir and Geok-tepe massacres."

The late Professor Huxley's name doubtless gave considerable weight to his avowal, that the world cannot be ruled by benevolence, because we hear, or may hear, so many sighs and groans of pain throughout the whole animal realm. But he has no greater right to be heard than Mr. A. R. Wallace, the co-originator of the doctrine of Evolution, who says—

"Now there is, I think, good reason to believe that all this is greatly exaggerated: that the supposed torments and miseries of animals have little real existence, but are the reflection of the imagined sensations of cultivated men and women in similar circumstances; and that the amount of actual suffering caused by the struggle for existence among animals is altogether insignificant.

"On the whole, then, we conclude that the popular idea of the struggle for existence entailing misery and pain on the animal world, is the very reverse of the truth. What it really brings about is the maximum of life and the enjoyment of life with the minimum of suffering and pain."

---

[1] See *Nineteenth Century*, Nov. 1890.

Furthermore, when we rise into the consideration of purely human suffering, we must never allow a false sentimentalism to blind us to the fact that an enormous proportion of this, at any given time, is due, not to the plan of nature, but to the manifest thwarting of that plan by the persistent vice and guilty folly of men and women. The mystery of pain may be great, but to honest eyes, there are always visible along with it two greater mysteries, namely, the mystery of painlessness incarnate in the overwhelming majority of living creatures alive at any moment, and the mystery of the human will which perversely turns into evil so much that would otherwise make for the good alike of the individual and the race.

Let it be granted, however, that when all these just deductions have been made, there yet remains an appalling amount of pain, in the natural history of humanity in particular, that can neither be avoided nor explained. Does the Nemesis of faith lighten this load upon our hearts, or dispel the darkness of such mystery?

The frank avowal of Strauss will serve for sufficient reply when, towards the end of his attempt at reconstruction,[1] he declares that

"The loss of the belief in Providence belongs indeed to the most sensible deprivations which are connected with a renunciation of Christianity. In the enormous machine of the universe, amid the incessant whirl and hiss of its jagged iron wheels, amid the deafening crash of its ponderous stamps and hammers, in the midst of this whole terrific commotion, man, a helpless and defenceless creature, finds himself placed, not secure for a moment that on an imprudent motion a wheel may not seize and rend him, or a hammer crush him to powder. This sense of abandonment is something awful."

---

[1] *The Old Faith and the New*, p. 435.

Even if it were wholly true, as he goes on to assert, that "the understanding clearly shows that the world indeed is such a machine," it would nevertheless remain manifest that in passing from Christian Theism to Atheism, there would be a reversion from the glimmer of dawn that promises day, to the hopeless blackness of eternal night. For the attitude of faith, however sometimes bewildered like the disciples on the tempestuous lake, is expressed in a word—

"Well roars the storm to those that hear,
A deeper voice across the storm."

The gospel of Jesus Christ assuredly counsels no callous Stoicism in face of the world's suffering. Rather does it bid men listen with sympathetic hearts and helping hands to the groans of creation as it "travaileth together in pain." Yet over all the storm, the reverent believer hears a voice that can be trusted, saying, "Peace, be still." The great facts upon which his faith is grounded warrant his looking forward, with a patience made possible by humility and love, to the day when not only he but "the creation itself also shall be delivered from the bondage of corruption into the liberty of the glory of the children of God."

No such vision of hope presents itself to the anxious and despondent gaze of unbelief. Neither for the intellectual difficulties which present themselves immediately upon the rejection of the supernatural, nor for the oppression of heart which, as Strauss affirmed, results from the loss of faith in God, is there any present relief or any future promise. Thus despair joins hands with difficulty to block the downward way of unfaith. An inevitable precipice, with a fathomless abyss yawning from its edge, terminates the bypath which under the guise of "naturalness" turns so seductively off the high road of a reasonable faith into the mazes of anti-supernaturalism.

The great objection, we are told, to the supernatural element in the Gospel, is the difficulty of accepting it in the face of the natural law which on all hands encompasses us. But when it is demonstrated that natural law, if taken alone as the adequate cause of all the manifest facts of the case, creates more difficulties than it removes, nothing is left for the persistent objector but the perpetuation of captivity in the meshes of a net of his own devising. Certainly if difficulty be a valid objection to the supernatural, then the very validity of the objection is the deathblow of naturalism.

CONCLUSION

It should be observed, finally, that the preceding considerations are not put forward as definite evidence of the Divine origin of Christianity. The positive reasons for accepting the Christian gospel constitute a distinct subject, and will be found elsewhere. Yet there cannot but be immense significance in the fact that events and realities so many and so great as are comprised in the history and essence of Christianity, should all be perfectly and naturally explicable upon one supposition, and utterly inexplicable rationally upon any other. That supposition is, of course, the simple truthfulness of the account given of them in the New Testament.

The modern aversion to the supernatural, on the other hand, can account for nothing, can elucidate nothing, can inspire nothing, can promise nothing. The final researches of the latest science do but bring us to the edge of "a great gulf fixed," where even the hardiest assertor has to own himself helplessly baffled. It is as true to-day as it was some three thousand years ago, that "the secret things belong to the Lord our God; but the things which are revealed, to us and to our children for ever."[1] Of all those "secret things," the persistent diligence of our vaunted modern knowledge has not succeeded in wresting one out of the Almighty hand. How evolution began to be, how the organic issued from the inorganic, how the living sprang from the non-living, how the highly organised came to pass, through no matter how many stages, from the not-at-all-organised, how the intellectual arose out of the physical, with the inherent potentiality of the moral and spiritual, our fullest knowledge no more informs us to-day than the opening chapters of Genesis.[2] Life may be as Mr. Herbert Spencer affirms, the "definite combination of heterogeneous changes, both simultaneous and successive, in correspondence with external coexistences and sequences"; but if so, we know less about it after it has been thus accurately defined for us than before. It was the late Dr. Carpenter who asserted, with an authority which he had assuredly earned, that we not only did not know, but were never likely to know, how any single gland or cell in the whole human body fulfils its appointed function. That we live, we feel assured, but we

[1] Deut. xxix. 29. [2] See Chapter XI., p. 343.

know no more.[1] That the brain works, we have sufficient reason to believe; but how the vibrations of its ultimate molecules—which are confessedly material—produce the immaterial ideas and emotions which we call consciousness, out of varying states of matter, is as far beyond our utmost modern analysis as the differential calculus is beyond the comprehension of a savage. No man living can explain, or is ever likely to explain, how it comes to pass that the black marks on white which form the printer's type on this page, become instantaneously intellectual perceptions. Even the late Professor Clifford acknowledged that if these miracle-working molecules of our brain could be magnified some sixty million times, so that we might see them in their uttermost actual working, we should be as far as ever from the secret we so long to grasp. Every time that the cry of an infant falls upon an anxious mother's ear, the love responding to the sound sets science the utterly insoluble problem as to how the immaterial can be brought into existence by means of the material.

Yet it is in these very things, which are denied us, that the essence of real knowledge consists. To know that a fact is, is nothing. It is merely the apprehension of phenomena. True knowledge comes only when we know how it is, *i.e.* when noumena are comprehended. Until science can unravel these mysteries for us, that is, until science can do that which its ablest representatives pronounce it never likely to do, it is utterly beside the mark to reject the supernatural on the ground of its

[1] Cf. Dr. Lionel S. Beale's *Life Theories and Religious Thought* (Churchill), and *Protoplasm* (Harrison), *passim*.

incomprehensibility. On the other hand, it is the very essence of the indictment which faith brings against unbelief, that by its *a priori* rejection of facts and truths which involve supernatural influence and action, it unnecessarily intensifies and complicates the mystery of human life, even to the point of wholesale and hopeless confusion. Hence, if it be a canon of the human mind that of two mysteries the lesser and easier should be accepted, according to the "law of parsimony," then a fair and full statement of the case for and against a supernatural Author of nature and Revealer of Himself to men in the Gospel, results in a manifest duty on the part of all thinking men to accept and abide by the former.

Whenever, therefore, what is now known as "naturalism" becomes, as it occasionally does, arrogant enough to vaunt itself to be a complete theory of the universe, to the utter exclusion of all that is super-natural, a triple failure must be alleged, namely, its intellectual insufficiency to solve the problems which relate to the past, to explain the realities of the present, to do anything else than crush human aspirations in regard to the future. In the very midst of this world's physical suffering and moral evil, naturalism, with all its dramatic pessimism, can give no rational account of the whence or the whither of either of these. It is therefore utterly disqualified on scientific principles from suggesting any fundamental cure. Surrounded, moreover, on all hands, by overwhelming sublimity and delicate beauty, together with manifest benevolence,—marvellously adapted to human needs, and in the richness of its profusion baffling all our powers of perception even when reinforced with the microscope and spectroscope,—naturalism can render no reason whatever as to the source and existence of all these things, save that they *developed themselves by chance, through a process of evolution which determined itself, out of ultimate atoms which caused themselves to be* the "manufactured articles" which science is compelled to own them. The plain and genuine records of history concerning the origin of Christianity, a mere fraction of which would suffice as evidence to establish other matters, it can only meet with laboured evasions which are more and more clearly seen to be fallacious in the light of exact scholarship. In face of mental facts which cannot be gainsaid, it is compelled to resort to such suggestions of wholesale delusion or downright fraud as would necessitate more miracle by far than the alleged Christian account. As regards the historic Christ, whilst it is constrained to acknowledge His transcendent greatness and goodness, it is driven in the next breath to accuse Him either of deliberate falsehood or superstitious fanaticism. And, finally, with reference to that deepest and finest instinct of humanity which leaps up in quick response to the promise of Christ—the yearning for blessed immortality—naturalism has nothing to hold out to the sore heart of man but the clammy hand of hopeless death, together with the sarcastic comfort that some day, when each individual in turn shall have become "a forgotten streak in the infinite azure of the past," a "golden age" for the race shall arrive which shall itself culminate in the eternal extinction of this whole planet.

Such, in brief but careful summary, is the solid

content of the system of thought which offers itself with growing audacity as a substitute for the "glorious gospel of the blessed God." Sometimes it stoops with pitying patronage from haughty heights of scientific eminence; sometimes it shrieks and howls from the deeps of coarse popularity. Its meaning and purpose are ever the same. No sheep's clothing can avail to conceal its true character. It is fairly judged neither by the hasty sentiments of Christian subjectivity, nor by the personal amiability and social influence of some of its representatives, but by actual facts and reasonable principles. These show that, so far from relieving the human heart from its anxieties, it does but add to them a hideous nightmare of despair; and instead of liberating the human mind from difficulties, it serves only to increase and aggravate and perpetuate them.

For sheer mental relief, therefore, no less than for comfort of heart, we "turn again home" to the actuality and working of the supernatural as postulated by Christian Theism, and asserted from beginning to end of the gospel of Jesus Christ. Neither by threats nor blandishments can the intellectual foundations of this highest hope of humanity be shaken. The more thorough the scrutiny with which these are examined, the more firm and clear becomes the conviction that "we have not followed cunningly devised fables" in accepting the Christ of the Gospels as the Saviour of the world, but are rather on the high road towards that farthest goal of human certainty so well expressed by Robert Browning [1]—

[1] "A Death in the Desert."

> "I say, the acknowledgment of God in Christ
> Accepted by thy reason, solves for thee
> All questions in the earth and out of it,
> And has so far advanced thee to be wise."

The only weapon forged against this trust which seems to have even the semblance of prospering, is the counter charge of inconsistency brought against those who profess to hold it. And it must freely be acknowledged to be, as Paley said, "a tremendous thing to believe in one God." It is confessedly no less tremendous to believe in the risen, ascended, ever-living Christ, and in an ever-present, ever-working Spirit, to Whom each individual is an object of tender care throughout all the march of history and amid the crush of our modern environment. Alas! that there should be any ground at all for the suggestion that average Christendom does not justify its avowed belief. It cannot be denied that the profession of a supernatural creed involves, as a logical result, the living of a life also—in some degree at least—supernatural: a life, that is, whose goodness truly exceeds the natural instincts of human beings, as Jesus Himself pointed out in His "Sermon on the Mount." The justification of the gospel, does not, indeed, call for a gross quantity of fanaticism, but it does demand the true quality of Christian holiness. It is to be feared that the ordinary professing Christian too often forgets that the test of genuine discipleship is not goodness but extra-goodness. Christ's own crucial question[1] was, "What *extra* do ye?" and His unmistakable insistence, "I say unto you, That except your righteousness shall *exceed* that of"

---

[1] See Matt. v. 47, τί περισσὸν ποιεῖτε;

the pious Jew, "ye shall in no wise enter into the kingdom of heaven."[1] Maybe it is too sadly true that, judged by this standard, Christendom has been, and yet is, to some extent, a failure. The opponents of the supernatural, baffled in their attacks upon its roots, may perhaps find some opportunity for revenging themselves upon its branches.

Yet even then, as a counter charge, every such attempt fails of its purpose. For however much the human side of the gospel, as seen in avowed Christians, may be open to criticism, its actual foundation in truth can only be attacked through Christ Himself. It is not the misrepresentation of the Divine ideal in men which has to be reckoned with, but the true representation in Him. The question whether Christians are everything that they ought to be, is one that really does not at all concern the unbeliever. "To his own master" every servant stands or falls.[2] Even the inquiry as to whether Christianity be true, is really meaningless until it is expressed in its ultimate terms—"Is Christ true?" This is the actual and transcendent demand which comes with ever-growing emphasis before the world for answer. Christ the Heaven-born Lord of life, the crucified Son of God, the risen Saviour of the world; or, Christ the son of an adulteress, the impostor of Galilee, the world's greatest disappointment and delusion—such is the awful dilemma before the mind and heart of humanity. Nor is there any more pressing need in the whole world of thought to-day, than that this dilemma should be unflinchingly stated and fairly faced.

That many sincere unbelievers and some avowed

[1] Matt. v. 20.   [2] Rom. xiv. 4.

believers persistently evade such a dilemma, is not to be wondered at. If anti-supernaturalism could but be driven to its only logical result, namely, the disowning and denunciation of Christ, it would be no small gain for the truth. For as not a few in the past have been saved from making utter shipwreck of faith by the contemplation of such an inevitable result, so might many who for the time being have gone under, like the late Professor Romanes, be rescued from despair, even as he was.

Meanwhile Jesus Himself stands before us, transfigured in the light of nineteen centuries. Fain we still may be to veil our eyes before the glory of the mystery of the veritable incarnation of God in our human midst, yet to troubled modern thinkers as earnestly as to His first perplexed disciples comes His own gentle remonstrance, "Will ye also go away?" And from the minds of men to-day, made clear and keen by later knowledge, no less than from human hearts grown heavier through a deeper apprehension of the whole world's sin and woe, there may well come the response, "To whom shall we go? Thou hast the words of eternal life."

But if now, as in the days of His earthly ministry, men should still be found disposed to turn upon their heel by reason of the difficulties of His doctrine, and say, "This is a hard saying, who can hear it?" one plea yet remains, as solemn as it is reasonable. If they deem Him in any degree wise or good, they should at least learn from Him to cast out the beam from the eye of their own philosophy before complaining of the mote in that of Christian doctrine.

It is and must ever remain most of all irrational, upon

COMPLICATION, CULMINATION, CONCLUSION 341

avowedly rational principles to "strain out the gnat" and then "swallow the camel." That being, however, the process to which the rejection of the supernatural inevitably leads, a certain French savant of high repute was well warranted in his retort, "In truth, I am not credulous enough to be an unbeliever."

That God the infinite and eternal and self-existent Spirit, whose boundless might and unmeasured benevolence are manifest on every hand, should in past eternity have created what we call "matter," and have ordained all those relations which we know as its "laws," whence follow worlds and systems, is just as naturally conceivable as it is necessarily incomprehensible. But that matter should have created itself, and that mere chance should have ordained the laws which have issued in evolution, is, and must ever be, utterly unthinkable by the powers of human reason.

That life and mind, with the correlative environment of this whole kosmos, should have come to pass in response to the creative fiat of the Eternal Mind, and in obedience to His will should continue to work upwards into all the intellectual and moral and spiritual capacities of human nature, is a perfectly rational conception. But that all these should ever have issued fortuitously out of a lifeless, mindless, self-created nebulosity, is a suggestion that can only find place where reason has been dethroned.

That the Christianity of the New Testament, with its lofty ethics and its hallowing influence, should have resulted from the incarnation of Divine pity and tenderness in the life and works, the suffering and death, the resurrection and ascension of Jesus Christ, and thenceforth through the power of the Holy Spirit, should have triumphed over all the bitter opposition of foes and the even deadlier injuries of friends, is a stupendous fact adequately accounted for. But that all its acknowledged purity and strength, its inculcation of truth and love, its inspiring motives and ennobling hopes, should have spontaneously generated themselves out of delusion, or fraud, or both combined, is a thesis that can only be pronounced monstrous by all sane men.

And, finally, that Christ, the Christ of the Gospels, at once supremely good and utterly true, equally Divine and human, should have created the Christian Church, is at least credible, whatever difficulties or failures may require consideration and tend to make Christian believers equally humble and charitable. But that the primitive Church, as it existed during the First Century, should have created, out of nothing but contemporary credulousness, ignorance, and bigotry, the Christ of the New Testament, so full of sublime goodness as to command the ever-growing adoration of humanity and become at this hour the holiest and mightiest power that makes for righteousness throughout the world, is so absolutely incredible, from whatever standpoint it is viewed, that the acceptance of such a preposterous notion could only bitterly intensify the problem of being, and land the human race in "permanent intellectual confusion."

Thus, in one word, the miracles of unbelief compared with those of faith, are as immeasurable enormities by the side of scarcely significant trifles. The latter we may learn to bear in the "patience of hope." The former are, now and evermore, intolerable.

XI

HAECKEL'S
"THE RIDDLE OF THE UNIVERSE"

"Let him, the wiser man who springs
    Hereafter, up from childhood shape
    His action like the greater ape,
But I was born to other things."

XI

HAECKEL'S "THE RIDDLE OF THE UNIVERSE"

IF this statement (*vid.* note 2, p. 333) should seem so strong as to need confirmation, the requisite support may be found in an unexpected quarter. Whilst these pages are passing through the press, there has appeared an English translation of *Die Welt-räthsel*, by Ernst Haeckel, of Jena. This is an uncompromising synopsis, in forceful language, of the most virulent opposition to Christianity on the part of Ultramontane science. From it the following acknowledgment may therefore be taken without suspicion (p. 388) :—

"We grant at once that the innermost character of nature is just as little understood by us as it was by Anaximander and Empedocles 2400 years ago, by Spinoza and Newton 200 years ago, and by Kant and Goethe 100 years ago. We must even grant that this essence of substance becomes more mysterious and enigmatic the more deeply we penetrate into the knowledge of its attributes, matter and energy, and the more thoroughly we study its countless phenomenal forms and their evolution. We do not know the thing in itself that lies behind these knowable phenomena."

To a thoughtful mind this extract is more than sufficient to warrant all that has been said above (p. 333). But the whole work from which it is taken calls for some further notice, both on account of the scientific eminence of the author, and the expectation evinced by the translator (an ex-Romish priest), that it will in England as in Germany find "an immediate and extensive circle of readers." Whether it deserves to do so is a matter open to question. The title scarcely conveys the writer's intention, which is to cast out at once and for ever, in the name of modern science, all thought of God, the human soul, free will, and immortality, as being nothing more than "creations of poetic mysticism and baseless dogma; and to substitute instead, a thoroughgoing 'monism,'" which consists in attributing everything to "the true and only cosmological law, the law of substance." This effectually rebukes the "false anthropism" which permits man to think himself of any importance at all in the universe, and assures him that he is absolutely nothing more than a protoplasmic automaton whose destiny is ruled by "eternal laws of iron," and issues only in utter extinction. Thus the book might more truthfully be entitled, "The Scientific Gospel of Despair." A more utterly one-sided polemic it would be impossible to imagine. All the writer's acknowledged eminence in the realm of biology is employed as a kind of *malleus hereticorum* to crush those who dissent from his dogmatic estimates and sentences of condemnation. It would be amusing if it were not pitiful, to mark how all whose findings in regard to the great "*Welt-räthsel*" differ from his own, are dismissed with a contemptuous wave of the hand. Even such workers as Newton, Bois-Reymond, Baer, Romanes, Wallace, etc., whose scientific acumen the author himself cannot deny, are credited with having become weak-minded, because they decline to adopt the monism which he so vehemently urges. To Darwin is accorded the "palm of victory," because he "gave us the key to the monistic explanation of organisation in his theory of selection forty years ago," whence "it has become possible for us to trace the splendid variety of orderly tendencies of the organic world to mechanical, natural causes, just as we could formerly in the organic world alone." Hence " the supernatural and telic forces to which the scientist has had recourse, have been rendered superfluous." This is a fair specimen of the author's style of completely ignoring all that has been advanced to the contrary, including the acknowledgments of Darwin himself. Which is all very well for those whose acquaintance with science is limited to what they find on his pages. But there are other workers and thinkers besides the few whom he admits into his pantheon, who will assuredly neither be annihilated nor silenced by these fulminations. Nor will the "dualism" for which he cannot find sufficiently scornful expletives, cease to be, because of these *ex cathedra* anathemas of scientific pseudo-infallibility. The translator opines that "it seems impossible to follow this broad survey of the psychic world from protist to man, without bearing away a conviction of the natural origin of every power and content of the human soul." But apart from the fact that, as is shown above, the Christian account of human origin and power is more "natural" than the anti - Christian, and that what is wanted is rather a true than a "broad" survey of the psychic world, the conviction which many will bear away is certainly, that when all which here deserves to be called science is extracted from the false statements, unwarranted inferences, misinterpretations and misrepresentations which are to be found on almost every page, there is left, in spite of all the energetic animus displayed, only another instance of the failure of pure naturalism, or monism, to explain even one power of the human soul, let alone its whole content, still less the contents of the universe. One leading reviewer has already well said concerning a portion of this book: "Nor would the author have written the amazing chapter on 'Science and Christianity' had he devoted to it a fraction of the critical care he has bestowed on the propagation of protozoa."

So far as the present work is concerned, this volume of Dr. Haeckel's serves rather to emphasise than to diminish the force of the main contention. No valid answer, alike rational and manifest, is here given to any one of the problems of unbelief shown to demand solution in each realm of thought, and the general position stated on p. 326, remains decidedly stronger rather than weaker.

Take but one instance. With specially repulsive baldness of speech, and gratuitous innuendoes which seem to show a kind of delight in his task, this well - known scientist commits himself utterly and contentedly to the ridiculous story of an apocryphal gospel, that the father of Jesus was a Roman officer, named Pandera, who seduced Mary of Bethlehem, about whom (says Dr. Haeckel) "other details are given which are far from being to the credit of the 'Queen of Heaven.'" The ruthlessness of this coarse and credulous slander is on a par with the sneering employment of a title which (according to critically reliable gospels) Mary herself would have repudiated as utterly as most thoughtful Christians in this country. But without subjecting this assumption to a critical inquiry which it does not merit, or pausing to ask this eminent biologist—in response to the perpetually reiterated impossibility and inconceivability of an immaculate conception — whether even in the lower reaches of life he has never heard of parthenogenesis, it must suffice here to point out that this puerile attitude of uncritical assertion only adds further weight and point to what has been advanced above (cf. pp. 247–276). The miracle of unbelief which from such a source can extract the Christ of the Gospels, or even the Christ of D. F. Strauss, is such as, by comparison, to make the "impossible thesis of a conception by the Holy Spirit" not only decidedly possible, but even easy.

To take seriously in hand, however, all the allegations and conclusions of this remarkable production, would require another volume of equal size. We must here be content to call attention to one or two main features which lie unmistakably upon the surface. All due respect should, of course, be paid to such a writer, when he avows that "my Monistic Philosophy is sincere from beginning to end—it is the complete expression of the conviction that has come to me after many years of ardent research into Nature, and unceasing reflection as to the true basis of its phenomena." But granting this, freely and deferentially, we are bound to ask how it comes to pass that the scientific sincerity which thus pleads for respectful consideration, should so utterly fail to accord the same to others. For, assuredly, the treatment meted out to dualistic philosophers (and these mentioned by name), as well as all branches of Christian believers, is disrespectful and contemptuous to the last degree. Waiving, however, this question of sincerity, is it truly scientific, is it Monistic Philosophy, to make definitely false statements, to multiply misrepresentations, to employ language which cannot but give unnecessary pain to those who think differently, to claim by a sweeping *ipse dixit*, in numerous cases, to have settled for ever that which is disputed, and even denied, by workers every whit as able and sincere as this author himself? Only space is needed to prove all these intimations to the utmost. A few typical instances may stand for many more.

Is it true that the "majority of believers" conceive of God as "a gaseous vertebrate"? (p. 295). The author should know that it is just as false as to assert that he himself worships a clod. Is it any more true that the Christian doctrine of a future life (p. 201) "teaches that the material body shall rise and dwell in a material heaven"? The writer confessedly shows small acquaintance with the New Testament, yet one might have thought that the apostle's words were sufficiently familiar and plain to give the lie to an assertion of this character—"But this I say, brethren, that flesh and blood cannot inherit the kingdom of God; neither doth corruption inherit incorruption." Where has this writer learnt (p. 323) that "the exclusive preparing for an unknown eternity, beyond the tomb, the contempt of nature, the withdrawal from the study of it, are essential elements of Christianity"? It were surely sheer waste to quote to such a one from the New Testament, if he is thus contemptuously blind to the myriad workers of his own age who, under Christian auspices, are exhibiting in every department of modern life, ability and devotion quite equal to that on which, in pleading for himself, he lays such stress. And when it is demonstrated, even beyond the denial of a monistic philosopher, that such earnest attention to present-life duties and opportunities is given by numbers around him, by what right does this man of science—who so strongly pleads for respectful regard on the ground of his own sincerity—assert that

(p. 331) "Liberal Protestantism" means that "there has arisen a widespread religious profession in educated spheres which we can only call Pseudo-Christianity, at the bottom of it a religious lie of the worst character"? We in return can "only call" this reckless rant, calumny, and opine that it is unworthy of the name of science. Some of the statements in regard to the Papacy are, no doubt, sadly true, but they do not constitute the whole case even as to Rome. Nor is it anything more than similar wholesale recklessness of vituperation to represent Constantine (p. 325) as being only "a worthless character, a false-hearted hypocrite, and a murderer."

Especially in regard to Christianity do we find misrepresentations so gross and glaring, as to make it extremely difficult to credit the writer at once with mental ability and sincerity. If similarly false or careless statements were made by theologians in regard to the Monera or Metazoa, it is easy enough to imagine how they would be dealt with by the author of *The natural history of Creation*. Here, however, we are told, without any qualification, that "Christian theologians deny the freedom of the will, because it is irreconcilable with their belief in the omnipotence of God and in predestination. God omnipotent and omniscient saw and willed all things from eternity—He must consequently have predetermined the conduct of man." Any tyro in theology to-day would reject this "consequently"; and the whole statement is just about as true as to affirm that modern chemists deny the atomic theory of matter, because it conflicts with their conception of the four elements as earth, air, fire, and water.

Again, we are informed that "all that we find in the life of man here below, all that is beautiful in art and science, in public and in private life, is of no real value to Christianity. The true Christian must avert his eyes from them, he must think only of a worthy preparation for the life beyond. Contempt of nature, aversion from all its inexhaustible charms, rejection of every kind of fine art, are Christian duties." Furthermore, it is roundly asserted that "Christianity has no place for love of animals, or sympathy with nearly related and friendly mammals": that "according to Christ's teaching our earthly life is valueless—that all earthly goods, such as technical science, hygiene, commerce, painting, sculpture, music, and poetry, are worthless, nay injurious": that "Christ thought as lightly of woman and the family, as of all other goods": that "he shared the idea which prevailed everywhere in the East, that woman is subordinate to man, and that intercourse with her is unclean." So we might continue in quotation. No comment is required upon such gross parodies. If wholesale misrepresentations like these *are* sincere, then the ignorance they display is alike culpable and pitiable.

Of similar calibre are the representations in regard to the four Gospels in our New Testaments. In one place (p. 320) the reader is informed that at the Council of Nicea "the three synoptic Gospels, Matthew, Mark, and Luke — all written *after* them, not *by* them, at the beginning of the second century—and the very different Fourth Gospel, ostensibly *after* John, written about the middle of the second century, leaped upon the table out of forty which had been placed underneath the altar, and so became canonical"; and "were thenceforth recognised, with their thousand mutual contradictions, as the inspired foundations of Christian doctrine." Meanwhile the Christian doctrines in regard to immortality, resurrection, and the Trinity are "dogmas that contradict pure reason no more and no less than that miraculous bound of the Gospel manuscripts." In another place we are told that "the four Gospels were deliberately chosen from a much larger number of gospels," but "the details which the apocryphal gospels give of the life of Christ have just as much claim to historical validity as the four canonical Gospels." Also, that "the most important sources after the Gospels are the fourteen separate and generally forged epistles of Paul." But the "genuine Pauline Epistles were *three* in number, to the Romans, Galatians, and Corinthians." Such quotations as these are confessedly nauseating to the modern "sincere" student of the New Testament; but it is well that they should be set forth, in order that the reader may see what—from quarters which boast the highest intelligence—is supplied to the world of unbelief by those who ceaselessly vaunt their quest of truth.

It is tempting, indeed, to turn to the scientific features of this diatribe, but detailed scrutiny is neither possible here nor necessary. It is interesting, however, to find that although we as human beings have neither wills nor souls, "the two fundamental forms of substance, ponderable matter and ether," have both. For these "are not dead, and only moved by extrinsic force, but they are endowed with sensation and will: they experience an inclination for condensation, a dislike of strain; they strive after the one and struggle against the other." This being categorical information, and in the author's own words, it is surely a false modesty which remarks, "I am myself too little informed in physics and mathematics to enter into a critical discussion—" For certainly men like James Clerk Maxwell, Sir G. G. Stokes, and Lord Kelvin, etc., who are confessedly well "informed" in these matters, have neither mentioned the love stories of the ether particles, nor recognized their wills and souls.

It is also somewhat perplexing to be told more than once that this little world of ours is by and by going just to drop into the sun and be lost for ever, and yet also, "The duration of the world (*sic*) is equally infinite and unbounded: it has no beginning and no end: it is eternity." What we are really to understand from this, must be left to each reader's judgement.

Meanwhile it is well to note that Dr. Haeckel utters no uncertain sound upon one important matter. He "entirely" agrees with Naegeli that "to reject abiogenesis is to admit a miracle." That is to say, in plain English, life certainly did create itself. "It is an indispensable thesis in any natural theory of evolution, that the first development of living protoplasm should be out of inorganic carbonates" purely by chance, without any influence *ab extra* save "the law of substance." "The monera which consist only of primitive protoplasm, arise by spontaneous generation from inorganic nitrocarbonates."

Such language has at least the merit of lucidity. As

the strength of any chain is but that of its weakest link, here is one link which may be tested in that of the Monistic philosophy. It is by no means the only faulty one, but it must suffice here. Monism stands or falls with spontaneous generation. Is it necessary, however, to call up Tyndall from the grave to express the attitude of modern science upon this matter? Are the names of Pasteur, Drysdale, Dallinger, Roscoe, Kelvin, Beale, and a host of others, to count for nothing? At all events, valid confirmation is hereby afforded of what has been said in the present work (Preface, p. ix, etc.), that the miraculous is inevitable. The choice is, manifestly, whether God, the Creator of life, shall be regarded as the miracle-worker, or whether it shall be accomplished by the nitrocarbonates. Now the consensus of modern science is unmistakably to the effect that the nitrocarbonates cannot naturally do this. In the more precise language of a well-known F.R.S., "new life is not generated in the absence of all living substances at least in a world constituted as ours now is." It is conceded (cf. p. 105, above) that to God the miraculous is easy enough. But that the nitrocarbonates, without God, should create life, is assuredly not easy. By all the difference, herefore, between inorganic salts and the infinite Mind postulated by Christian Theism, the miracle of unbelief therein is greater than that of faith. So that on principles of sheer mental economy, we are constrained to prefer Christian dualism to Dr. Haeckel's monism.

Under all the circumstances, one can understand how such an author, however sincere, is obliged at last to take refuge in sheer assertion. A good bold *ipse dixit* is like a bomb-proof shelter, invulnerable. Of such a character one cannot but pronounce the following to be. They are merely specimens. "Man is not distinguished from apes, dogs, etc., by a special kind of soul, or by any peculiar and exclusive psychic function, but only by a higher degree of psychic activity, a superior stage of development." Would Mr. A. R. Wallace, the co-discoverer of evolution, endorse this? It matters not. Dr. Haeckel has spoken.

Again (pp. 207–9), as regards the immortality of the soul. "The theological proof is a pure myth. The cosmological proof is a baseless dogma. The teleological proof rests on a false anthropism. The moral proof is only a pious wish. The ethnological proof is an error in fact. The ontological proof is a spiritualistic fallacy." So it is all settled, at once and for ever. What Dr. Salmond and a score of other writers, quite as able and sincere as our author, have set forth, amounts to nothing worthy of regard. "The monistic view definitely rules out the three central dogmas of metaphysics, God, freedom, and immortality." That is enough. Upon the tomb of Christian truth and hope, *Requiescat in pace* has been cut by Dr. Haeckel's own hand.

Again (p. 275, etc.), as regards design in nature. "Nowhere in the evolution of animals and plants do we find any trace of design, but merely the inevitable outcome of the struggle for existence, the blind controller, instead of the provident God, that effects the changes of organic forms by a mutual action of the laws of heredity and adaptation." The reader of Chap. IV. above, will, it is hoped, know how to estimate this magisterial dogma. Could the Vatican say more?

"Religious faith," we are further told, "means always belief in a miracle, and as such is in hopeless contradiction with the natural faith of reason. In opposition to reason it postulates supernatural agencies, and therefore may be justly called superstition. The so-called revelations on which the mythical dogmas of Christianity are based, are incompatible with the firmest results of modern science." But if incompatibility with the firmest result of modern science constitutes a myth, certainly the doctrine of biogenesis is such a result. Now monism is confessedly incompatible with that. Monism, therefore, is the myth hereby condemned. The rest of this quotation is, as every youthful student will see, simple *petitio quæstionis*.

An exhaustive list, however, of such dogmatic settlements would be as wearying as unprofitable. It only remains to ask what is the human issue of this monism, *alias* determinism, concerning which the writer modestly claims that "the great struggle between the determinist and the indeterminist, between the opponent and the sustainer of the freedom of the will, has ended to-day, after more than two thousand years, completely in favour of the determinist"? Assuming for the moment as true what many deem to be manifestly false, we may at least appraise the answer to "the riddle of the universe" which pure monism offers to humanity.

The source of the most dangerous errors, in the eyes of this eminent biologist, is "anthropism"; *i.e.* the human conceit which falsely and foolishly thinks a man, not to say mankind, worth something in the sight of the great Creator, as being gifted above other animals and dowered with the potentiality of an eternal destiny. Monism pronounces this to be mere fatuity. "Our own human nature which exalted itself into an image of God in its anthropistic illusion, sinks to the level of a placental mammal, which has no more value for the universe at large than the ant, the fly of a summer's day, the microscopic infusorium, or the smallest bacillus. Humanity is but the transitory phase of the evolution of an eternal substance, a particular phenomenal form of matter and energy, the true proportion of which we soon perceive when we set it on the background of infinite space and eternal time."

From this cheerful prospect, the dogmatism of which was rightly characterised as "Philistinism," years ago, by Professor Huxley, it is easy to deduce the difference between Christian dualism and Haeckelian monism. The one asks—"How much is a man better than a sheep?" and answers, "Immeasurably." The other inquires how much a man is better than "the smallest bacillus," and answers, "Not at all." Whether this involves the exaltation of the bacillus or the degradation of the man, students of bacteriology will be best able to estimate. According to such a view, the hope of the twentieth century is that it will bring about "the construction of a system of pure monism, and so spread far and wide the long-desired unity of world conception." And the solid contents of this conception, the gospel of monism, in the "perfect poetic expression" of Goethe, adopted by Dr. Haeckel, is simply this—

> "By eternal laws
> Of iron ruled
> Must all fulfil
> The cycle of
> Their destiny."

Clearly therefore the "antitheses" which the next century "will complete the task of resolving," are, anthropism and misanthropism. In regard to which we may safely aver that whatever be the faults of the former, it is as much better as truer than the latter. For the science which dogmatises to man that, in spite of all his convictions, feelings, sufferings, struggles, hopes, he is less than a chance drop in an ocean of spray, coming through nothing, from nothing, *en route* to nothing, bears its own sentence of refusal writ large across its brow. It is not poetic imagination, but the valid science of the heart which, in such case, cries out against Goethe's helpless and hopeless determinism—

> "Not only cunning casts in clay:
> Let science prove we are, and then
> What matters science unto men,
> At least to me? I would not stay."

But when it is further demonstrated that the road to this abyss of despair is blocked by greater and grosser miracles of unbelief than those which bar the way of faith, the man possessed of equal head and heart may well pause before flinging away his only hope, and committing himself to the blackness of darkness which Strauss from sad experience pronounced to be "something awful." The mysteries of Providence and of human life, of pain and of moral evil, upon which Dr. Haeckel and others seem almost to gloat, may bring him even bewilderment and tears, but the voice which bids him wait, in "the work of faith, the labour of love, and the patience of hope," is that of One whom he can afford to trust, though it be in the dark, when He says: "Let not your heart be troubled, neither let it be afraid: believe in God, believe also in Me." Such faith is but the noblest expression of the highest reason.

XII

APPENDIX

THE following list of books is appended, not as being by any means exhaustive, but as affording useful suggestions to those who may wish to study the subject more carefully from the Christian standpoint. At the same time, although they are simply works most familiar personally to the writer, and taken from his own shelves, they represent beyond question the researches and conclusions of men thoroughly well qualified to speak in their own departments. They therefore deserve the earnest and unbiassed attention of all those who sincerely desire to face with honest care the grave questions at issue. They can be obtained from any bookseller. Not one of them will be found to be either superficial or superfluous. A few are marked with an asterisk as meriting especial notice.

I. GENERAL

TITLE.	AUTHOR.	PUBLISHER.
*Cumulative Evidences of Divine Revelation. (A small volume not nearly so well known as it ought to be.)	Phillips, L. F. M.	Christian Evidence Society
Apologetics; or, Christianity defensively stated	Bruce, Dr. A. B.	T. & T. Clark
*The Basis of Faith. Congregational Union Lecture for 1877	Conder, Dr. E. R.	Hodder & Stoughton
The Christian's Plea against Modern Unbelief	Redford, R. A.	,, ,,
Christian Evidences in Relation to Modern Thought. Bampton Lectures for 1877	Row, C. A.	Norgate

APPENDIX

Title.	Author.	Publisher.
*The Foundations of Faith. Bampton Lectures for 1879	Wace, Dr. H.	Macmillan
Modern Doubt and Christian Belief	Christlieb, Dr.	T. & T. Clark
The Logic of Christian Evidences	Wright, G. F.	Dickinson
Christian Theism	Row, C. A.	H. & S.
Manual of Christian Evidence	,, ,,	,,
Modern Scepticism } Faith and Freethought } Popular Objections to Revealed Truth }[1] Strivings for the Faith } Credentials of Christianity }	Various authors	Chn. Ev. Soc.
Boston Monday Lectures — on Transcendentalism, Biology, Orthodoxy, Labour, Marriage, Conscience, Heredity, Socialism	Cook, Dr. Joseph	H. & S.
Religious Doubt	Diggle, J. W.	Longmans
Christian Instincts and Modern Doubt	Craufurd, A. H.	James Clarke
*Theistic Problems	Sexton, Dr. G.	H. & S.
Nature and the Supernatural	Bushnell, H.	Strahan
Popular Handbook of Christian Evidences	Kennedy, Dr. J.	London Sunday School Union
Defence of the Christian Faith	Godet, Dr. F.	T. & T. Clark
Credentials of the Gospel. Fernley Lecture for 1889	Beet, Dr. J. A.	Ch. Kelly
Reasonable Orthodoxy	Ballard, F.	James Clarke
Critical History of Free Thought. Bampton Lectures for 1882	Farrar, T.	Macmillan
In Relief of Doubt	Welsh, R. E.	James Clarke
Christian Dogmatics	Martensen, Dr.	T. & T. Clark
Reason in Revelation	Caillard, E.	Nisbet
Christian Evidences	Fisher, Dr. G. P.	Dickinson
Thoughts on Religion	Romanes, G. J.	Longmans
Christianity Vindicated by its Enemies	Dorchester	Hunt & Eaton
Some Modern Religious Difficulties	Various	S.P.C.K.
*Present-Day Tracts. A series of nearly 100 monographs, brief but by the best authors. (An exceedingly valuable collection, meriting a much more attractive name.)		Religious Tract Society
God, the Soul and a Future State	Cooper, Thos.	H. & S.

II. PHYSICAL

Paley's Natural Theology. Latest edition, with special Introduction by Professor le Gros Clark, F.R.C.S.	Edited by Prof. le Gros Clark	S.P.C.K.

[1] These five volumes are all of exceptional interest and value, and merit most careful study.

APPENDIX

Title.	Author.	Publisher.
Christian Prayer and General Laws. The Burney Prize Essay for 1873	Romanes, G. J.	Macmillan
The Supernatural in Nature	Reynolds, J. W.	Kegan Paul
*Science and the Faith	Moore, Aubrey L.	,, ,,
Does Science aid Faith?	Cotterill, Dr.	H. & S.
Life Theories and Religious Thought	Beale, Dr. L.	Churchill
Protoplasm	,, ,,	Harrison & Sons
Natural Theology. Gifford Lectures for 1891	Stokes, Prof. G. G.	A. & C. Black
*Natural Theology and Modern Thought	Kennedy, J. H.	H. & S.
Scientific Obstacles to Christian Belief. The Boyle Lectures for 1884	Curteis, G. H.	Macmillan
Christian Doctrine and Modern Thought	Bonney, Prof. T. G.	Longmans
The Creator and Method of Creation. Fernley Lecture for 1887	Dallinger, Dr. W. H.	Charles Kelly
*Origin of the Laws of Nature	Lord Grimthorpe	S.P.C.K.
The Unseen Universe	Stewart and Tait	Macmillan
*Baseless Fabric of Scientific Scepticism	Sexton, Dr. G.	Smart & Allen
Aspects of Theism. Baird Lecture	Flint	Blackwood
Anti-Theistic Theories	,,	,,
Nature and Revelation	Pritchard, Dr. C.	Murray
Scientific Sophisms	Wainwright, Dr.	H. & S.
Burnett Lectures on Light. 3 vols.	Stokes, Prof. G.G.	Macmillan
Moral Teaching of Science	Buckley, A.	Stanford

III. MIRACLES

*Miracles. Bampton Lectures for 1865	Mozley, Dr. J. B.	Rivingtons
Can we believe in Miracles?	Warington, G.	S.P.C.K.
*Miracles: An Argument and a Challenge	Cox, Dr. S.	Kegan Paul
Are Miracles Credible?	Lias, J. J.	H. & S.
The Mystery of Miracle	Reynold, Dr. J.	Kegan Paul
*Review of Hume and Huxley on Miracles	Lord Grimthorpe	S.P.C.K.
The Christian Miracles, and Conclusions of Science	Thomson, W.	T. & T. Clark.
The Verity and Value of Miracles	Cooper, Thos.	H. & S.

IV. EVOLUTION

*Evolution in Relation to Religious Thought	Le Conte, Prof.	Chapman & Hall
Evolution and Religion	Henslow, Prof.	Macmillan
*Christianity and Evolution	Iverach, Dr. J.	H. & S.
Christianity and Evolution: Symposium	Various	Nisbet
The Basis of Evolution	Croll, Dr. J.	Stanford
Modern Ideas of Evolution	Dawson, Sir W.	Rel. Tr. Soc.
Darwinism and Design	St. Clair	H. & S.

Title.	Author.	Publisher.
Darwinianism: Workmen and Work	Stirling, Dr. J. H.	T. & T. Clark
The Theology of an Evolutionist	Abbott, Dr. L.	James Clarke
Preorganic Evolution and the Biblical Idea of God	Chapman, Dr. C.	T. & T. Clark
The Ascent of Man. Lowell Lectures	Drummond, H.	H. & S.
*The Ascent through Christ	Griffith-Jones, E.	James Bowden
Evolution of the Universe	Howard, W. W.	Nisbet & Co.

V. HISTORICAL

*The Divine Origin of Christianity	Storrs, Dr. R. S.	H. & S.
The Witness of History to Christ. Hulsean Lectures for 1870	Farrar, Dr. F. W.	Macmillan
The Preparation for Christianity	Wenley, Dr.	R. & R. Clark
Fragmentary Records of Jesus of Nazareth	Wynne, E. R.	H. & S.
*Plain Proofs	,, ,,	,,
Gesta Christi	Brace, C. L.	,,
Religion and History in Modern Life	Fairbairn, Dr.	,,
Historic Doubts concerning Napoleon Buonaparte	Whately, Dr.	Putnams
The Bridge of History	Cooper, Thos.	H. & S.

VI. CHRIST

The Christ of History	Young, Dr. J.	Strahan
Our Lord's Divinity. Bampton Lectures for 1866	Liddon, Dr.	Rivingtons
Christ in Modern Theology	Fairbairn, Dr.	H. & S.
Mohammed, Buddha, and Christ	Dods, Dr. M.	,,
*The Self-Revelation of Jesus Christ	Kennedy, Dr. J.	Isbister
Pilate's Question	,, ,,	D. Douglas
The Jesus of the Evangelists	Row, C. A.	Norgate
The Gospel and its Witnesses	Wace, Dr. H.	Murray
*Ecce Homo	Seeley, Prof.	Macmillan
*Christ not a Product of Evolution	Henslow, Prof.	Nisbet
Gleanings about Christ and Early Christianity	Alexander, J. H.	,,

VII. THE RESURRECTION

This subject is dealt with continually in other books referred to. But the following merit special mention :—		
*The Resurrection of Jesus Christ	Kennedy, Dr. J.	Rel. Tr. Soc.
*The Gospel of the Resurrection	Westcott, Dr. B. F.	Macmillan
The Verity of Christ's Resurrection	Cooper, Thos.	H. & S.
Witnesses of the Resurrection	Milligan, Dr.	,,

VIII. BIBLICAL

(1) GENERAL

TITLE.	AUTHOR.	PUBLISHER.
*The Superhuman Origin of the Bible. Congregational Union Lectures for 1893	Rogers, Dr. H.	H. & S.
What is the Bible?	Ladd, Dr. G. T.	Chas. Scribner's Sons
The Impregnable Rock of Holy Scripture	Gladstone, W. E.	Isbister
Scripture and its Witnesses	Banks, J. H.	Charles Kelly
Guide to Biblical Study	Peake, Prof.	H. & S.
The Bible in the Church	Westcott, Dr. B. F.	Macmillan
Inspiration. Bampton Lectures for 1893	Sanday, Dr. W.	Longmans
History of the English Bible	Westcott, Dr. B. F.	Macmillan
Bible Dictionary. Edited by Dr. Hastings, containing most valuable articles by ablest men, on modern lines.		T. & T. Clark.

(2) NEW TESTAMENT

The Canon of the New Testament	Westcott, Dr. B.	Macmillan
Canonicity	Charteris, Dr.	Blackwood
*Introduction to the New Testament	Salmon, Dr.	Murray
The New Testament Scriptures	Charteris, Dr.	Nisbet
*The Moral Teaching of the New Testament	Row, C. A.	S.P.C.K.

(3) GOSPELS

*Introduction to the Gospels	Westcott, Dr. B. F.	Macmillan
The Genuineness of the Gospels	Norton, Andrews	Norgate
The Gospels: their Age and Authorship	Kennedy, Dr.	Sunday School Union
*Christianity and Agnosticism	Wace, Dr. H.	Blackwood
Authorship and Historical Character of the Fourth Gospel	Sanday, Dr. W.	Macmillan
The Apocryphal Gospels	Cowper, B. H.	Norgate

IX. PSYCHOLOGICAL

Title.	Author.	Publisher.
Spencer's Structural Principles Examined	Ground, W. D.	Parker
The Philosophy of Religion	Lotze, Prof. H.	Dickinson
The Supernatural in the New Testament	Row, C. A.	Norgate
The Conversion of Paul	Lyttleton, Lord	Rel. Tr. Soc.
The Whence and Whither of Man	Tylor, Prof. J. M.	Blackwood

X. MORAL AND SPIRITUAL

Title	Author	Publisher
*Christianity and Morality. Boyle Lectures for 1874	Wace, Dr. H.	Macmillan
Physical and Moral Law. Fernley Lectures for 1883	Arthur, W.	Charles Kelly
Christian Ethics	Smyth, Newman	T. & T. Clark
The Christian Ethic	Knight, Prof. W.	Murray
The Moral Teachings of Science	Buckley, Ara.	Stanford
*Burning Questions	Gladden, Dr. W.	James Clarke
The Ascent of Faith	Harrison, A. J.	H. & S.
The Teachings of Experience	Barker, Jos.	,,
Autobiography	,, ,,	,,
Social Evolution	B. Kidd	

XI. COMPARATIVE RELIGION

Title	Author	Publisher
Christ and other Masters	Hardwick, Archdeacon	Macmillan
*The Mohammedan Controversy	Muir, Sir W.	T. & T. Clark
Mahomet and Islam	,, ,,	Rel. Tr. Soc.
Notes on Muhammadanism	Hughes, T. P.	Allen
Islam	Stobart, J. W. H.	S.P.C.K.
Hinduism	Monier-Williams	,,
The Unknown God,	Brace, C. L.	H. & S.

XII. ESCHATOLOGICAL

Title	Author	Publisher
*The Christian Doctrine of Immortality	Salmond, Dr.	T. & T. Clark
The Hope of Immortality	Welldon, Dr. J.	Seeley
The Natural History of Immortality	Reynolds, J. W.	Longmans
The World to Come	,, ,,	Kegan Paul
Physical Theory of another Life	Taylor, Isaac	
*Human Immortality	James, Prof.	Constable
The Witness to Immortality	Gordon, Dr.	Putnams
A Scientific Demonstration of the Future Life	Hudson, T. J.	,,
Man's Destiny.	Fiske, J.	Macmillan

ADDENDA

The following works, inadvertently omitted in First Edition, also deserve notice :—

Title.	Author.	Publisher.
Chrétien ou Agnostique	Abbé Picard	
Foundations of the Creed	Dr. Harvey Goodwin	
Grammar of Assent	Dr. J. H. Newman	Longmans
Scientific Aspects of Christian Evidences	G. F. Wright	C. A. Pearson
The Mystery of God	T. V. Tymms	Elliot Stock
Christianity and Agnosticism	Wace, Dr. H.	Blackwood
Modern Realism Examined	T. M. Herbert	Macmillan
*Witnesses to Christ	Dr. Wm. Clark	T. & T. Clark
Christian View of God and the World	Dr. Orr	Andrew Elliot
The Evolution of Christianity	Dr. Lyman Abbott	Jas. Clarke & Co.

Note to p. 39.

Nor can it be truly said that during the last half-century, the trend of modern textual criticism—with all respect to Ritschlian developments—is definitely in the direction of the sweeping and dogmatic conclusion asserted above.

The standpoint, for example, of the author of the recent Commentary upon Luke's Gospel in the "International Critical Commentary" Series, or the article on "Gospels" in Hastings' *Bible Dictionary*, is quite as really abreast of modern knowledge in this regard, as anything assumed or asserted by Dr. Abbott, or Dr. Schmiedel and the *Encyclopædia Biblica*.

APPENDIX

NOTE TO THE PRESENT EDITION

SINCE the issue of the Second Edition only two adverse notices have appeared. One from an avowed Secularist prefaces its animadversions by thanking the author "for his recent humorous contribution to literature." Such a critic cannot reasonably complain if his objections are treated as too "humorous" for further consideration.

A courteous and thoughtful reviewer in the *Literary Guide* hints at replies which would, he says, if elaborated, reduce the miracles of unbelief "to modest and natural proportions." If, however, we may judge of the elaboration from the synopsis, it would seem to tend rather to the magnification than the diminution of unfaith's monstrosities. After a simple assertion that the attitude of the foregoing pages is "at variance with the indisputable results of modern science and modern criticism," he proceeds to defend Haeckel's unworthy sneer at God, in Christian parlance, as "a gaseous vertebrate," on the ground that an "Infinite Mind" is a nebulous phrase. Is this philosophy? He regards all Biblical predictions as simply post-dated history. Is this valid modern criticism? He reaffirms Haeckel's assumption of spontaneous generation, avowing that "*life arises from the non-living* by some natural process at present unknown." Is this science? If it be, then such names as Tyndall Huxley, Carpenter, Drysdale, Dallinger, Beale, Wallace, and a host of others, must be set aside as of no account. Again, "the universe," it appears, "was never originated" at all, it simply "*resulted inevitably* from the interaction of Matter and Energy" (why spelt with capitals?) which "are eternal and self-existent." There is "nothing singular in the rise and rapid spread of Christianity"; the "Christ of the Gospels was *the slow creation of the first and second centuries,* and many widely-spread Churches contributed their quota to the stream of myth and tradition which slowly crystallised into the Four Gospels." Christ's resurrection is "absolutely disproved by *the one fact* " that He appeared only to chosen witnesses. Paul, the only authentic witness, "either knew nothing of the discourses, parables, and miracles of Jesus, or he thought it right to treat them with silent contempt." "The Gospels declare that Jesus was not the son of His mother's husband. The story that He was begotten by the Holy Spirit is incredible and absurd, He *must therefore* have been illegitimate. Thus if there be any substratum of truth at all in the New Testament narratives, the Talmudic account of Jesus, son of Pandera, becomes the natural explanation of the alleged birth of Jesus Christ." The italics are mine. The logic would be "humorous" if it were not so desperate. The Gospels, it seems, are reliable so far as subserves the anti-supernatural pre-determinations of Agnosticism; beyond that all is "incredible and absurd"! Very simple, but hardly sufficient to an unprejudiced mind. At all events the argument of the preceding pages is hereby strengthened. From the merely human son of an adulteress, Christianity, with all that it includes and involves, has to be evolved. Knowing what we do of the first and second centuries, if they accomplished this feat, then the literal miracle is greater than ever.

It cannot, however, be too plainly pointed out, whether this reviewer is or is not aware of it, that *all* these points of his, and many others, have been fairly and squarely met in the volumes enumerated in the foregoing list. To these, therefore, I must be content, for the present, to refer the scrutiny of the honest inquirer, in support of the assertion that, for all its courtesy, such criticism as this does but serve to throw up into more lurid relief the monstrosity of the miracles of unbelief.

INDEX

ABBOTT, Dr. E. A., as to spiritual Resurrection, 157.
Abbott, Dr. Lyman, on Miracles, 105.
Acts, as related to the Epistles, 191.
Adaptation to environment, 69.
Agnosticism, a witness to true progress, 6.
   Modern forms, 30–54.
   Contrary to reason, 63.
   Alternative in rejecting Christianity, 243.
Akoustics, wonders and beauties of, 99.
Alger, Mr., on life after death, 294.
Allen, Mr. Grant, as to Christianity, 311.
   As to Immortality, 313.
Alternatives of Belief and Unbelief, 341.
Ammianus, as to Julian's Edict, 126.
Anderson, Dr., on the Ascension, 168.
Annihilation, repulsive and degrading, 308.
Anthropism, denounced by Haeckel, 346–355.
Anti-Supernaturalism, its logical result, 340.
Apocrypha, Old Testament, as to life after death, 295.
Apocryphal Gospels compared with the New Testament, 237.
Apologetics, neglected and ignored in the pulpit, 18–21.
Appendix, list of books, 359.
Arabian Nights' Entertainment, 315.
Argument, a necessity of Gospel teaching, 24.
Armenians, 113.
Arthur, Rev. William, on Positivism, 282.

Ascension, the, 168.
Assumption, one only in this work, 36.
Assumptions of Mr. Clodd's Evolution, 58.
Attitude of the Christian Church, 11.
Avebury, Lord, on *The Beauties of Nature*, 92, 94.

BAKER, Sir Samuel, as to cruelty in Nature, 329.
Bartlet, Professor Vernon, on early Christian persecution, 122.
   As to Paul's belief in Christ's Resurrection, 164.
   As to authorship of Acts, 179.
Baur, as to the Resurrection, 155.
Beale, Dr. Lionel S., on Life, 60, 62, 334.
Beauty, a witness for the Divine Existence, 65.
   Showing design in Nature, 87.
   Involving mind, 89.
   Impossible from chance, 90.
   And the struggle for existence, 92.
   Crystalline, 98.
   Of human face and character, 100.
Beet, Professor J. A., on Christology, 28.
Belfast Address, Dr. Tyndall's, on Crystalline Beauty, 98.
Bennett, Sir Risdon, as to the power of Christianity, 203.
Besant, Mrs., on Christian Apocryphal writings, 195.
Bias of Scepticism against the Supernatural, 267.
Bible; its ethics, 111.
   Influence, 112.
   Superhuman origin, 112.

366   INDEX

Bible, more miraculous on premises of Atheism, 113.
   Vitality of, 197.
Bible Dictionary, Hastings', quoted, 28, 108.
"Big carpenter," the, theory of Creation, 70.
Birth stories of Gospels not discredited, 39.
Blaikie, Dr., on the Vitality of the Bible, 197.
Blasphemy, human, 266.
Blavatsky frauds in India, 127.
Body of Christ, the, what became of it, 146.
   Stolen, an absurdity, 147.
Bolingbroke, Viscount, Deist, quoted, 216.
Books, list of useful, 359.
Boxers, Chinese, as illustrations of fanaticism, 184, 208, 233.
Brace, G. Loring, *Gesta Christi*, 204.
Brooks, Dr. Phillips, on the influence of Jesus, 204.
Browning, Robert, on the life to come, 297.
   On the reasonableness of Christianity, 338.
Bruce, Dr. A. B., as to the Resurrection, 143, 172.
Buonaparte, Napoleon, historic doubts concerning his existence, 272.
Butler, Bishop, on the ridicule of Christianity, 3.

CAMEL swallowed after straining out gnat, 63, 341.
Candid examination of Theism, by Physicus, 290, 311.
Canon of the New Testament unalterable, 196.
Carlyle, Thomas, on Jesus of Nazareth, 230.
Carpenter, Dr. W. B., as to miracles, 105.
   On the ignorance of modern Science, 333.
Cell, the ultimate, as a product of chance, 62.
Certainty in the Christian promise of Immortality, 299.
Cessation of animal sacrifices, explanation of, 225.

Channing, Dr., on Christ's character, 252.
Character of Christ, the only valid method of attack on the Supernatural, 274.
Chinese not similar to Jews, 113.
Christ, His origin and character, 247.
   His personality and influence extreme, 248.
   The lowest estimate possible, 250.
   Estimates of well-known unbelievers, 251–253.
   Evolution as an explanation of, 254–258.
   His goodness inseparable from His truthfulness, 259.
   His claim to sinlessness, 262.
   His claim to royalty, 264.
   The dilemma concerning Him, 339.
Christendom, partial failure of, no disproof of Christianity, 339.
Christian Evidence lectures, 22.
Christian inconsistencies and their significance, 200.
   Intensification of sin, 226.
   Appreciation of Christ not irrelevant, 249.
Christianity, its first appeal to the judgement, 23.
   The *sine quâ non* of, 33.
   More incredible without the Supernatural than with, 35.
   Existence and diffusion, 116.
   Unique, 117.
   Origin, 118.
   Triumph over enemies and friends, 127.
   Third triumph, 128.
   More vigorous than ever, 128.
   Compared with Mohammedanism and Buddhism, 130, 226.
   Its elevating influence, 199.
   To be accounted for, 233.
   Adequately explained by New Testament account, 241.
   Its early programme inexplicable, 239.
Cicero, as to the universal notion of gods, 219.
   As to future existence, 294.
Clark, Sir Andrew, as to Christian faith, 23.
   As to effect of Gospel, 203.

INDEX

Clark, Prof. Le Gros, on Paley's *Natural Theology*, 85.
Clarke, Dr. W. N., as to Evolution, 108.
  On the Resurrection, 173.
  On the Personality of God, 278.
Clifford, Prof. W. K., as to belief in God, 281.
  As to Christianity, 311.
  On the mystery of brain action, 334.
Clodd, Mr. E., *Plain Account of Evolution*, 57–64.
  As to Christianity, 311.
Cobbe, Miss F. P., on Christ's character, 252, 265.
Comparative insignificance of Christian miracles, 315.
Complication and culmination of argument, 319.
Concluding summary, 332.
Conditionalists and the future life, 305.
Congreve, Dr., on Positivism and Christ's character, 253.
Consensus of New Testament writings, 192.
Consolatory religion insufficient, 20.
Constantine and early Christianity, 125.
Conviction *versus* Denunciation, 17.
Conversion of Paul, 177–186.
  Natural explanations of, contradictory, 324.
Cowper, B. Harris, as to the Christian Apocrypha, 195.
Crafts, Dr., on practical Christian Sociology, 204.
Craufurd, Rev. A. H., *Christian Instincts and Modern Doubt*, 20, 71.
Credentials of Gospels not disproved, 273.
Credibility of Gospels, 267.
Credulity of primitive Christians estimated, 211, 238.
Critical notes, 37.
Cruelty in Nature exaggerated, 75, 328.
Cumming, Miss Gordon, as to Christianity in Fiji, 206.

Daily Chronicle, Testimony to vitality of Christianity, 129.
Dallinger, Dr., Fernley Lecture on the Creator and Creation, 84.

Darwin, confession in his later years, 68.
  As to teleology, 68.
  Concerning orchids and adaptation, 79.
  As to influence of Christianity in New Zealand, 205.
Davids, Mr. Rhys, as to the Buddhist Trinity, 284.
Debates on religion unsatisfactory, 22.
Design, as proof of God's existence, 65–104.
Destructive criticism, 267.
Deuteronomy xxviii. and xxix., 114.
Differences of Doctrine amongst Christians exceeded amongst Unbelievers, 269.
Difficulties in connection with Christianity, 7, 8, 31.
  Of unbelief greater than those of belief, 32.
  Of unbelief in regard to Christ's character, 260.
  Of unbelief in construction, 321.
  Aggravated and perpetuated by Naturalism, 337.
Dilemma of unbelief hopeless, 261.
  Inevitable, 275.
  As to Christian philosophy and its origin, 293.
  As to Christian ethics, 312.
  As to Immortality, 313.
Dilemmas of Naturalism, 310, 311.
Diocletian, his persecution of the early Christians, 123, 125.
Discordant explanations of unbelief, 324.
Discrepancies in the Gospels and their significance, 189.
Disharmony of Rationalism as to the Gospels, 268.
Distinction between the difficulties of belief and unbelief, 327.
Dods, Dr. Marcus, On Mohammed, Buddha, and Christ, 222.
Dreyfus Trial, The, and modern anti-Semitism, 115.
Drummond, Prof. Henry, on Evolution, 56.
Dudgeon, Dr., as to missions in China, 208.

EBRARD, quoted as to the Lord's Supper, 134.
Ecce Homo, as to Christ's miracles, 44, 108, 261.
  As to Christian holiness, 227.
  As to Christ's character, 246, 253.
  As to Christian philanthropy, 287.
  As to Christian influence, 289, 290.
Ectopic gestation, as a comment, 52.
Effect of modern preaching upon preachers, 15.
  Christian Scriptures, 202.
  Christianity upon humanity, 288.
Elimination of the supernatural as an intellectual panacea, 319.
Environmental conditions of Christ's birth and life, 256.
Epistles, as related to the Acts, 191.
Essenism, as an explanation of Christ, 257.
Ethics of Christianity, not derived from Romans, Greeks, Jews, 240.
Evangelicalism, and its work, 4.
Evolution, the modern word, 54.
  Herbert Spencer's final formula, 80.
  Out of the question in regard to Christian morality, 241.
  As an explanation of Christ's character, 254-258.
  Contradicting itself as to Christian philosophy, 293.
Experience of Christians, a valid argument, 209.
Explanation of all difficulties required from unbelief, 326.
Eye, the human, 51-53, 78, 79.

FACTS of the same order as to the Resurrection, 162.
Fanaticism, characteristics of, well-known, 183, 236.
Fathers, writings of the, compared with the New Testament, 237.
Fetish worship, rightly estimated, 219.
Fichte's estimate of Christianity, 202.
Fifth Gospel, the, Paul's acknowledged letters, 290.
First Principles, Mr. Herbert Spencer's, 81.
Fiske, Mr. John, on teleology, 48.
  Cosmic Philosophy, quoted, 48.
  As to the immortality of the soul, 278, 298, 308.

Footman, Rev. H., on "reasonable apprehensions," 128.
Foraminifera, beauty of, 95.
Fourth Gospel, the, as to miracles, 45.
Fragments of Science, Tyndall's, quoted, 97.
Frere, Sir Bartle, as to missions in India, 207.
  On Christianity's adaptation to all forms of civilisation, 237.
Future life, scientific demonstration of, by Mr. T. J. Hudson, 297, 306, 309.

GALAHAD, Sir, 102.
Galerius, persecution and edict of toleration, 123.
Gardner's *Exploratio Evangelica*, note on, 46.
Gibbon's explanations of early Christian triumphs, 125, 173, 234.
Gipsies, no parallel to the Jews, 113.
Gladstone, Prof. J. H., F.R.S., on the Divine purpose in Nature, 67.
Gladstone, W. E., as to the worth of Christianity, 204.
God, idea of, universal, 218.
Goethe, as to genuineness of Gospels, 176.
  As to Christianity, 221, 278.
  As to Christ's character, 251.
  Quoted by Haeckel, 356.
Goodness in Christ's character inseparable from truthfulness, 259, 274.
Gospel, the, more miraculous without miracles, 36.
  Of John dismissed, 268.
Gospels, their characteristics, 188.
  Their credibility, 267.
Gray, Dr. Asa, as to teleology, 68.
Greeks, attitude of, towards the Gospel, 121, 126.
Greg, Mr. W. R., as to Christ's character, 252.
  As to Christ's Resurrection, 322.
Grimthorpe, Lord, on Agnostic Evolution, 71, 80, 81, 83, 86.
  On Huxley and Hume, 234.
Ground, on Spencer's structural principles, 71.

HAECKEL, *History of Creation*, 67.
  Theory of Evolution, 72.

Haeckel, on *The Riddle of the Universe*, 345.
　Emphasises main contention of this work, 347,
　Assertion of sincerity, 348.
　Contemptuous *ipse dixit*, 349, 353, 354.
　False statements, 349–352.
　Pledged to abiogenesis, 352
Hamlet, and the sequence of death, 304.
Happiness, in the animal world, 76.
Harnack, Adolf, *Das Wesen des Christentums*, 278.
Harrison, Rev. A. J., quoted, 108.
　Mr. Frederic, as to the need of religion, 288, 289.
Hastings' *Bible Dictionary*, referred to, 140.
Hausrath, Dr., as to Christ's character, 252.
Helmholtz, Professor, as to the primitive nebulosity, 58.
　As to the human eye, 78.
Henslow, Professor, as to Evolution and Christ's character, 256.
Herschel, Sir John, quoted, 48.
Higher Criticism, the, and its influence, 5.
　Irrelevant here, 110.
Hirst, Mr. J. Crowther, as to Nature's cruelty, 76.
History, realm of, 109 *et seq.*
Holiness, as a Christian conception, 228.
Hope, Christian, in face of the mystery of pain, 331.
Horæ Paulinæ, Paley's, instanced, 191.
Hudson, Dr., on animal happiness, 76.
　Mr. T. J., scientific demonstration of a future life, 297, 306, 309.
Hughes, Rev. T. P., on Mohammedanism, 285, 290, 302.
Hull, Professor E., F.R.S., as to the origin of life, 60.
Human eye, the, related to moral causes and effects, 74.
Hume, as to Christianity, 130.
Hutton, Mr., on human sacrifices in India, 206.
Huxley, Professor T. H., as to the basis of life, 61.
　As to teleology, 68, 69, 71.

Huxley, as to development of the tadpole, 78.
　As to miracles, 105.
　As to Bible ethics, 111.
　As to Christ's Resurrection, 139.
　As to the effect of Bible teaching, 203.
　As to Positivism, 282.
　As to suffering in Nature, 329.

Ideas of Christianity compared with those of other religions, 286.
Ignorance of modern Science, 334.
　Attested by Haeckel, 345.
Immortality, its significance in human thought, 293–295.
　Its certainty in Christian thought, 299.
　Its simplicity in Christian thought, 300.
　Its individuality and nobility, 301.
　Reserve in the Christian doctrine of, 303.
　Not derived from Judaism, 304.
　As a corollary to Evolution, 308, 309.
　Most desired by the best, 309.
Imperfection, the, of human eye no disproof of design, 79.
Inconsistencies of Christians, 287.
Individuality in the Christian promise of immortality, 300.
Inevitable conclusion, from rejection of Supernatural, 242.
Inferior eyes of lower creatures consistent with design, 80.
In Memoriam, quoted, 102, 296, 305, 307, 331, 344, 356.
Intelligence, required for greater marvels, if for lesser, 78.
Introductory Chapter, 1.
Involution necessary to Evolution, 55.
Irrational to reject the Supernatural, 341.
Islam, 117, 285, 289, 290, 299, 302.
Iverach, Dr., on Evolution, 54, 56, 66.

Jevons, Professor S., quoted, 25.
Jewish idiosyncrasies inexplicable by natural Evolution, 116.
　Well known, 119.
　Early belief of, only explained by New Testament account, 120.

Jews, the, 109-116.
Jones, Rev. Griffith, as to the Resurrection Body of Christ, 151, 164, 156.
   As to the Ascension, 168.
Judgement, the true basis of emotion, 24.
Julian, and early Christianity, 126.

KANT's avowal, 279.
Karma, Buddhist doctrine of, 301.
Keim, as to Christ's Resurrection, 140, 143, 155.
   As to Paul's conversion, 182, 185.
Kelvin, Lord, atheistic idea nonsensical, 64.
   As to design, 86.
Kennedy, Dr., on the Resurrection of Christ, 136.
Kennedy, Rev. J. H., on *Natural Theology and Modern Thought*, quoted, 48.
Kernel and the Husk, The, quoted, 2.
   As to a non-miraculous Christ, 37.
   As to the Fourth Gospel and the Miraculous Conception, 40.
   As to the Supernatural, 152.
   As to a spiritual Resurrection, 156, 172.
Keshub Chunder Sen, as to Christianity in India, 207.
Kidd, Mr. Benj., *Social Evolution*, quoted, 28.
Kidd, Dr. W., F.Z.S., as to Creation, 63.
   As to Design, 70.
Knight, Professor, on Christian Ethics, 312.
Koran, compared with the New Testament, 237.
Kropotkin, Prince, as to suffering in Nature, 329.

LACTANTIUS, as a witness of early Christian persecution, 123.
Law of Parsimony, 335.
Lawrence, Lord, as to missions in India, 208.
Lawrence, Rev. Eric, on the Resurrection, 163, 170.
Leaders of modern Science not necessarily Agnostic, 86.
Lecky, *History of European Morals*, 121, 125, 130.

Lecky, as to Christ's character and influence, 246, 253.
Le Conte, Professor, Evolution and Religious thought, 48.
   On Design, 84.
   As to beauty, apart from use, 95.
Le Gallienne, Mr. R., as to personal identity, 301.
Lias, Dr., on miracles, 35.
   As to Christ's influence, 176.
   As to the whole body of evidence for Christianity, 326.
Liddon, Dr., on the belief in Immortality, 295.
Lightfoot, Dr., on the Acts of the Apostles, 194.
   As to Essenism, 257.
Lord's Supper, The, and its significance, 131-234.
Luke's Gospel and its date according to McGiffert, 273.
Lyttleton, Lord, on the Conversion of Paul, 177-180.

MACAULAY, Lord, political estimate of Christianity, 202.
Maccabees, Second Book of, references to Immortality, 305, 306.
Maclaren, Dr., as to the Resurrection, 150.
Maclear, Dr., on the historical fidelity of New Testament, 193.
Madagascar, effect of Christian missions in, 206.
Maharajah of Travancore, as to missions in India, 207.
Man, a moral being assumed, 217.
Maronites, 113.
Martyrs, early Christian, 121.
McGiffert, Dr., as to Paul's belief in Christ's Resurrection, 163.
   As to the Acts of the Apostles, 178.
   As to Gospels of Luke and John, 273.
Mental obliquity of unbelief, 25.
Mill, James, on the origin of things, 308.
Mill, John Stuart, as to miracles, 105.
   As to character of Christ, 189, 257.
   As to Gospels, 195.
   As to Christianity, 231, 286.
   Indictment of Nature, 329.
Milligan, Dr., on a spiritual Resurrection, 157, 161.

INDEX

Mind, involved in the universe, 51.
Mineral world, inexplicable and useless beauty of, 96.
Minimum, an irreducible, for Christianity, 33.
Miracles, cannot be detached from the Gospel, 38, 41.
  In the New Testament, 42.
  And mighty works, 43, 44.
  Not violations of cause and effect, 44.
  Not incredible, 45.
  And the Fourth Gospel, 45.
  Not impossible or incredible, 65.
  Rejection of, only necessary for the Atheist, 105.
  Purely a question of evidence, 106.
  Inevitable in connection with the Resurrection, 151.
  Intensified by withdrawal of the Supernatural, 240.
Miracles, of unbelief, in regard to Christ, summarised, 274, 275.
Miraculous conception, 40, 41.
Miraculous and supernatural compared, 43.
Missions, Christian, and their effects, 118, 129, 204, 233.
Modern life and its influences, 18.
Mohammed and Christ, 222.
Mohammedanism, 117, 284, 289, 290, 299, 302.
Momerie, Dr., on belief in God, 64, 318.
  On belief in immortality, 295.
Monism, failure of, 347.
Monstrosities of Naturalism, 315.
Moral realm, the, 217.
Muir, Sir Wm., as to Mohammedanism and Christianity, 285, 289.
Müller's *Fertilisation of Flowers*, quoted, 77.
Mystery of pain exaggerated, 73.
Myth, futility of appeal to, 271.

NAPOLEON BUONOPARTE, as to Christ's character, 254.
  Doubts as to existence of, 272.
Natural difficulties worse than miraculous, 37.
Natural Religion, Seeley's, quoted, 318.

Naturalising, the, of Christianity mistaken, 34.
Naturalism, its difficulty as to Christ, 260.
  Its influence, 308.
  Its dilemmas, 312, 315.
  Its contradictory solutions of Christian difficulties, 320.
  Creates more difficulties than it removes, 332.
  Treble failure of, 335.
  Summary of its contradictions, 336.
Nature, "red in tooth and claw," a misrepresentation, 72.
Necessity for other Christian methods besides preaching, 18.
Neglect of Apologetics in the pulpit, 18, 21.
Newman, F. W., acknowledgment of, as to New Testament, 192.
New Testament and its miracle portions, 42.
  As to its nature and origin, 186-213.
  Its foundation on fraud psychologically inconceivable, 211.
Newton, Sir Isaac, as to the Being of God, 64.
Nitro-carbonates, the, as workers of miracle, 353.
Nobility of Christian promise of Immortality, 301.
Notes on *The Kernel and the Husk*, 37.
Number of believing men of science greater than of unbelieving, 67.
Numbers as an estimate of moral worth, 232.

OBJECTIVE and Subjective, as to Christ's Resurrection, 163.
Occult phenomena, 297.
Omissions of New Testament calling for explanations, 234, 237.
Open conferences unobjectionable and profitable, 22.
Opening century, three portentous facts, 9.
Orchids, cultivation of, 103.

PAIN, value of, to the race, 74.
  Mystery of its mitigation and alleviation 75.

Paine, Thomas, 118.
   As to Christ's character, 229.
Painlessness, the greater mystery of, 75.
Paley's *Natural Theology* not antiquated, 50.
   Scorn cast upon, 65.
   Happiness of this world, 72.
   On belief in God, 338.
Paracelsus, Browning's, quoted, 297.
Parker, Prof. Kitchen, on Evolution, 85.
Parker, Theodore, as to Christ's character, 246, 252.
Paul's acknowledged letters, 270.
   Their date, 271.
Paul's conversion, 177–186.
   Supernatural, 176.
   Contrary explanations of, 324.
Persecution of early Christians, 122.
   And increased enthusiasm, 123, 124.
Persistence of religious notions, 225.
Personal sincerity insufficient, 43.
Philistinism, modern, 30.
Phillips, L. F. March, 154.
   Lectures on Cumulative Evidences of Divine Revelation, 154.
Physical Science, realm of, 47.
Plato, as to the need for God, 220.
Pliny's rescript to Trajan, 122.
Political economy not noticed in New Testament, 235.
Preaching, modern, compared with Apostolic methods, 14.
Present - Day Tracts, commended, 112, 115, 119, 193, 197.
Pressensé's *Early Years of Christianity, Martyrs and Apologists*, 119, 122.
Proctor, Mr. Richard A., quoted as to Divine intervention, 154.
Psychical Research Society, 306.
Psychology, realm of, 175.
Pulpit logic, 16.
Pyramid, poised on nothing, 56.

RADIOLARIA, beauty of, 95.
Reason before faith, 14, 24.
   And faith, their relations, 25.
Renan, M., as to Christ's character, 251, 257.
Renouf, M., on life after death, 294.

Reserve of New Testament as to future life, 303.
Response, the Christian, to the longing for Immortality, 299.
Results of timid conservatism in pulpit, 19.
Resurrection of Christ, the, 135–151.
   Indisputable facts as to the, 141.
   Its immediate results unparalleled, 145.
   Actuality of, 155.
      Spiritual, considered, 156–172.
   Varying theories of unbelief concerning, 322.
   The only rational explanation of, 323.
Reynolds, Dr., on Buddhism, 283.
Rogers, Prof. Henry, on the Bible, 112, 197.
   On the conversion of Paul, 177, 181.
Romanes, G. J., quoted, 28.
   As to sudden creation, 66.
   Thoughts on Religion, quoted, 108.
   On Christianity, 291, 311.
Romans, attitude of, towards the early Gospel, 120.
Roscoe, Sir Henry, on Protoplasm, 61.
Rousseau, 117.
   As to origin of New Testament, 213.
   As to Christ's morality, 239.
   As to Christ's character, 251.
Row, Rev. C. A., on the Resurrection, 135, 165.
Royalty, Christ's claim to, 264, 265.

SACRIFICES, meaning and cessation of, 224.
Salmon, Dr., as to non-miraculous Christianity, 39–42.
Salmond, Dr., as to the Jewish conceptions of Immortality, 305.
Sanday, Dr., as to the Resurrection, 140, 172.
Sartor Resartus, Carlyle's, quoted, 230.
Scientific demonstration of a future life, by T. J. Hudson, 297, 306, 309.
Secretary of State, as to effect of missions in India, 207.
Secularist ribaldry, 3, 250, 276.
Seeley, Prof., as to Christian holiness, 227.
   As to Christ's character, 246, 253.

INDEX

Seeley, Prof., as to miracles, 261.
   As to Christian philanthropy, 287.
   As to Christian influence, 289, 290.
   As to natural religion, 318.
Selby, Rev. T. G., on the resurrection body, 171.
Self-confutation of sceptic explanations of Christianity, 320.
Severity, Christ's, towards the Pharisees, 29.
Shairp, Principal, on miracles, 105.
Shallow sentimentality as to the course of nature, 74.
Shaw, Mr. D., on converging proofs of Christianity, 327.
Silencing of modern hearers, 15.
Simplicity of Christian hope of Immortality, 299.
Sin, conviction of, in Christianity, 223.
   Conviction of, strongest in best men, 262.
Sinlessness, Christ's claim to, 262–264.
Slavery, not prohibited in the New Testament, 235.
Smith, Prof. Goldwin, as to Secularist ribaldry, 3.
   As to progress and Christendom, 289.
Socrates and the Christian hope of Immortality, 304.
Sound, beauty and significance of, 98.
Speed and purpose incommensurable, 70.
Spencer, Mr. Herbert, as to religion, 281.
    Appropriate conditions, 55.
    Redistribution, 59.
    "Big carpenter" theory, 71.
    Evolution, 80.
    Definition of life, 333.
Spinoza, as to Christ's character, 251.
Spiritual resurrection, 156, 172.
   Realm, the, 279.
Spontaneous generation asserted by Haeckel, 352.
Standard, testimony of, as to Christian missions, 205.
Statement of the case, 27.
Stephen, Sir James F., as to Positive Humanity, 282.

Stevens, Dr., *Theology of New Testament*, quoted, 176.
Stirling, Dr. Hutchinson, on Darwinianism, 72.
Stokes, Sir G. G., on Design, 53, 67.
Storrs' *Divine Origin of Christianity*, 119, 232.
Strata, no two distinct in Gospel narratives, 38.
Strauss, as to Christ's resurrection, 139.
   Mythical theory, 141.
   Character of Christ, 221, 230, 251
   As to loss of faith, 330.
Stuckenberg, Dr., on *Christian Sociology*, 204.
Subjective criticism, 209.
   And objective, as to Christ's Resurrection, 163.
Sublimity in Nature and the Design argument, 87.
Suddenness as proof of Design, 69, 70.
Suffering as an argument against Christianity, 328.
   Largely due to vice and folly, 330.
Supernatural *versus* Miraculous, 43.
Supernatural, the, in history of Jews, 111.
   Meaning of, 152-154.
   Modern aversion to, 333.
Supernatural Religion, author of, as to subjective impressions, 165.
   As to the Ascension, 168.
   As to Christ's character, 253.
   His final construction, 321.
   As to Christ's resurrection, 322.
Suppositions of Mr. Greg, as to Christ's Resurrection, 322, 323.
Synoptic Gospels discredited, 268.
Synthesis of gems and the inevitable inference, 97.

TALLYRAND referred to by Prof. Seeley, 318.
Testimonies of unbelief to Christ's character, 250, 253.
Theism assumed by the New Testament, 49.
Theodoret, as to Julian's laws, 126.
Theology of an Evolutionist, Dr. Lyman Abbott's, 106.
Thoughts on Religion, by J. G. Romanes, quoted, 68, 108, 291, 311.

Tragedy of loss of faith growing, 21.
Triple opposition to Christianity and triple triumph, 119.
"Triple tradition," 268.
Tübingen School, 5.
"Two Voices," Tennyson's, quoted, 307.
Tylor, Dr., on the longing for a future life, 294.
Tyndall, Prof., as to beauties of crystallisation, 97, 98.

UNBELIEF unreasonable, 25.
 Its dilemma as to Christ, hopeless, 261.
 Its difficulties of construction, 321.
Unbelievers, well known, worth of their testimony, 200.
Unconvincedness, 19.
Unseen Universe, The, authors of, on science as a supporter of Christianity, 310.

VERBAL inspiration untenable, 194.
Voltaire, 118.
 As to belief in God, 288.

WACE, Dr., Boyle Lectures, quoted, 2, 12, 48.

Wace, Dr., on natural explanations of the New Testament, 211.
 As to miracles, 216.
 Christianity and Morality, 229.
Wainwright, Dr. S., quoted, 108.
Wallace, Dr. A. Russell, as to the exaggeration of suffering in Nature, 329.
Weakening of Christian Conviction, 9.
Well-known unbelievers and their testimony, 200.
Wells, Mr. H. G., and the *War of Worlds,* 128.
West, Gilbert, on the Resurrection of Christ, 178.
Westcott, on the nature of Christ's Resurrection, 161, 166, 170.
Whately, Abp., *Historic Doubts concerning Napoleon,* 272.
Wilkins, Prof. A. S., on Induction, 45.
 As to Christian ethics, 230.
Worship, its object and influence, 280.
Wright, Dr. G. F., *Scientific Aspects of Christian Evidences,* 176, 216.

ZIONIST Movement, 116.

A GREAT BIBLICAL ENCYCLOPÆDIA.

'If the other volumes come up to the standard of the first, this Dictionary seems likely to take its place as the standard authority for biblical students of the present generation.'—*Times.*

In Four Volumes, imperial 8vo (of nearly 900 pages each).
Price per Volume, in cloth, 28s.; In half morocco, 34s.,

A DICTIONARY OF THE BIBLE,

Dealing with its Language, Literature, and Contents, including the Biblical Theology.

Edited by JAMES HASTINGS, M.A., D.D., with the Assistance of J. A. SELBIE, M.A., and, chiefly in the Revision of the Proofs, of A. B. DAVIDSON, D.D., LL.D., Edinburgh; S. R. DRIVER, D.D., Litt.D., Oxford; and H. B. SWETE, D.D., Litt.D., Cambridge.

Full Prospectus, with Specimen Pages, from all Booksellers, or from the Publishers.

'We offer Dr. Hastings our sincere congratulations on the publication of the first instalment of this great enterprise. . . . A work was urgently needed which should present the student with the approved results of modern inquiry, and which should also acquaint him with the methods by which theological problems are now approached by the most learned and devout of our theologians.'—*Guardian.*

'We welcome with the utmost cordiality the first volume of Messrs. Clark's great enterprise, "A Dictionary of the Bible." That there was room and need for such a book is unquestionable. . . . We have here all that the student can desire, a work of remarkable fulness, well up to date, and yet at the same time conservative in its general tendency, almost faultlessly accurate, and produced by the publishers in a most excellent and convenient style. We can thoroughly recommend it to our readers as a book which should fully satisfy their anticipations. . . . This new Dictionary is one of the most important aids that have recently been furnished to a true understanding of Scripture, and, properly used, will brighten and enrich the pulpit work of every minister who possesses it. . . . We are greatly struck by the excellence of the short articles. They are better done than in any other work of the kind. We have compared several of them with their sources, and this shows at once the unpretentious labour that is behind them. . . . Dr. A. B. Davidson is a tower of strength, and he shows at his best in the articles on Angels, on Covenant (a masterpiece, full of illumination), and on Eschatology of the Old Testament. His contributions are the chief ornaments and treasure-stores of the Dictionary. . . . We are very conscious of having done most inadequate justice to this very valuable book. Perhaps, however, enough has been said to show our great sense of its worth. It is a book that one is sure to be turning to again and again with increased confidence and gratitude. It will be an evil omen for the Church if ministers do not come forward to make the best of the opportunity now presented them.'—EDITOR, *British Weekly.*

'Will give widespread satisfaction. Every person consulting it may rely upon its trustworthiness. . . . Far away in advance of any other Bible Dictionary that has ever been published in real usefulness for preachers, Bible students, and teachers.'—*Methodist Recorder.*

'This monumental work. It has made a great beginning, and promises to take rank as one of the most important biblical enterprises of the century.'—*Christian World.*

EDINBURGH: **T. & T. CLARK,** 38 GEORGE STREET.

T. & T. CLARK'S PUBLICATIONS.

ST. PAUL'S CONCEPTION OF CHRIST; or, The Doctrine of the Second Adam. Being the Sixteenth Series of the 'Cunningham Lectures.' By Rev. DAVID SOMERVILLE, D.D., Edinburgh. In demy 8vo, price 9s.

'By its keen and profound insight, by its sanity, and by its fulness of knowledge, the volume will at once take its place as the best authority on that department of New Testament theology with which it deals.'—*Critical Review.*

ST. PAUL'S CONCEPTION OF CHRISTIANITY. By the late Professor A. B. BRUCE, D.D., Glasgow. Post 8vo, price 7s. 6d.

'There need be no hesitation in pronouncing it the best treatment of Paulinism we have. . . . A book of first-rate importance.'—*Expositor.*

THE HUMILIATION OF CHRIST, in its Physical, Ethical, and Official Aspects. By the late Professor A. B. BRUCE, D.D., Glasgow. In demy 8vo, Fourth Edition, price 10s. 6d.

'These lectures are able and deep-reaching to a degree not often found in the religious literature of the day; withal, they are fresh and suggestive. . . . The learning and the deep and sweet spirituality of this discussion will commend it to many faithful students of the truth as it is in Jesus.'—*Congregationalist.*

THE RELATION OF THE APOSTOLIC TEACHING TO THE TEACHING OF CHRIST. By Rev. ROBERT J. DRUMMOND, D.D., Edinburgh. 8vo, Second Edition, price 10s. 6d.

'No book of its size has taken such a hold of us for many a day. . . . It is a strong book, the book of a scholar and thinker, fearless yet reverent, new and yet built on a solid foundation of faith and experience.'—*Expository Times.*

A HISTORY OF CHRISTIANITY IN THE APOSTOLIC AGE. By Professor A. C. MCGIFFERT, D.D., New York. Post 8vo, price 12s.

'A reverent and eminently candid treatment of the Apostolic Age in the light of research.'—*Literary World.*

CANON AND TEXT OF THE OLD TESTAMENT. By Professor Dr. FRANTS BUHL, Leipzig. *Authorised Translation.* In demy 8vo, price 7s. 6d.

'By far the best manual that exists on the subject of which it treats.'—Professor A. B. DAVIDSON, D.D., in the *Expositor.*

EDINBURGH: T. & T. CLARK, 38 GEORGE STREET.

TWO NEW VOLUMES now ready.   Dr. C. H. TOY on PROVERBS.
Dr. H. P. SMITH on I. & II. SAMUEL.
[*See page* 3.]

The International Critical Commentary

on the Holy Scriptures of the Old and New Testaments.

UNDER THE EDITORSHIP OF

THE REV. SAMUEL ROLLES DRIVER, D.D.,
Regius Professor of Hebrew, Oxford;

THE REV. ALFRED PLUMMER, M.A., D.D.,
Master of University College, Durham;

AND

THE REV. CHARLES AUGUSTUS BRIGGS, D.D.,
*Edward Robinson Professor of Biblical Theology,
Union Theological Seminary, New York.*

The time has come, in the judgment of the projectors of this enterprise, when it is practicable to combine British and American scholars in the production of a critical, comprehensive Commentary that will be abreast of modern biblical scholarship, and in a measure lead its van. The Commentaries will be international and inter-confessional, and will be free from polemical and ecclesiastical bias. They will be based upon a thorough critical study of the original texts of the Bible, and upon critical methods of interpretation.

NINE VOLUMES OF THE SERIES ARE NOW READY.—*See following pages.*

'The publication of this series marks an epoch in English exegesis.'—*British Weekly.*
'We can sincerely congratulate the authors and the publishers upon producing one of the most epoch-making theological series of the day.'—*Church Bells.*
'"The International Critical Commentary" promises to be one of the most successful enterprises of an enterprising age. . . . So far as it has gone it satisfies the highest expectations and requirements.'—*Bookman.*
'This series seems likely to surpass all previous enterprises of the kind in Great Britain and America.'—*Methodist Times.*
'"The International Critical Commentary" has vindicated its claim to stand in the front rank of modern English exegesis. Every volume that has hitherto appeared has ranked with the foremost on the book expounded.'—*Methodist Recorder.*

EDINBURGH:
T. & T. CLARK, 38 GEORGE STREET.

LONDON AGENTS:
SIMPKIN, MARSHALL, HAMILTON, KENT, & CO. LTD.

To be had from all Booksellers.   [P.T.O.

✻

The International Critical Commentary

In post 8vo, Second Edition (pp. 530), price 12s.,

DEUTERONOMY

BY THE

Rev. S. R. DRIVER, D.D.,

REGIUS PROFESSOR OF HEBREW, AND CANON OF CHRIST CHURCH, OXFORD.

Professor G. A. SMITH (in the *Critical Review*) says: 'The series could have had no better introduction than this volume from its Old Testament editor. . . . Dr. Driver has achieved a commentary of rare learning and still more rare candour and sobriety of judgment. . . . It is everywhere based on an independent study of the text and history . . . it has a large number of new details: its treatment of the religious value of the book is beyond praise. We find, in short, all those virtues which are conspicuous in the author's previous works, with a warmer and more interesting style of expression.'

'There is plenty of room for such a comprehensive commentary as that which we are now promised, and if the subsequent volumes of the series come up to the standard of excellence set in the work that now lies before us, the series will supply a real want in our literature. . . . The Introduction is a masterly piece of work, and here the Oxford Professor of Hebrew is at his best. It gives by far the best and fairest discussion that we have ever seen of the critical problems connected with the book.'—*Guardian.*

'We have said enough, we hope, to send the student to this commentary. . . . To the diligent miner there is a wealth of gold and precious stones awaiting his toil and industry.'—*Church Bells.*

'The commentary on the text of Deuteronomy is characterised by the highest learning and fulness of research, and will be of great value, not only to the ordinary student, but to the mature scholar.'—*Record.*

'The work will be not less a treasure to the English student than a credit to English scholarship.'—*Christian World.*

In post 8vo (pp. 526), price 12s.,

JUDGES

BY THE

Rev. GEORGE F. MOORE, D.D.,

PROFESSOR OF HEBREW IN ANDOVER THEOLOGICAL SEMINARY, MASS.

Professor H. E. RYLE, D.D., says: 'I think it may safely be averred that so full and scientific a commentary upon the text and subject-matter of the Book of Judges has never been produced in the English language.'

'Dr. Moore's "Judges" will come as a deep surprise to many in this country. It is not in any respect, so far as we have been able to judge, of lighter weight than the two great volumes of the series which appeared before it.'—*Expository Times.*

'It is unquestionably the best commentary that has hitherto been published on the Book of Judges.'—*London Quarterly Review.*

'Professor Moore of Andover follows up Canon Driver's volume on Deuteronomy with a commentary on Judges, marked by as great learning—it could not be greater—and perhaps by somewhat more freedom of expression. . . . He has examined every word, every letter, of the original text under the microscope.'—*Academy.*

EDINBURGH: T. & T. CLARK, 38 GEORGE STREET.

The International Critical Commentary

Just published, in post 8vo (pp. 460), price 12s.,

THE BOOKS OF SAMUEL

BY

HENRY P. SMITH, D.D.,

PROFESSOR OF BIBLICAL HISTORY AND INTERPRETATION IN AMHERST COLLEGE.

'The commentary is the most complete and minute hitherto published by an English-speaking scholar.'—*Literature.*

'This latest volume of "The International Critical Commentary" is in nowise behind its predecessors in thoroughness and scholarship. We have only to compare it with any earlier English commentary on the same books to see how much our knowledge in every department of biblical scholarship has advanced during the past few years . . . The new light gained from Semitic folk-lore and the comparative study of Eastern customs and traditions is very welcome, and has been employed to illustrate the history, as also that coming from our modern geographical and archæological research.'—*Church Bells.*

Just published, in post 8vo (pp. 590), price 12s.,

THE BOOK OF PROVERBS

BY

C. H. TOY, D.D.,

PROFESSOR OF HEBREW, HARVARD UNIVERSITY.

'The commentary is full, though scholarly and business-like, and must at once take its place as the authority on "Proverbs."'—*Bookman.*

'It is difficult to speak too highly of this volume. . . . The result is a first-rate book. It is rich in learning.'—*Jewish Chronicle.*

In post 8vo (pp. 375), price 10s. 6d.,

ST. MARK'S GOSPEL

BY THE

Rev. EZRA P. GOULD, D.D.,

PROFESSOR OF THE NEW TESTAMENT LITERATURE AND LANGUAGE, DIVINITY SCHOOL OF THE PROTESTANT EPISCOPAL CHURCH, PHILADELPHIA.

'This commentary is written with ability and judgment; it contains much valuable material, and it carries the reader satisfactorily through the Gospel. Great care has been spent upon the text.'—*Expositor.*

'Everything relating to the department of criticism on these points is more thoroughly explained and illustrated here than has ever been done before in an English commentary.'—*Methodist Times.*

EDINBURGH: T. & T. CLARK, 38 GEORGE STREET.

The International Critical Commentary

In post 8vo, Third Edition (pp. 678), price 12s.,

ST. LUKE'S GOSPEL

BY THE

Rev. ALFRED PLUMMER, M.A., D.D.,

MASTER OF UNIVERSITY COLLEGE, DURHAM;
FORMERLY FELLOW AND SENIOR TUTOR OF TRINITY COLLEGE, OXFORD.

'It is distinguished throughout by learning, sobriety of judgment, and sound exegesis. It is a weighty contribution to the interpretation of the Third Gospel, and will take an honourable place in the series of which it forms a part.'—*Critical Review*.

'The best commentary on St. Luke yet published. Dr. Plummer's gifts for the work were already well known and appreciated, and he has not disappointed us in this his latest work.'—*Church Bells*.

'Marked by great learning and extreme common sense. . . . Altogether the book is far and away the best commentary on Luke we yet have in English.'—*Biblical World*.

'We feel heartily that the book will bring credit to English scholarship, and that in its carefulness, its sobriety of tone, its thoughtfulness, its reverence, it will contribute to a stronger faith in the essential trustworthiness of the gospel record.'—*Guardian*.

In post 8vo, Fourth Edition (pp. 562), price 12s.,

ROMANS

BY THE

Rev. WILLIAM SANDAY, D.D., LL.D.,

LADY MARGARET PROFESSOR OF DIVINITY, AND
CANON OF CHRIST CHURCH, OXFORD;

AND THE

Rev. ARTHUR C. HEADLAM, B.D.,

FELLOW OF ALL SOULS' COLLEGE, OXFORD.

Principal F. H. CHASE, D.D., Cambridge, says: 'We welcome it as an epoch-making contribution to the study of St. Paul.'

'This is an excellent commentary, scholarly, clear, doctrinal, reverent, and learned. . . . It is a volume which will bring credit to English scholarship, and while it is the crown of much good work on the part of the elder editor, it gives promise of equally good work in the future from both.'—*Guardian*.

'A most valuable gift to the student of Romans. . . . It is the fullest and freshest in learning, the most patient, the most willing to be intelligible, and to make the Apostle so; and it need not be added, in any work of Dr. Sanday, that in textual criticism it will be a standard authority.'—*British Weekly*.

'Will at once take its place in the front rank of similar works. Its rich fulness of learning, its careful and dispassionate statement of difficulties, and its candour, which will not affect an undue positiveness, call upon us to give it a very hearty welcome.'—*Record*.

'It stands easily at the head of English commentaries. It has qualities, especially in what concerns the text, in which it is superior to the best works of Continental scholars.'—*Critical Review*.

EDINBURGH: T. & T. CLARK, 38 GEORGE STREET.

The International Critical Commentary

In post 8vo (pp. 368), price 10s. 6d.,

EPHESIANS AND COLOSSIANS

BY THE

Rev. T. K. ABBOTT, D.Lit.,

PROFESSOR OF HEBREW, FORMERLY OF BIBLICAL GREEK, TRINITY COLLEGE, DUBLIN.

'For long to come this summary of the results of modern criticism applied to these two Pauline letters is, for the use of scholarly students, not likely to be superseded.'—*Academy*.

'There is no work in all the "International" series that is more faithful or more felicitous.'—*Expository Times*.

'All is done in a clear and easy style, and with a point and precision which will make his commentary one that the student will consult with satisfaction. . . . A strong book, with a certain marked individuality.'—*Critical Review*.

In post 8vo (pp. 240), price 8s. 6d.,

PHILIPPIANS AND PHILEMON

BY THE

Rev. MARVIN R. VINCENT, D.D.,

PROFESSOR OF SACRED LITERATURE IN UNION THEOLOGICAL SEMINARY, NEW YORK.

'It is in all respects such a commentary as is needed for the profitable study and right understanding of these two Epistles. . . . Dr. Vincent has produced a book which may be considered as summing up all that has been previously done for the elucidation of this Epistle of Paul and the shorter one which seems to have been written about the same time. . . . It is, in short, in every way worthy of the series which was so well commenced [in the New Testament] with Dr. Sanday's and Mr. Headlam's admirable commentary on the Romans.'—*Scotsman*.

'He has given us an edition of "Philippians" that takes its place beside its fellows in the very front rank of modern theological literature.'—*Expository Times*.

'Business-like, full, and competent.'—*British Weekly*.

N.B.—*For List of other Volumes in preparation, see page 8 of this Prospectus.*

EDINBURGH: T. & T. CLARK, 38 GEORGE STREET.

THE INTERNATIONAL CRITICAL COMMENTARY.

NINE VOLUMES NOW READY.—*See preceding pages.*

The following other Volumes are in course of preparation:—

THE OLD TESTAMENT.

Genesis.	T. K. CHEYNE, D.D., Oriel Professor of the Interpretation of Holy Scripture, Oxford, and Canon of Rochester.
Exodus.	A. R. S. KENNEDY, D.D., Professor of Hebrew, University of Edinburgh.
Leviticus.	J. F. STENNING, M.A., Fellow of Wadham College, Oxford; and the late Rev. H. A. White, M.A., Fellow of New College, Oxford.
Numbers.	G. BUCHANAN GRAY, M.A., Lecturer in Hebrew, Mansfield College, Oxford.
Joshua.	GEORGE ADAM SMITH, D.D., Professor of Hebrew, Free Church College, Glasgow.
Kings.	FRANCIS BROWN, D.D., Professor of Hebrew and Cognate Languages, Union Theological Seminary, New York.
Isaiah.	A. B. DAVIDSON, D.D., LL.D., Professor of Hebrew, Free Church College, Edinburgh.
Jeremiah.	A. F. KIRKPATRICK, D.D., Regius Professor of Hebrew, and Fellow of Trinity College, Cambridge.
Minor Prophets.	W. R. HARPER, Ph.D., President of Chicago University.
Psalms.	C. A. BRIGGS, D.D., Edward Robinson Professor of Biblical Theology, Union Theological Seminary, New York.
Job.	S. R. DRIVER, D.D., Regius Professor of Hebrew, Oxford.
Daniel.	Rev. JOHN P. PETERS, Ph.D., late Professor of Hebrew, P. E. Divinity School, Philadelphia, now Rector of St. Michael's Church, New York City.
Ezra and Nehemiah.	Rev. L. W. BATTEN, Ph.D., Professor of Hebrew, P. E. Divinity School, Philadelphia.
Chronicles.	EDWARD L. CURTIS, D.D., Professor of Hebrew, Yale University, New Haven, Conn.

THE NEW TESTAMENT.

Synopsis of the Four Gospels.	W. SANDAY, D.D., LL.D., Lady Margaret Professor of Divinity, Oxford; and Rev. W. C. ALLEN, M.A., Exeter College, Oxford.
Matthew.	Rev. WILLOUGHBY C. ALLEN, M.A., Chaplain, Fellow, and Lecturer in Theology and Hebrew, Exeter College, Oxford.
Acts.	FREDERICK H. CHASE, D.D., Christ's College, Cambridge.
Corinthians.	ARCH. ROBERTSON, D.D., Principal of King's College, London.
Galatians.	Rev. ERNEST D. BURTON, A.B., Professor of New Testament Literature, University of Chicago.
The Pastoral Epistles.	WALTER LOCK, D.D., Dean Ireland's Professor of Exegesis, Oxford.
Hebrews.	T. C. EDWARDS, D.D., Principal of the Theological College, Bala; late Principal of University College of Wales, Aberystwyth.
James.	Rev. JAMES H. ROPES, A.B., Instructor in New Testament Criticism in Harvard University.
Peter and Jude.	CHARLES BIGG, D.D., Rector of Fenny Compton, Leamington; Bampton Lecturer, 1886.
The Johannine Epistles.	S. D. F. SALMOND, D.D., Principal, and Professor of Systematic Theology, Free Church College, Aberdeen.
Revelation.	ROBERT H. CHARLES, D.D., Professor of Biblical Greek in the University of Dublin.

Other engagements will be announced shortly.

EDINBURGH: T. & T. CLARK, 38 GEORGE STREET.
LONDON: SIMPKIN, MARSHALL, HAMILTON, KENT, & CO. LTD.

Reprint Publishing

FOR PEOPLE WHO GO FOR ORIGINALS.

This book is a facsimile reprint of the original edition. The term refers to the facsimile with an original in size and design exactly matching simulation as photographic or scanned reproduction.

Facsimile editions offer us the chance to join in the library of historical, cultural and scientific history of mankind, and to rediscover.

The books of the facsimile edition may have marks, notations and other marginalia and pages with errors contained in the original volume. These traces of the past refers to the historical journey that has covered the book.

ISBN 978-3-95940-079-4

Facsimile reprint of the original edition
Copyright © 2015 Reprint Publishing
All rights reserved.

www.reprintpublishing.com

www.ingramcontent.com/pod-product-compliance
Lightning Source LLC
Chambersburg PA
CBHW071944220426
43662CB00009B/988